Welcome to the EVERYTHING®

These handy, accessible books give you all you need to tackle a difficult project, gain a new hobby, comprehend a fascinating topic, prepare for an exam, or even brush up on something you learned back in school but have since forgotten.

You can read an *EVERYTHING®* book from cover-to-cover or just pick out the information you want from our four useful boxes: e-facts, e-ssentials, e-alerts, and e-questions. We literally give you everything you need to know on the subject, but throw in a lot of fun stuff along the way, too.

We now have well over 100 *EVERYTHING®* books in print, spanning such wide-ranging topics as weddings, pregnancy, wine, learning guitar, one-pot cooking, managing people, and so much more. When you're done reading them all, you can finally say you know *EVERYTHING®*!

FACTS

Important sound bytes
of information

SSENTIALS

Quick handy tips

ALERT

Urgent warnings

QUESTIONS?

Solutions to
common problems

Dear Reader,

Having a deep-rooted love of literature, it is only natural that classical mythology takes its place among my passions and interests. If you have any interest in literature or art whatsoever, it is advisable to have a solid foundation in classical mythology to fully appreciate and understand these mediums of expression. Indisputably, the myths of ancient Greece and Rome influence and inspire the literature and artists of the Western world. But this knowledge and groundwork is merely an added bonus; what matter most are the myths themselves.

While academia has its own numerous reasons for the study of classical mythology, I advise you to look at it from a nonacademic standpoint. I think that first and foremost, you should derive enjoyment from the myths. Once you are won over—and you undoubtedly will be—you can then take your time to explore the myths as you see fit. Classical mythology offers something for everyone—whether you are interested in romance, drama, tragedy, war, monsters, or vengeance. The myths are so very rich in excitement, intrigue, and imagination that it is hard to dispute their appeal.

Read on. You won't be disappointed.

Sincerely,

Lesley Bolton

THE
EVERYTHING®
CLASSICAL MYTHOLOGY BOOK

Greek and Roman gods, goddesses,
heroes, and monsters from Ares to Zeus

Lesley Bolton

Adams Media Corporation
Avon, Massachusetts

EDITORIAL
Publishing Director: Gary M. Krebs
Managing Editor: Kate McBride
Copy Chief: Laura MacLaughlin
Acquisitions Editor: Allison Carpenter Yoder

PRODUCTION
Production Director: Susan Beale
Production Manager: Michelle Roy Kelly
Series Designer: Daria Perreault
Layout and Graphics: Arlene Apone,
Paul Beatrice, Brooke Camfield,
Colleen Cunningham, Daria Perreault,
Frank Rivera

An Everything® Series Book.
Everything® and everything.com® are registered trademarks of F+W Publications, Inc.

Published by Adams Media, an F+W Publications Company
57 Littlefield Street, Avon, MA 02322 U.S.A.
www.adamsmedia.com

ISBN: 1-58062-653-X
Printed in the United States of America.

J I H G F E D

Library of Congress Cataloging-in-Publication Data
Bolton, Lesley.
    The everything classical mythology book : Greek and Roman gods,
godesses, heroes and villians from Ares to Zeus / by Lesley Bolton
        p.   cm.
    Includes bibliographical references (p. 277) and index.
    ISBN 1-58062-653-X
    1. Mythology, Classical. I. Title.
BL723 .B65 2002
292.1'3—dc21   2001055214

This publication is designed to provide accurate and authoritative information with regard to the subject
matter covered. It is sold with the understanding that the publisher is not engaged in rendering legal,
accounting, or other professional advice. If legal advice or other expert assistance is required, the services of a competent professional person should be sought.
                —From a *Declaration of Principles* jointly adopted by a Committee of the
            American Bar Association and a Committee of Publishers and Associations

Illustrations by Barry Littmann.
Additional illustrations reprinted with permission from Dover Publications, Inc.

This book is available at quantity discounts for bulk purchases.
For information, call 1-800-872-5627.

Visit the entire Everything® series at everything.com

Contents

Introduction

What do you know about classical mythology? You know it's important. *Everyone* knows it's important. But why? How can stories created more than 2,000 years ago possibly influence your life? Just wait, you'll see.

If you haven't yet been formally introduced to classical mythology, now is the perfect time! Allusions to Greek and Roman mythology are everywhere today. Look around you—billboards, museums, and libraries are just a few of the places that have welcomed the ancient myths.

Perhaps you think your only encounter with classical mythology so far was that stressful six-week crash course in high school followed by the traumatic final exam that held the power to make or break your GPA. But this isn't true. You have had a direct connection with mythology your entire life, regardless of whether or not you studied it in school. For instance, did you know that many names for plants and animals were taken directly from Greek and Roman mythology? These words we use every day help create that invisible link.

There's no doubt about it; classical mythology surrounds us. Yes, it may be thousands of years old, but it is alive and thriving today. Though it is no longer considered a religion, mythology is useful in other forms. All mediums of Western art have incorporated the characters and scenes of classical mythology. Allusions are made by public speakers all the time. Movies, cartoons, and theater have all tried to capture the passion and drama of ancient myths.

As you read through these captivating myths, consider their characters and scenes and then take a look around. Your eyes will be opened to the many colorful analogies and inside jokes present in today's world that pay tribute to the beliefs of an ancient world. This foundation will help to heighten your appreciation of all forms of Western art, including literature, sculpture, and even advertising.

Of course, classical mythology also allows us a sneak peak into the everyday lives of the ancient Greeks and Romans. If you enjoy history, mythology is a fun and interesting way to learn about the culture, beliefs, and religious rituals of these peoples. Woven into the myths are clues as to how these people lived and what was important to them.

If you fancy science and origins, the myths are sure to intrigue you. You will find the meaning behind the names of planets, animals, constellations, and plants. Even today, we look to mythology to give names to our spacecraft such as Apollo, Mercury, and Zeus. The ancient Greeks and Romans used mythology to explain the mysteries of nature that weren't able to be explained using the technology of the day, providing an interesting look at how the ancients were able to answer those broad and fundamental questions that every society must answer.

Classical mythology can be a pretty intimidating subject. It *can* be, but it doesn't have to be. What you have to keep in mind is that regardless of all the intellectual hoopla associated with Greek and Roman mythology, what it all boils down to are just good old-fashioned stories. And who doesn't love a good story? Consider classical mythology to be one huge book with hundreds of chapters nestled between its covers. Each chapter can stand alone as its own intriguing story or be combined with others to create one of the most awe-inspiring, fantastic tales ever told.

CHAPTER 1
The Myth and Its Function

Before diving into stories of passion, tragedy, war, and heroism, you must first build a foundation on which to procure the most meaning from these stories. Though you may find these stories simply entertaining, and that's all you're looking for, the question of how these stories were created will surely enter your mind at some point. This chapter will answer that question so you can continue with your pleasurable reading with greater understanding.

What Is a Myth?

Myth, defined simply, is a fictitious story or half-truth, but it goes much deeper than that. Scholars of mythology have struggled to pinpoint an exact definition that encompasses all of the attributes contained within a myth. It's funny how such a small word holds the weight of defining and giving purpose to lofty ideas such as the meaning of life. It's no wonder an accurate definition has not been settled on!

Though this book concentrates on Greek and Roman mythology, these of course are not the only myths in existence. Many other cultures—including Japanese, Native American, Indian, Chinese, Norse, African, Celtic, and Egyptian—have their own myths. While the stories themselves may be wildly different, the characteristics are similar. Using these attributes, the myth can be outlined if not completely defined.

What Makes a Myth?

The myth has several characteristics that set it apart from the run-of-the-mill fictitious story. First, you have to keep in mind that these characteristics apply to the creation of the myth, and may not necessarily be viewed in the same way in today's world.

The origin of the myth is without one single author. The story evolves through the telling of it by many people. In other words, the mythology of a particular culture is created through the oral renderings of its people. Therefore, there is often more than one version of the same story.

ESSENTIALS

Much like modern religions, classical mythology tells of the relationship between mankind and a higher power. Myths often center around stories of direct interaction between man and the gods and goddesses. However, unlike most modern religions, the gods and goddesses are often driven by emotion more so than reason. Because of this, the interaction between man and deity isn't always pretty and is almost always dramatic.

A myth is a religious story. A higher power or entity is always involved in the plot. The gods, goddesses, or other supernatural beings are often worshipped or revered by humankind. Believed to be true, the myth is considered sacred to those within the culture of the mythology.

The myth will offer explanation for the unknown, such as the creation of the universe and Earth. It also attempts to answer those broad and fundamental questions we all ask ourselves, such as the meaning and purpose of our existence.

The myth is part of a larger mythology, which incorporates several myths all tied together by a similarity or common theme. In so doing, the mythology then becomes a socially accepted truth.

While the above characteristics are the essential elements of a myth, there are also a few other elements that are not necessarily recognized to be essential, but are nonetheless evident in the mythology of several cultures. For instance, nearly every myth will highlight activities that break the laws of nature people will change into inanimate objects, the dead rise and live again, and so forth. Also, myths often convey the different planes of existence and the interaction between them—heaven, hell, the future, and the past.

Legends and Folktales

Quite often the words myth, legend, and folktale are used interchangeably. Granted, all three connote some type of story and do share similarities, but from there they branch out with their own purposes. In order for a myth to be a myth, it must have all the essential characteristics you just read about. If it doesn't have all these attributes, it can be called a legend or folktale. But even so, there are still differentiating elements.

A legend is a story handed down through the generations, which has no hard evidence backing it up. Its roots are founded regarding a specific person, place, or historical event. Legends are grounded in their association with one particular thing. They are different from myths in that they do not incorporate all the essential elements of a myth. A myth can be a legend, but a legend is not necessarily a myth.

QUESTIONS?

So then what is a fable?
A fable is a fictitious story that often has a supernatural element to it. The differentiating feature of a fable is that it is intended to teach practical lessons, or morals. Though myths do sometimes teach lessons, this is only an added bonus; they aren't constructed with this purpose in mind.

Folktales are also a bit different. They are pure fiction and are not founded on a particular person, place, or event. Folktales use symbolism to convey concepts and meaning, therefore anything is possible—animals take on the actions of humans, for example. Like legends, folktales do not have the essential elements of myths and a myth can be a folktale, but a folktale is not necessarily a myth.

The Sacred Myth

The myth served several purposes for the ancient Greeks and Romans, one of the foremost being religion. As you know, one of the essential elements of a myth is a religious significance. In these cultures, the myth explained the religious beliefs as well as justifying religious rituals. This heavily influenced the behavior of the Greeks and Romans. Though the society of today no longer partakes in mythology as a religion, it is important and interesting to recognize that they once did.

Protect Yourself—Pray!

The Greeks and Romans were very religious peoples. The gods and goddess, even the lesser deities, all held powers the people believed to be supreme. The myths defined which god or goddess the people should turn to in times of need. For instance, those wanting safe voyage on the seas would pray to the Greek god Poseidon or the Roman god Neptune; those in need of a successful hunting endeavor would pray to the Greek goddess Artemis or the Roman goddess Diana; or before a battle, it was common to pray to the Greek god Ares or the Roman god Mars.

With so many deities to pay reverence to, one had to be careful to keep them all straight. You certainly wouldn't want a prayer meant for the god of justice to be directed toward the god of wine; the outcome could easily turn disastrous.

Appeasing the gods and goddesses isn't always as easy as a simple prayer. These deities often expected more than just prayer from mankind. In ancient times, if you wanted results, you often had to make a sacrifice or perform a religious rite along with your prayers.

The deities weren't always steady in their support of the human race and often were very moody and temperamental toward mankind. As part of a religion, the inconsistent behavior and temperament of the gods was accepted by the people, and they altered their own behavior accordingly. After all, these deities held the power of creation and destruction—it was best to be on their good side as often as possible.

Read Your Rites

Like any religion, the ancients had particular religious rites beyond prayer. The myths gave these rituals meaning or sometimes even spawned new rites. One ritual in particular that is explored in several myths is that of sacrifice.

The ritual of sacrifice was devised by Prometheus, a Titan god who was considered to be the champion of mankind. Prometheus was called in to settle a dispute between the gods and man—which portion of the sacrifice would be given to the gods and which kept for man? Prometheus carved up a sacrificial bull and divided it into two parts. The first part was the flesh wrapped in skin, with the stomach placed on top; the second was the bones covered in the animal's fat. He then offered the parts to Zeus (ruler of the gods) and told him to choose which portion he wanted. Zeus chose the fat covering the bones. Of course, upon discovering the bones, Zeus became very angry, but alas the decision had been made. The ritual of sacrifice would require man to burn the bones of an animal and keep the flesh for himself.

FACTS

The Olympic Games were founded in ancient Greece. However, unlike today, the games were then part of a huge religious festival that took place to honor Zeus. Athletes offered not only prayer, but also sacrifices to the gods and goddesses. A special sacrifice to Zeus of 100 oxen was an important part of the ritual.

Of course, there were rituals aside from sacrifice that are described by myths, some of which were even created because of myths. Furthermore, certain rituals were reserved for only one deity. For example, rites associated with the worship of Dionysus, the Greek god of wine, are unlike those of any other god. The rituals performed to honor Dionysus were kept secret so not much is recorded about them. However, from allusions made, a pretty clear picture can be carved. Let's just say there was a lot of drinking, dancing, and wild behavior taking place. Take heart, this party god will be discussed in greater detail later.

The religious rituals were an important part of not only the religion itself, but also of social order. Because the myths explained and justified these rituals and actions, the ancients relied heavily on myths to guide them along the correct path; they needed myths in order to appease the gods and to maintain an organized community.

Mystery Solved

An important function of the myth is to explain the unknown. It is human nature to pose questions and not simply accept things for the way they are. We always want to know "why." Many of the world's mysteries have been explained to us through science. However, clearly the ancients did not have the technological advancements available today with which we can experiment and prove theories. Instead, they relied on myths to give them the answers they sought.

The Questions

The ancients, just like us, hungered for knowledge. Most wanted explanations for what they considered to be phenomena they encountered in their daily lives. Others went beyond that and wanted reasons for the structure of the universe. Regardless of the importance or size of the question, a curiosity drove them to begin asking questions. And myths were formed to provide explanation for these otherwise unanswerable questions.

Some myths are solely dedicated to providing reason, such as the creation myth (which will be discussed in greater detail later). This myth answers big questions such as "How was the universe and earth created?" and "Where did man come from?" Another explanatory myth is that of the Underworld which answers the question, "What happens when we die?"

In ancient times, if you were a mighty hero or favored by the gods, you might end up in the Elysian Fields after death, a blessed place in the afterlife. A forever-happy land, the Elysian Fields were certainly where you wanted to end up.

Myths not only take on the challenge of tackling these colossal questions, but also venture to answer the more everyday wonderings. For instance, can you give a reason for the existence of the hyacinth? A Greek myth can. Apollo, god of archery, fell in love with a youth named Hyacinthus. Hyacinthus was accidentally killed when he and Apollo were practicing throwing a discus. Apollo was so heartbroken that he changed Hyacinthus' blood, which fell to the ground, into a new flower: the hyacinth. The flower returns every spring to honor the memory of the youth.

Some other subjects explored by the ancient myth include:

*   The origin of certain constellations
*   Why the sun disappears at night

- Why certain creatures behave the way they do (for instance, why the spider weaves a web)
- How the evils—sickness, death, grief—were released upon the world
- How fire came to man
- The changing of the seasons

The Answers

The Greeks and Romans answered these questions through myths. This explanatory element of the myth is quite important to its structure. Just like any other religion, classical mythology sought to provide definitive answers to these ever-looming questions. The stories tell their tale and that's that.

Because the ancients were not constrained by the truths of science and technology, they were free to develop stirring and sometimes outrageous tales to explain these phenomena. If you think about it, this was beneficial in many ways. The entertaining nature of the myths promoted their transmission and retention. In other words, the oral tradition of the ancients was able to thrive in part because of the interest these stories aroused. This helps to secure the longevity of the myth.

Establishing Order

Another important role of the myth, though not as direct as providing explanation or religious structure, is that of creating both natural and social order. As you will soon see, creation begins with Chaos, but from there the myth works to give a specific order to the universe. After order is created within the cosmos, the myth can then bring order down unto the lesser beings—humankind and its society. There's even order in the order of bringing order!

Natural Order

Most myths confirm that Zeus, ruler of the gods, was held responsible for creating order in the natural world. However, by the time he came to power, some sense of order already existed. The earth, heaven, seas, sky, and space were already set in their respective places. So, we shouldn't give Zeus *all* the credit.

FACTS

You will often see the ruler of the gods and men referred to as Zeus. This was the name used by the ancient Greeks. However, the Romans gave a different name to the same character—Jupiter. For a comparison of Greek and Roman names given to the gods, check out Chapter 21.

However, the affairs of the universe were in Zeus's domain; he presided over the natural world. He was believed to have placed the stars and planets in their individual places. But he didn't stop at the celestial beings. Zeus was also sometimes referred to as the weather god for he gave rain, snow, thunder, and lightning to the earth.

Zeus, though he held highest command, wasn't the only one involved with maintaining order in the natural world. The universe was divided up amongst the gods (the goddesses were left out of this bit), each having jurisdiction over a particular domain. For instance, Poseidon became god of the seas and Hades became god of the Underworld.

And there were more players in the ultimate order of things. For instance, Zeus conceived children who helped to establish this natural order. The three Horae were the goddesses of nature: Eunomia (Discipline), Dike (Justice), and Eirene (Peace). Zeus also sired the Moirai, who represented destiny. There were three Moirai: Atropos, Clotho, and Lachesis. These three sisters determined the length of an individual's life by first spinning a thread, then winding it, and finally cutting it.

All these key players, who held power over the maintenance of the natural world, were often helped by various lesser deities. Although not much credit is given to them, it is worth mentioning that there were river gods, nymphs, satyrs, sirens, and the various gods and goddesses of light, moon, darkness, dawn—all of whom played a role. But don't worry! They will be given their due, as an entire chapter is devoted to these lesser gods later in the book.

Social Order

Now that order has been created in the universe and the big picture is under control, it's necessary to make sure the lesser beings understand their roles and rules so as not to upset the order of the natural world. Just as we have laws today, the ancients had their own set of rules—established through the myths—that worked to maintain order in society by showing what was and what was not acceptable behavior.

Once again, the burden of creating order was laid upon the shoulders of Zeus. To reign over immortals and mortals alike was a huge responsibility. But Zeus took his duty very seriously and also came to be known as a god of justice. He created laws that were fair and sensible, and recognized and respected his responsibility of maintaining order and justice. Having a strain of diplomacy, he often used compromise to settle disputes and watched very closely that his laws were not broken. Specifically, he made sure oaths were not broken and the laws of hospitality were observed—by both the host and the guest alike. Because Zeus never really warmed to mankind, it was easy to lose his favor. Therefore, it was best to abide by his laws—the wrath of Zeus was the last thing you wanted.

If you are going to swear by the gods, it is best to know what you are doing. Oaths were often sworn to Helios, the sun god, because he was able to see everything that happened on earth (and he had no qualms about telling on you!). However, for the very serious oaths, swear to Styx. It was proclaimed that no one could ever break an oath to Styx, not even the gods. If you did so, you would essentially be placed in a coma for nine years.

Though Zeus set the laws and quite often carried out the harsh punishments for those who broke them, he wasn't the only deity concerned with maintaining order. All the gods and goddesses placed their own demands upon humankind, most of which were concerned with sacrificial rites and due respect. Crimes never went unpunished. The thought of dodging or escaping a deity was almost laughable. To put it simply, the ancients had a lot of rules to follow, but did so willingly so as to avoid the wrath of not just their fellow countrymen (as is common today), but that of the gods!

Emotion Overload

Now that we've covered the respected and obligatory function of myths, let's get to the heart of the matter. One thing that makes us human and makes us *feel* human is our range of emotions. Even the most stoic person feels emotion. We can't escape it. It is a natural, and sometimes disruptive, part of our lives. It just makes sense that the myths, designed to help the ancients understand themselves and their place in the world, would cover the wide range of emotions we experience.

The gods and goddesses were superior beings, wielding powers beyond our ability and sometimes comprehension. But even they, in all their glory, could not escape emotion. They suffered from emotion just as mankind did—at times on even more extreme levels, it seems.

Perhaps the deities were granted the privilege of feeling to help make the myths more accessible to the people—to help them relate on a personal level. Or maybe the myths' creators understood that to really make an impact, it's best to appeal to the emotions of people, therefore making the myth memorable and lasting. Regardless of the reasoning behind forcing the deities to bow to emotion at times, the myths certainly do not hold back when it comes to exploring the complications and power of emotion.

If you have ever felt an emotion so powerfully that it overwhelmed you, then you will relate to several experiences the myths describe. Immortals and mortals alike share the weakness of allowing an emotion to take control. The outcome isn't always pretty; at other times, it works out for the best. What's more, unlike some modern tales, you really can't guess the ending to most myths. So if your emotional stability is easily influenced by drama, be prepared to have your mood altered as you explore the stories of classical mythology.

Look out for the moodiness of the gods and goddesses! Combine emotional instability with the power of the heavens, and the outcome can be quite disastrous. You will see the effects emotions have on the deities as you read further into the ancient myths.

If you are expecting to learn a lesson about the destructive power of jealousy or the brighter side to sadness, think again. Though myths give accounts of emotion as part of human (and deity) nature, rarely do they offer lessons or teach morals. This isn't to say that you won't learn anything from reading these myths. On the contrary. Though lessons aren't spelled out for you as they are in fables, due to the epic nature of myths you will no doubt discover things on your own and on a personal level.

The Ideal

Because myths were created by a collective people, they evolved and changed in small ways, depending on whom was recounting the tale and whom the audience was. Therefore, the myth reflected not only the cultural views and ideas, but also those of individual people.

On that note, the myth served to paint the portrait of the ideal human behavior and being. This shows us what the people of a particular culture viewed as admirable, upright, and worthy of recognition and explains why some within that culture maintained a higher social standing than others.

Man's Shining Moment

Most often, the ideal human attributes shine brightly through the character of a hero. The hero plays an important role in classical mythology. Amidst all the grandiose stories of gods, goddesses, and lesser deities, a few humans find praise and admiration for their own feats. In a sense, man is elevated to the level worthy of the same esteem as the deities—perhaps even more so considering that man does not have the same power as the immortals. These chosen human heroes became models for good and appropriate behavior.

We will explore the individual heroes later in this book, but for right now, let's focus on their behavior. What made these men heroes while still in the shadows of the gods? What actions were worthy enough to repeat over and over again? Why were they singled out as exemplary?

Good Behavior Rewarded

Characteristics deemed ideal by the ancients weren't so different from those of today. Read through the following characteristics and see if you can identify any attributes evident in the heroes of today.

Obviously, when conjuring up the image of a hero, adventure comes to mind. Yes, in ancient times, the adventure story was one of the most popular. But a hero must display certain behaviors during his adventure to warrant admiration. For instance, the hero must be brave and not just brave as in "I killed that spider without a second thought!" but rather by displaying a fearlessness that can only be derived from confidence. The hero's ambition drives him to succeed when faced with a challenge.

FACTS

The definition of today's hero isn't quite as concrete as in ancient times. Even dictionaries vary on the definition. A hero can be anything from a distinguished warrior to the central figure in an event to a submarine sandwich.

Amidst all this confidence (sometimes amounting to outrageous egomania), the hero must have a loyalty to something that keeps him grounded. Even when faced with the most tempting of treacheries, the hero must stay true and loyal to his allies and/or creed.

Outside of the adventures and battles, the hero must be devoted to his family. With adultery running rampant in classical mythology, cheating on one's spouse is often overlooked as simply a force outside the control of the hero. However, for those few who did remain faithful to his or her spouse, the admiration granted them was astounding.

THE EVERYTHING CLASSICAL MYTHOLOGY BOOK

Let's not bypass the means by which the hero is successful in his quest. The hero will also often exhibit a mastery of a particular skill, sometimes several. Now, whether that skill is mastery of archery or the art of seduction doesn't matter. The point is: the hero exercises an undeniable skill.

Oh, but let's not forget about the admirable qualities of women revealed in the myths. Though not always as celebrated as the male heroes, several women throughout classical mythology are esteemed for their attributes. The most important is the virtue of loyalty to family—even to the point of staying faithful to a husband she thinks is dead. Other common characteristics of a good woman are her cleverness, wisdom, and hospitality.

All of the above traits, in both women and men, were deemed respectable and worthy of the highest esteem by the ancients. We are led to believe that these traits are what shaped social standing and manner of these people. The myth not only allows us to get a clearer picture of the times, but it helped to create a uniform ideal throughout the entire culture in ancient times.

The Right to Rule

Speaking of social standing, did you know that myths also beget kings and rulers? Roman mythology, in particular, accounted for the succession of several kings and emperors. Myths validated rulers' claims to have been descended from gods. What people wouldn't want a ruler with the power of the gods running through his veins? Or on the flip side of that, what people would dare challenge a ruler who held family ties with a deity?

If you ever doubted the power of the myth, withdraw that doubt now. Granted, it would seem ludicrous to the society of today if our president's campaign centered around his claim to be a descendant of Zeus. However, in the time of classical mythology, the myth was the authoritative standard and taken seriously to provide the functions we have discussed in this chapter.

Entertaining the Masses

Amidst all these serious and important functions of the myth lies the one function that has withstood the test of time, technology, and progression: entertainment. Yes, classical mythology is important and quite a serious study, but that doesn't mean it can't be fun as well! Had these stories been any less lively, do you really think they would have made it to the point of being recorded?

Then and Now

The ancients enjoyed entertainment just as much as we do—and the oral tradition was one of the foremost sources of entertainment. And their society—just like ours of today—was full of individualists, all with slightly differing views. Therefore, it is likely that not everyone accepted all myths to be literal truths, and therefore took them a little less seriously. Although there were varying degrees of doubt, the myths have endured and are now a part of our lives. The entertaining quality of myths no doubt helped to carry them into the present day.

FACTS

The ancient myths were often told to the people by bards, storytellers who were well versed in heroic tales. Bards often relayed these stories through song and poetry. Because they were under pressure to please the audience, stories were sometimes altered according to the audience's wishes, yet another reason why the same story will vary a bit from myth to myth.

It is obvious that for our purposes, mythology is a source of great entertainment and academic study. We do not accept the myths as literal truths and therefore do not study them to gather answers. Even so, that doesn't mean that we can't find our own truths within the tales, though less literally.

Better Than Any Soap Opera

Remember that these myths are, above all else, stories. And what stories they are! Much like Shakespearean plays, mythology presents all the faces of human experience, from love to tragedy to comedy. Let's take a look.

The adventure stories are probably the most favored. Here we have tales of heroic deeds, mortals going up against gods, rescues, and long journeys and quests. Several myths come to mind in this category: Heracles (*Heracles* is the Greek version, while *Hercules* is the Roman), Odysseus, and Perseus are just a few of the more popular heroes to get you started.

Tragedies, though sometimes upsetting, always have an addictive quality. The Greeks and Romans certainly weren't shy about throwing tragedy about. There are numerous myths for which you are best prepared with a box of tissue. For example, it is likely you will cry along with Demeter as she searches relentlessly for her kidnapped daughter.

Perhaps you prefer the shoot-'em-up-kill-'em-all form of entertainment. If this is the case, check out the battle scenes of classical mythology. If you are impressed by the wars of recent history, you will be amazed by what the ancients could do. And don't worry, there's plenty of blood-guts-and-gore to keep you occupied. The story of the Trojan War alone has more than enough violence to keep your attention.

Do you like monsters? Classical mythology can offer you a variety of monsters that you never dreamed might be lurking beneath your bed. But beware, once you know them, there's no forgetting them! From Typhon with its hundred serpentine heads to Minotaur who regularly fed on children, the monsters of classical mythology might very well keep you up at night.

Also included are tales of witchcraft and revenge, murder and mystery, crime and punishment, and don't forget the all-encompassing passionate love stories. As you will soon learn, love plays a major role in mythology, so if this is your interest, you're in luck! You have a litter of love stories to linger over, including both scandalous affairs such as that of Aphrodite and Ares, and true love stories such as the myth of Perseus and Andromeda.

With such a wide variety of tales to choose from, classical mythology is guaranteed to have a little bit of something for everyone!

CHAPTER 2

Sources of Classical Mythology

If classical mythology descended the generations through oral tradition, how on earth did it reach us? Fortunately, people had the foresight to copy these myths down in written form. This chapter will introduce you to those we have to thank for our knowledge of classical mythology.

Homer

You will never study classical mythology without hearing the name of Homer. Homer is regarded as not only the greatest poet of the ancient world, but also one of the greatest—and certainly one of the most influential—artists of the literary world. But did Homer truly exist? This question has been debated among scholars, historians, and the common man alike for centuries. What is not argued though is the prominence of the *Iliad* and the *Odyssey*, literary tombs attributed to Homer.

Homer as a Man

For the moment, let's just assume that the popular theory of Homer's existence is correct, and that he was in fact a man and the author of these two great epic poems. After all, the ancient Greeks and Romans believed in his existence.

Although the information regarding Homer's birth date and place aren't secure, historians believe he was born somewhere around 750 B.C. Homer was a bard, which means he traveled around telling stories and performing poetry for audiences. The Greeks believed him to be a blind man, presumably concluded from one of his poems in which he speaks of a blind bard.

FACTS

Seven cities claim to be the birthplace of Homer: Argos, Athens, Chios, Colophon, Rhodes, Salamis, and Smyrna. However, historians have not yet settled on an exact location.

Homer's epic poems are not the typical poems of today. The *Iliad* and the *Odyssey*, both approximately 12,000 lines each, might require several evenings to perform in their entirety . But if you think the ancients tired of such long encounters with poetry, think again. These two poems speak of the Trojan War (discussed in greater detail in Chapter 20), a defining moment in the lives of the Greeks and the catalyst for the foundation of Rome. Because the poems center on such a pivotal historic event, and because Homer is such a gifted storyteller, they became an integral part of the Greek culture. In fact, the Greeks were said to have introduced the study of these works into their schools around 400 B.C.

Homer as a Myth

With the extensive study of Homer's works, several theories are afloat regarding the idea that Homer wasn't the single author of all his works—some even question whether or not he really existed. Debates on the subject run rampant among scholars and historians, each of whom holds his or her own ideas as to the creator of these famous works.

One theory is that several people were involved in the composition of these poems and that the collection was later attributed to Homer. From here it branches out into different ideas. Some believe Homer composed the first part of the *Odyssey* and that someone else or several others concluded it. Others believe that there wasn't a man named Homer at all and that the word Homer referred to bards in general, thus encompassing all the different authors. Yet another theory is that Homer was the name of the scribe who took on the task of writing down all these works. By signing his name to them, he wound up with credit of authorship.

Why all the skepticism? Most likely because the works of Homer have come under such scrutiny. By comparing the poems to each other, especially the *Iliad* and the *Odyssey* (though the lesser poems were also taken into account), differences are obvious. Granted, they are two separate poems, but if the author were the same for both, wouldn't there be quite a few similarities?

The differences stand out between them. For instance, the use of vocabulary suffers from an extensive range. Dialects change within the same work. Adding to the mystery, an extreme difference in social settings and conditions is present, implying that the two works were composed during different time periods. However, nothing has yet been proven. But you can bet that scholars will not rest until the mystery is solved.

Though these differences lay a foundation for doubt and skepticism, we still attribute our knowledge of classical mythology to Homer—whether we are honoring a single man or a group of several different authors.

Hesiod

You can't talk about Homer without talking about Hesiod. Though it is suspected that Hesiod lived after Homer, around 700 B.C., the two figures go hand in hand when learning about classical mythology. Hesiod is often referred to as the Father of Greek Didactic Poetry. Whereas Homer is famous for his epic poetry, Hesiod holds the reins when it comes to ancient didactic poetry. The difference is that epic poetry is typically a narrative poem that recounts the tale of a hero or event, whereas a didactic poem is one that is meant to teach a moral lesson and to serve as entertainment at the same time. Before you learn about the works of Hesiod, it's good to have a little background information.

Bio Breakdown

While Hesiod is shrouded in mystery as well, we do know a bit more about his life than that of Homer. Most of what we know of him was taken directly from his works. The best guess is that he lived sometime around 700 B.C. in the village of Ascra in central Greece. According to his poems, he was a shepherd in his youth and grew to become a poor farmer when his father died. However, Hesiod wasn't your average, everyday peasant.

While tending his flock one day, Hesiod was visited by the Muses. They appeared to him in a mist and gave him a poet's staff and a poet's voice. They told him to use these gifts to spread the word about the immortal gods. Hesiod did as he was told. Honoring the Muses, he even went so far as to compete in contests using this skill! What came of his mystical visitation are the famous works *Theogony* and *Works and Days*, as well as some lesser-known poems.

QUESTIONS?

What are the Muses?
The Muses were the nine daughters of Zeus (ruler of the gods) and Mnemosyne (Memory). As the goddesses of music, poetry, literature, and art, the Muses were said to provide inspiration and enlightenment to artists.

There aren't any cold, hard facts relating to Hesiod's death. But, according to legend, Hesiod was murdered by the sons of a family he stayed with during his travels. However, no motive or blow-by-blow account is given about the murder. His bones were then taken to Orchomenus and a statue was built to honor him in the middle of the marketplace.

The Works

Like Homer, Hesiod had two famous poems—poems that descended the years and are still studied and enjoyed today. Also like Homer, debate surrounds Hesiod as the sole author of his works. Unlike Homer, most scholars agree that Hesiod was indeed a living, breathing individual, and that he authored *most* of *Theogony* and *Works and Days*. Only bits and pieces of these works are under question and are believed to have been added later by other poets.

Theogony

Theogony is the first of the two famous poems and was composed following the Muses' command. The poem centers around the history of the gods, beginning with creation, and provides us with a foundation on which to build the stories of the gods and goddesses. Without this account of creation and the succession of the deities, we might not have ever known the ancients' basis for mythology as a religion. A story can't be a story without a beginning, after all.

Works and Days

Works and Days is a bit different from *Theogony*. This poem reflects the didactic nature of Hesiod's work in that it teaches lessons and morals—it was for this particular quality that it was so highly valued by the people of ancient times. *Works and Days* is essentially a disagreement between Hesiod and his brother concerning the inheritance of their father's estate, but is filled with fables and myths as the two brothers debate the issue. Rich with description, this work also gives us an account of the rituals and superstitions of the Greeks.

Aeschylus

We are now going to skip ahead a few hundred years to cover some other important sources of classical mythology. Please keep in mind, however, that even though we are leaping ahead, there were several lyric poets who maintained the mythological subject matter during this time. However, these poets simply didn't have the impact that Hesiod and Homer did.

During the fifth century B.C., Greece experienced an inclination toward tragedy and theater. Three famed Greek tragedians rose to fame during this time period, the first of which was Aeschylus.

Life

Aeschylus was born into an aristocratic family near Athens, presumably in either 525 or 524 B.C. Unlike the two former authors we've discussed, we know several facts concerning the life of Aeschylus. Aeschylus was quite the busy man—fighting in battles, creating timeless plays, participating in the Great Dionysia. The Great Dionysia was part of a festival honoring Dionysus, the Greek god of wine. During the Great Dionysia, three dramatists would create and perform three tragedies and a satyr play. Aeschylus took part in this competition several times. His first competition was thought to have taken place around 499 B.C. with his first victory in 484 B.C. From then on, he was nearly untouchable (though he was bested once by his own protégé, Sophocles. Ouch!)

Aeschylus died in either 456 or 455 B.C. in Gela, Sicily. His cause of death is unknown, although a rumor thought to have been started by a comic writer claims that Aeschylus was killed when an eagle dropped a tortoise on his bald head. Regardless of how he died, Aeschylus was honored with a public funeral in which sacrifices and performances were carried out.

ESSENTIALS

If you are or wish to be a writer, you should become familiar with not only the works of Aeschylus, but also with his gravesite. Located in the town of Gela in Sicily, his grave has been known as a pilgrimage destination for both budding and experienced writers alike.

Works

So why all the fuss about Aeschylus? If you read his works, you'll know. Aeschylus is estimated to have written ninety plays during his lifetime, approximately eighty of which are known from the bits and pieces that managed to survive. However, only seven of these plays remain intact today, all of which are tragedies: *Persians, Seven Against Thebes, Suppliants, Agamemnon, Libation Bearers, Eumenides* (these three make up the famous trilogy *Oresteia*), and *Prometheus Bound*.

These tragedies all focus on the theme of justice. Aeschylus believed that the gods and goddesses often resented the rise of mankind to standards considered "great." Therefore, they often tricked man into devising his own downfall through the means of haughtiness or pride, which would then be considered a form of divine justice. Zeus, being the god of justice is quite often a central figure in helping to weave the theme.

Justice does not only prevail through the physical and emotional downfall of man, though. Aeschylus also relates a form of justice that does not directly affect the culprit himself. Rather, the innocent descendants of the unjust are punished, creating a guilt complex that stands out in many of his plays.

There is no doubt that the works of Aeschylus are important to our knowledge of classical mythology today. Although Aeschylus believed in the gods as a religious order, his works are not full of the bias and glorification often awarded to the deities. Instead, his plays work out themes with clarity and neutrality. And it is because of this that we are able to better reach an understanding.

Sophocles

The second great Greek tragedian is Sophocles. But don't let his order in succession fool you. He is considered to be the most successful of the three. Like Aeschylus, Sophocles lived during a time in which there were many wars being fought. The Persian Wars (546–479 B.C.) followed by the Peloponnesian War (431–404 B.C.) made wartime a constant in the life of this man. And the effects of these wars evidently influenced his work as an artist.

Life

Sophocles was born around 496 B.C. in a village outside the city of Athens. Born into a wealthy family (his father manufactured armor), Sophocles was sent to Athens to receive a good education. He studied military techniques, science, mathematics, philosophy, government, law, astronomy, and, of course, the arts. It is widely believed that as part of Sophocles' excellent education, he studied under Aeschylus. Small world, huh?

Sophocles was one of those people you wish you could hate. He excelled in nearly everything he did, was known to be quite handsome, and earned the respect of all who knew him. He held many public offices during his life and was also a patron of the arts. To say the least, he was a very popular man.

Sophocles also took part in the Great Dionysia, winning his first victory in 468 B.C. at the age of twenty-nine. He went on to win this competition eighteen (some say twenty-four) times throughout the course of his life, even beating out his tutor Aeschylus one year.

The seven plays of Sophocles survived because someone had the foresight to group these together and publish them as a set along with seven plays by Aeschylus and ten by Euripides. Since Sophocles' other plays weren't published in such a manner, they eventually faded from existence.

Sophocles' lifespan covered the Athenian Golden Age—a good time to be alive indeed. He certainly made the most of his life. He lived to the ripe old age of ninety, which simply didn't happen often during those times. There isn't much recorded concerning his death except an approximate year of 409 B.C., but we are probably safe in assuming that time finally got the best of him.

Works

Yes, Sophocles excelled in nearly everything, but what he is best known for is his artistic and philosophic skill. Sophocles produced an estimated 123 plays during his lifetime—no small feat. However, like the works of Aeschylus, sadly only seven survived intact: *Oedipus the King, Oedipus at Colonus, Antigone, Ajax, Trachinian Women, Philoctetes,* and *Electra.* Each one of these used mythology as its foundation.

Sophocles, as stated before, was greatly influenced by war and wartime deeds. This backdrop is directly reflected in the thematic schemes of his plays, as well as by some of the identities of his main characters. In the works of Sophocles, war goes hand in hand with negativity, pain, and suffering. But it is through this pain and suffering that humans are able to become more human. We learn to accept the natural order of things and strive to recognize reality.

Let's not forget the mythology part! It is because of Sophocles that Oedipus is now a widely known character of Greek mythology. He took this myth and expanded on it, creating three of his most famous tragedies. The gods are also used quite extensively in his works. The gods were the higher beings, and mankind was subject to their decisions. For instance, if the gods felt a man should be punished, he was indeed brought to justice. If the gods felt a man should be rewarded for his pain and suffering, then he was aptly rewarded. The gods also had a hand in making things even and fights fair.

Tragedy is the means by which Sophocles gets his message across. And because tragedy always seems to strike close to the heart, it normally makes a bigger and more memorable impact. Perhaps this is one of the reasons Sophocles' works are still so popular today.

Euripides

The third of the great Greek tragedians is Euripides. Though held in company with Aeschylus and Sophocles as far as playwright talent and notoriety go, Euripides was in a class of his own. He did not partake in famous battles, nor did he ever hold public office. He didn't even wholly and blindly believe in the religious beliefs of his fellow Greeks. No, Euripides was a philosopher and constantly questioned all that the Greeks held sacred. It was because of this that Euripides was not a very popular man and became quite controversial in his day. In fact, he was openly disliked and criticized during his lifetime.

Life

Euripides was born around 480 B.C. on the island Salamis. No one really knows for sure from what type of background he came, though it can be assumed that his family was pretty well-off, for Euripides was obviously well educated. It is likely that he studied the same topics as did Sophocles, but Euripides found a particular passion for philosophy. Being a philosopher, Euripides began asking questions and was outwardly skeptical of all that the Greeks held to be true.

He began writing plays around the age of eighteen. He had a talent that far surpassed the criticism and alienation he received from his fellow countrymen. He, too, competed in the Great Dionysia, beginning in 455 B.C. He is said to have competed twenty-two times, but won only four times, once posthumously. He attributed his "failures" to the bias of the judges.

Euripides eventually separated himself from the Athenians and their city. He died in Macedonia around 406 B.C. at the age of seventy-seven.

Works

It is estimated that Euripides wrote ninety-two plays in all, but unfortunately only seventeen tragedies survived—still, more than what remains of Aeschylus and Sophocles combined. These plays also use mythology as a foundation. The seventeen include: *Andromache, Hecuba, Iphigenia at Aulis, Bacchants, Alcestis, Medea, Children of Heracles, Hippolytus, Suppliants, Electra, Madness of Heracles, Ion, Trojan Women, Iphigenia Among the Taurians, Phoenician Women, Helen,* and *Orestes.*

Being a philosopher, Euripides was a big fan of realism and his plays reflect this. The works introduce characters—main characters—who are common, everyday people. Even the deities are more on the common level and often equal man in their level of importance. He also brings women to the forefront, making them the main characters and worthy of as much recognition as the traditional war hero. Euripides blatantly uses his works to portray his own thoughts and ideas with very little regard for the traditional acceptability of dramatic content.

FACTS

Even though the main characters in Euripides' plays are common people, his views of these people in general were rather pessimistic. He felt that the people blindly accepted the answers religion offered without seeking answers for themselves and through science.

We know that tragedy is meant to use emotion as a tool. Euripides recognizes this, but takes it a step further. Yes, we can feel sympathy, sorrow, and compassion toward the characters in these plays, but Euripides often uses innocent children as the suffering victims in his plays to augment these feelings. Can you think of a better way to gain an audience's empathy?

Virgil

The Greeks weren't the only ones to have great poets of mythology within their culture. We are now going to skip ahead to the Augustan Age of Rome to take a look at two poets who are often compared to Homer and Hesiod—Virgil and Ovid. These two Roman poets are held in the highest esteem for bringing immortality to Roman mythology. As before, there is a succession we must follow. Therefore, we will start off with Rome's greatest poet, Virgil.

Life

Virgil was born on October 15, 70 B.C., as Publius Vergilius Maro in the village of Andes. He was born to a farmer who sent his son to Cremona, Milan, and Rome for an education. Virgil studied both Greek and Roman literature and poetry, as well as the other natural studies of the day. Completely devoted to his studies, Virgil had no interest in taking part in a military or political lifestyle. World affairs didn't concern him, and he was all but a recluse during the first half of his life, and a sickly one at that.

Though he wasn't much interested in the world outside his studies, eventually his rising fame as a poet sucked him into the glories of Rome, and he formed some very significant friendships with influential people. However, even with all the splendor of Rome, he never abandoned his love of the countryside and this love is evident in all his poetry.

Virgil died of a fever on September 21, 19 B.C., on his way to Greece before his final revision of the *Aeneid* was completed. He is buried in Naples and, like Gela, this too became a destination for religious pilgrimages.

Works

Virgil is best recognized for his epic poem the *Aeneid*. If you have ever studied Latin, you are most likely familiar with this work. This poem follows the course and actions of the hero Aeneas after the fall of Troy, his settling in a new land, and the founding of a new race. It introduces all the great characters of ancient Roman mythology, mortal and immortal alike, including Dido, Romulus, Jupiter, and Venus, just to name a few. The Aeneid is a timeless classic that has served as inspiration for many past and present authors over the course of hundreds of years.

The *Aeneid* is a must-read for anyone even remotely interested in the classics or mythology. Due to great demand, annual printings of at least one version of the *Aeneid* has been conducted for the past 500 years. Surely the masses can't be wrong!

Although the *Aeneid* is Virgil's most famous work, we mustn't let his other works fall by the wayside. His earliest work is a collection of ten pastoral poems entitled *Eclogues*. Some of these poems speak of the ideal but unrealistic life, others move forward to bring these ideas into the real world, and some even mourn the eviction of farmers from their farms.

Yet another poem, *Georgics,* reflects Virgil's love of the Italian countryside (and may have served as political propaganda). In this work,

Virgil begs for the farmers to come back to their land and restore the agricultural lifestyle.

Virgil was essentially Rome's national poet. Needless to say, he and his works are very important to the study of Roman culture. It is because his work has so successfully transgressed the times that we know so much about Roman mythology today.

Ovid

Rome's other great poet, Ovid, is renowned for his fantastic storytelling abilities. Ovid was a hit with not only the ancients, but also with readers of today. It is said that Ovid is read more than any other ancient poet, even his predecessor Virgil. His works have influenced and inspired famous writers of both Roman and English literature. And most importantly, he provided us with several of the very best sources of classical mythology.

Life

Ovid was born on March 20, 43 B.C., as Publius Ovidius Naso. He was born in the small, country town of Sulmo, which is about 90 miles east of Rome. He came from a fairly affluent and respectable family and his father sent him and his older brother to Rome for their education.

SSENTIALS

To take a closer look at the life of Ovid, read his poem *Tristia*. This autobiographical work describes the main events that took place in Ovid's life in his own words. Hint: *Tristia* means sorrow.

Ovid became a member of the Roman knightly class and used this position to travel around before officially taking on any duties. However, once he did settle down and take up some of the duties necessary for his career in public life, he found he didn't have the stomach for it. Instead he abandoned his post, settled in Rome, and took up with a society of poets. Obviously, he made the right decision, for once he began producing, he immediately became a great success. Just like that. Don't we all wish it were that easy!

Ovid enjoyed immense popularity during his lifetime and his popularity is still going strong today. However, his life wasn't entirely full of glory. In A.D. 8 he was exiled to Tomis on the Black Sea. The reasons behind his banishment are still a mystery, but rumor states that it involved an adulterous affair with the emperor's granddaughter. He died in A.D. 17, still begging to be allowed to return to Rome.

Works

Ovid wrote several works, though by far the most popular is the narrative poem *Metamorphoses*, which is often called "the major treasury of classical mythology." Consisting of approximately 12,000 lines, this poem is a collection of Roman mythological stories. It covers everything from the creation theory to the death of Julius Caesar. Needless to say, this work is an amazing masterpiece, chock full of pretty much all you want to know about Roman mythology.

Now, you'd think that a project that size would take one an entire lifetime to complete, but no, Ovid had time for several other compositions as well. The *Amores*, a series of poems describing a love affair, were his first published poems. Keeping with these passionate lines is *Heroides,* which is a series of imaginary love letters written by mythological characters to their lovers. And of course we can't forget *Fasti,* which describes the various religious festivals upheld by the Romans on a month-to-month basis. Unfortunately, only the first six books—the first six months—have survived.

Last but Certainly Not Least

There is no question that all of the aforementioned writers greatly contributed to our knowledge of classical mythology. Though these names often take the spotlight in mythology, several others have also played a role in bringing mythology to the modern world. These people should not be forgotten and deserve honorable recognition.

Don't forget the artists! Though the most noted contributors are those who wrote and recorded works of literature about classical mythology, there are also the numerous sculptures, painters, and other artists who certainly made their mark in ancient Greece and Rome by depicting characters and scenes taken directly from classical mythology.

Greek Contributors

The following people are often shadowed by comparison with the great Greek poets and dramatists. But nonetheless, had it not been for these people, we might not have the extensive knowledge of Greek mythology that we have today.

- **Apollodorus:** A Greek mythologist and historian. His work *The Library* serves as a guide to classical mythology covering everything you would want to know about the history of the gods.
- **Apollonius Rhodius:** A Greek epic poet who lived in the second century B.C. He is best known for his poem *Argonautica*, which tells the story of Jason and his quest for the Golden Fleece.
- **Herodotus:** Better known as the "Father of History," Herodotus was a Greek historian living during the fifth century B.C. His work *History* is comprised of nine books named after the Muses and is a narration of the Persian Wars.
- **Musaeus:** A Greek poet who lived during the fifth century A.D. He is best known for his poem about the myth of Hero and Leander.
- **Pausanias:** A Greek writer and traveler who lived in the second century A.D. His work *Description of Greece* is exactly that—a description of Greece including mythology, religious rites, art, and history.
- **Pindar:** A Greek poet who lived in the fifth century A.D. He is often called "the greatest of the Greek lyric poets." His collection of lyric odes celebrates the winners of the Olympic, Pythian, Nemean, and Isthmian Games.

- **Plutarch:** A Greek biographer and essayist who lived during the first and second century A.D. He wrote biographies of both mythological and historical Greeks and Romans.
- **Stesichorus:** A Greek lyric poet who lived during the sixth century B.C. His works consist of the story of Thebes and Troy.

Roman Contributors

Though much of Roman mythology was taken from the Greeks—just a few names changed here and there—they did have their own mythology as well. The following people helped to make that mythology known to us today.

- **Horace:** A Roman lyric poet whose works *Odes* and *Epodes* offer information about both Greek and Roman mythology.
- **Livy:** A Roman historian whose work *History of Rome* tells of not only the history of Rome, but also of the legends of Rome as well.
- **Propertius:** A Roman poet whose works consist of elegies and mythological poetry.
- **Seneca:** A Roman tragedian whose plays focus on Greek mythological characters.
- **Statius:** A Roman epic poet who is best known for his work *Thebaid*, which relays the story of Oedipus trying to gain control of Thebes.

CHAPTER 3

Creation:
A Chaotic Theory

I t's time to move forward and get straight to the heart of the matter—the myths themselves. No doubt about it, this is the fun part. And what better place to start than at the beginning? This chapter will tell you the story of how it all started, relaying the similarities and differences in the various myths.

In the Beginning There Was Chaos

Today, we have several theories about the creation of the universe, religiously based theories as well as scientifically based ones. You can study these theories and pick and choose which you feel most comfortable with, but the ancients didn't have such an option. No, they were steadfast in their belief that the universe and all that was known to them sprang from one source—chaos.

You may think that nothing pretty could come from chaos, but if you think about it, it makes sense. In order to recognize order, you have to have disorder to counteract it. And creation is simply a process of bringing order and placement to the objects of the universe.

To explore the creation theories of classical mythology thoroughly, you must familiarize yourself with Hesiod's *Theogony* and Ovid's *Metamorphoses*. These two works serve as our main sources of creation as viewed by the ancients.

Chaos as a Being

Before there was the earth or sky or seas, all the elements of the universe were one, and this oneness was called Chaos. Chaos was a shapeless void of confusion, but held the seeds of the universe, so to speak. Contained within Chaos were the elements—earth, sky, sea— all jumbled together, yet no one element had its own identity. The earth didn't have its shape, the sky didn't have air, and the sea was not watery.

The elements constantly fought with each other until an unknown force put an end to the disorder. This force is not truly identified in the myths—some consider it to be nature, others speak of it as a divine being or a god. Some myths even leave out this force entirely, simply stating that the elements sprang from Chaos on their own. Regardless, the elements were separated—heaven from earth, sea from sky, heat from cold, and so on. This separation brought the order needed to create a universe. Thus we have creation.

Outlining the Elements

These elements still needed shape and definition. According to one popular myth, an unnamed force (we'll call it the Creator) first laid shape to the earth. The Creator designated water to its appropriate places: marshes, rivers, oceans, brooks, lakes, and seas were settled. He then raised the mountains, smoothed out the plains, and shoveled out the valleys, distributing forests, rocky terrain, and fertile fields.

Next came the sky. The Creator spread out air like a blank canvas on which to paint his masterpiece. He added clouds, thunder, lightning, and winds. The stars, however, he did not place. He simply drew them out from the confines of darkness.

Having the sky and earth initially set up, the Creator went back to add a few more things. This is when the fish came to the seas, the birds to the air, and beasts to land. Ah, but not all beasts. Man was not yet created. But we will get to that in a moment. First, we need to give names and personalities to all of the above elements.

Giving Personality to Nature

Because the ancients believed that anything moving and changing must be alive, the elements of the universe were thought to be living and therefore must have names and personalities. The previous explanation of creation is one of the more popular and basic myths, but another version exists in which the elements not only sprang from Chaos but were born into existence.

Back to the Beginning

Again, we have Chaos. But from there, things change a bit. This myth does not name a Creator; instead the first elements simply sprang into being. No explanation is given, and obviously none is needed, for this myth was quite popular with the ancients. It is also one of the foremost historical theories on creation, having been taken from Hesiod's *Theogony*.

From Chaos came the five elements: Gaia (Earth), Tartarus (the Underworld), Nyx (Night), Erebus (Darkness), and Eros (Love). Gaia gave birth to three children without the traditional mating with another being. These were Uranus (Sky), Pontus (Sea), and the Mountains. Now we have the earth and sky set up as a stage, but there is still more to come. From here on out, nearly all else is born as a result of good ol'-fashioned lovemaking.

ALERT

Don't forget to pay homage to Eros, the god of love, for his role in creation! Though Gaia is often the one most credited with giving life to the universe (which she did by giving birth to the elements), Eros served as the catalyst in that he urged the movement forward by prompting the elements to mate.

The Unions

Uranus, said to have been born to Gaia in her sleep, mates with his mother (yes, incest seems to run rampant throughout classical mythology) to create the rest of the earth's elements such as the waters, forestry, and the beasts. Uranus and Gaia also produced other children, including the Titans and Titanesses, the Cyclops, and the Hundred-Armed giants, but we will discuss these characters in greater detail in the next chapter.

FACTS

The Moirai, or Fates, were three sisters responsible for the lives of mortals. One sister would spin the thread of life, the next would measure its length, and the third would cut the thread to bring about death. Some myths say that even Zeus, the ruler of the gods, was subject to the Moirai.

Nyx mated with Erebus to produce Hemera (Day) and Aether (Air). Nyx also bore several other children, though the paternity test results still haven't come in. These are Thanatos (Death), Hypnos (Sleep), Moros (Doom), Nemesis (Retribution), Oizys (Pain), Momus (Sarcasm), Eris (Strife), the Keres (the female spirits of death), Geras (Old Age), Oneiroi (Dreams), and the Moirai (Fates). Obviously, she was quite busy.

Of course, the unions did not end there. Many more are yet to come. However, this helps to define the elements of the universe a little bit further. Think of it as adding a little more detail with each birth.

And Then There Was Man

With all the hard work put into it, you'd think the universe was complete. But no, a more magnificent animal was needed, one that would be superior to the other mortals—man. The ancient myths vary on exactly how man was created. Let's take a look at two of the most popular theories.

A myth that is popular, not only with the Greeks and Romans but also with other cultures, is that man simply sprang up from the earth. Remember the seeds of the universe buried in Chaos? Well, think of it that way. The seeds of man were buried in the earth. Without any further explanation, these seeds simply produced man, and they were considered the children of Gaia.

Another theory is that Prometheus was the creator of man. Prometheus was a Titan (the Titans will be discussed in the next chapter) and one of Gaia's many grandchildren. Prometheus and his brother Epimetheus were given the task of not only creating man, but also of giving the other beasts of earth protection. Epimetheus took it upon himself to present the beasts with gifts of preservation and Prometheus was to supervise his work. Therefore, Epimetheus is credited with giving the turtles their shells, the leopards their spots, and the bears their claws.

When it came time to create man, Prometheus performed this task himself, using earth and clay as his materials. He kneaded this with water and fashioned the form of man, which was molded in the likeness of the gods. But the first man was not what we know as the man of today. The mortal man went through several stages before reaching the final desired effect.

The Gift of Fire

Epimetheus did such a good job of distributing gifts that by the time he was finished with his task, all the gifts of protection were accounted for. But wait, man was left out of the loop.

Prometheus was considered the champion of mankind not only because he gave fire to man, but also because he contributed to the survival of mankind in several ways. For instance, he taught man how to plant seeds and harvest crops, how to domesticate animals such as the horse, and how to use herbs and other plant life for poultices and medicinal uses.

Prometheus decided that man also needed a gift of protection, one that went beyond all the others—and that gift was fire. But Zeus, ruler of the gods, was quite angry with mankind and refused to give them this fire. Prometheus was adamant though and resolved to steal fire from the heavens. According to one account, he stole fire from the forge of Hephaestus, the smith of the gods. Another account states that he stole the fire from the wheels of Helios's (the sun) chariot and concealed it in the stalk of a fennel plant. Regardless of how it happened, the quest was successful. Prometheus bestowed the gift of fire unto mankind.

When Zeus looked down upon the earth at night and saw it shining with firelight, his anger shook the heavens. He sent for his servants and ordered them to arrest Prometheus. The punishment of Prometheus was rather severe. Zeus ordered that Prometheus be bound by steel chains to a rock far from mankind. Zeus then sent an eagle to feed on his liver every day. The liver would regenerate every night. Vowing to never release Prometheus, Zeus left him to endure this torturous punishment.

Welcoming the Woman

To counteract the strength that mankind gained from the gift of fire, Zeus devised a scheme to give them a weakness just as powerful as this strength. Enter the woman. Until this time, mortal women did not exist.

Zeus ordered Hephaestus to create a woman of clay and water. What resulted was the greatest sculpture ever fashioned. Just as man was molded in the image of the gods, woman was molded in the image of the goddesses. As if this weren't enough, every deity contributed to this creation. She was given beauty along with lust, splendid clothes, lustrous jewelry, the gift of music, grace, dexterity, and charm. All these make for one hell of a woman, but that wasn't all she was given. She was also given the art of lies, seduction, deceit, and guile. These contributions simply made her a dangerous temptation that man was sure to fall for. Her name was Pandora.

Pandora's Box

As his gift to mankind, Zeus ordered Hermes, the messenger of the gods, to deliver Pandora to Epimetheus. Awestruck by her beauty and charm, Epimetheus accepted Pandora as his bride, though his brother Prometheus had warned him to not accept gifts from Zeus.

The ancient myths vary a bit concerning the story of Pandora's box. One myth says that Pandora was given a sealed jar by the gods to give as a gift to man. She had not been told what it carried, and she wasn't on earth very long before her curiosity got the better of her. She opened the jar and out flew the plagues of mankind. These included such afflictions as disease, pain, sorrow, insanity, envy, and death. Hastily replacing the lid, Pandora trapped the one member left behind—hope.

Another myth states that the box containing all the evils of the world was kept in a jar or box in the house of Epimetheus. Whether it belonged to Epimetheus or Prometheus is not known. Pandora, overcome by her feminine curiosity, stole to the room and removed the lid. Again, out poured all the ills of mankind, leaving behind hope, which did not escape.

The myth of Pandora's box is well known to even those who haven't the faintest idea who Pandora was. Pandora's box is often used today as an expression to describe danger, confusion, or trouble. If you ever come across something described as Pandora's box, it is best to suppress your curiosity and simply leave it be. You certainly don't want to be responsible for bringing pain to the world as Pandora did!

Yet other myths say the box or jar did not contain evils at all. Instead it contained only goodness and blessings, and was meant to be a wedding present from Zeus. Again, Pandora's curiosity overcame her and she opened the box carelessly. All the blessings escaped and returned to the heavens, save one—hope. Therefore, mankind was sentenced to endure all the hardships and evils of the world with only hope as a consolation.

Regardless of which myth you choose to favor, Pandora ultimately becomes the cause of weakness among men. In the end, Zeus's plan worked and he got his revenge.

Other Deities Affecting the Universe

You may have noticed that certain elements of the universe aren't accounted for. For example, we have the day, but no sun; we have the night, but no moon. These deities do in fact exist although they weren't part of the original offspring during creation; they came a bit later and were born of the Titans. Though we will discuss the Titans in the next chapter, it's best to take a look at the deities now as they certainly affect the way the universe was made whole.

The Sun

The god of the sun was Helios. He wasn't considered to be one of the great gods, but rather one of the "lesser" ones. Regardless, he was held in great esteem by the other deities and his purpose was no small matter.

Helios was responsible for giving light to the earth during the day. He accomplished this by driving his chariot of fire, pulled by four flaming steeds, east to west across the sky during the day. Nightfall comes as Helios crosses over the western horizon and lasts as long as it takes him to return to the east. It is said in later myths that Helios made his way back to the east in a huge golden cup that floated along the river Oceanus, which encircled the world.

Helios, though admired, was also feared. No one, mortal or immortal, could escape his eye during the day. He looked down upon the world and saw everything as he passed over. And to make matters worse, he was a bit of a gossip. So all that he saw, he rarely kept to himself. If you were raised with an overprotective father, just be glad you weren't born of Helios!

The Dawn

The dawn was the sun's sister and she was called Eos. It was her duty to rise every morning from her golden throne to open the gates of heaven and to announce the coming of the sun. But her day didn't end there. She accompanied Helios in his journey across the sky during the day. Some myths say she rode alongside him in his chariot of fire; others state she rode in her own chariot in front of Helios, announcing his arrival all day long.

Eos was also well known for her amour addiction. It would take hours to reveal the tales of all her lovers, but do know that of these lovers, she bore some rather well-known children. Eos was the mother of the Winds: Boreas (North), Notus (South), and Zephyrus (West). She also bore Eosphorus (the Morning Star), as well as all the other stars in the heavens.

FACTS

There are certainly many others who represent the elements of the universe, though they aren't as prominent in the myths. For instance, there were 3,000 river gods and 3,000 ocean goddesses, not to mention the various demi-deities of the forests and mountains, which will be explored further in Chapter 17.

The Moon

And of course, we can't forget the other sister of Helios—Selene, the moon. She also drove a chariot across the sky, though hers was made of silver and driven by two horses. She was responsible for providing the light of the moon to shine through the night.

Not much is known about Selene. The myths state that she was quite a beautiful girl and was rather well known for her own love affairs, though she may not have been quite as *eager*, shall we say, as her sister. It was said that Pan, god of shepherds and flocks, tried to seduce her with either a beautiful fleece or a herd of white oxen—the myths vary.

She was also involved with Zeus at one point and bore him a daughter named Pandia.

However, her most famous love affair took place with Endymion, king of Elis. Legend has it she looked down upon his sleeping body and fell instantly in love with him. She came down from the heavens and made love to him in his dreams. Some even say she bore him fifty daughters. At Selene's request, Zeus offered to grant Endymion one wish. He wished for eternal youth—and some say eternal sleep so as to keep reliving his amorous dreams—and was granted immortal sleep.

Giving Definition to Life

A fundamental question that nearly everyone has asked him or herself at least once is that of "Where did we come from?" The answer to this question would help us to understand why we are what we are and why we are where we are. It is because of this need to understand that creation stories are so important. Not only do they provide a simple—though not always straightforward—explanation, but they also provide us with definition of life.

Every religion has a creation story. Because we don't practice classical mythology as a religion today, the chaos theory is mainly just for fun. But you should recognize that this myth does have some similarities to the creation stories of other religions. For instance, as you were reading the story of Pandora, did the Biblical Eve ever cross your mind?

CHAPTER 4

The Children of Mother Earth

As you learned in the last chapter, Gaia (Mother Earth) was part of the original offspring during creation. She had a huge responsibility to the universe, being the earth and all, but above all else, she was a mother. This chapter is dedicated to the children of Mother Earth and their respective roles in classical mythology.

Children by Pontus

As you recall, Gaia gave birth to three children without the aid of a man. One of these was Pontus, the Sea. Gaia, although quite busy creating elements for the universe, took time out to then mate with Pontus. This union produced five children: Ceto, Eurybia, Nereus, Phorcys, and Thaumas.

ESSENTIALS

Pontus was recorded in mythology as the personification of the sea. Although you would think this character would show up time and time again throughout the myths, he doesn't. It seems as though his shining moment was the union with Gaia, after which he fades into the background.

Ceto

Ceto was considered to be the deity of large marine beasts. The Greeks use her name informally to refer to sea monsters. Ceto married her brother, Phorcys. Together they produced several children.

- **The Graeae:** These three daughters were born as old women, never able to enjoy the freshness of youth. Their names were Dino, Enyo, and Phephredo. The sisters were always portrayed together in the myths, and they weren't the prettiest of sights. Between them they had only one eye and one tooth, which they shared in turns. They lived in darkness away from the sunlight (some myths say they lived in a deep cave).
- **The Gorgons:** These three daughters were even less to look at than their sisters. They were monsters with snakes for hair, tusks, bronze claws, wings, and a stare that could turn men to stone. Both mortals and immortals feared these creatures. Only two of the Gorgons were immortal—Euryale and Stheno. The third and most recognizable to us, Medusa, was mortal. (Medusa will be featured in the myth of Perseus in Chapter 19.)
- **The Hesperides:** These daughters were nymphs. Their number varies from myth to myth (as do their parents), but most often they were

known as three: Aegle, Erythia, and Hesperarethusa. The Hesperides were quite a bit better looking than their sisters and they each had the gift of song. They lived in the Garden of the Hesperides and protected a tree with golden apples that grew there.

- **Ladon:** This son was a hundred-headed dragon. He lived with his sisters in the Garden of the Hesperides and was the prime guardian of the golden apples. After he is killed, he is turned into a great constellation of stars.

- **Echidna:** Yet another monster of a daughter, Echidna had the body of a beautiful woman and instead of legs, a serpent's tail. She is best known in classical mythology for giving birth to several monstrous offspring. She also is said to have laid in wait for people passing through her territory. She would then attack and devour them.

Eurybia

Eurybia isn't quite as popular as her sister Ceto. Most myths involving Eurybia simply mention her as the wife of Crius (a Titan) and mother of three Titan sons: Astraeus, Pallas, and Perses. Astraeus would later father the winds and the stars; Pallas would become the father of Victory, Valor, and Strength; Perses would later father Hecate, a triple goddess you will get to know better in Chapter 17.

Nereus

Nereus was a marine deity and was sometimes known as the "Old Man of the Sea." Though Poseidon is most often thought of first as the god of the sea, Nereus had this title well before Poseidon was even born. He had the ability to shapeshift—to take on various forms in different places—and also had the gift of prophecy. He is best known for fathering the Nereids (sea goddesses).

Phorcys

Like his brother, Phorcys was also a sea deity. However, he isn't often regarded for this attribute, but rather is best known for his offspring. As you know, Phorcys fathered several children by Ceto. However, some myths also claim that he was the father of the Sirens, which were sea deities: half woman, half bird. He is also rumored to be the father of Scylla, the famous sea monster.

The Sirens were great musicians with very beautiful voices. But beware—their songs were quite dangerous. They used their intoxicating songs to lure sailors close to the rocky coast, causing their ships to wreck. The Sirens would then attack and devour the poor, unsuspecting sailors.

Thaumas

Thaumas, also a sea deity, does not have a myth all to himself. He simply stood on the sidelines and was known only for his siring ability. He married Electra (an ocean deity) and fathered Iris and the Harpies. Iris was the personification of the rainbow as well as a messenger of the Olympian gods and goddesses. The Harpies were birdlike women who carried off the souls of the dead. They were also said to be responsible for anything that had gone missing, including children.

Need a Hand?

The most famous of Gaia's unions was with her other son, Uranus (Sky). The first children born of Gaia and Uranus were the Hecatoncheires. Hecatoncheires means "hundred handed" and that they were. These creatures are referred to as giants, though they differ from the giants we will encounter in later myths. There were three Hecatoncheires, each having one hundred arms and fifty heads. Perhaps "giant" isn't such a bad name for them.

These three were named Cottus, Briareus (or Aegaeon), and Gyges (or Gyes). The myths don't really distinguish between these three, except one myth that claims that Briareus later becomes Zeus's bodyguard.

Needless to say, the Hecatoncheires had incredible strength. They were able to throw boulders at such a speed and so many at a time as to make mountains crumble. Because of their outrageous strength, most feared these creatures upon sight—even their very own father, Uranus, ruler of the universe. And because Uranus was so intimidated by his sons, he had them imprisoned in Tartarus (the Underworld), where we will visit them later on. First, let's move on to the next set of children.

One-Eyed Wonders

Gaia then gave birth to three Cyclopes, sired by Uranus. The Cyclopes were not small creatures themselves. Giant in build, they possessed great strength and dexterity. However, each had only one eye, centered in the forehead. Even with their limited vision, they were still quite intimidating.

Traditionally, Cyclopes were feared as shepherd monsters said to eat men, and that is true in later myths. But these first Cyclopes were not like that. Instead they were known as the first smiths.

FACTS

Historians and mythographers have categorized the Cyclopes into three separate groups: the Uranian Cyclopes, the Sicilian Cyclopes, and the Gasterocheires Cyclopes. The Cyclopes discussed in this chapter belong to the first race, the Uranian Cyclopes. They are not to be confused with the savage Sicilian Cyclopes who were known to eat men and each other.

Unlike the Hecatoncheires, the three Cyclopes were distinguished from one another. Brontes became known as Thunder or Thunderer. Arges became known as the Shiner or Thunderbolt. And Steropes (or sometimes Asteropes) became known as Lightning or the Maker of Lightning. You get the idea. Just consider them storm deities.

Recognizing—and sometimes flaunting—their power and strength, the Cyclopes had a bit of a problem with authority. But Uranus took matters into his own hands and threw them into Tartarus to join their brothers. What it comes down to is, it seems that Uranus was afraid of his own offspring. Kind of cowardly for the supposed ruler of the universe, don't you think? We'll leave them there for a while to cool off and move on to the next group of children.

The Imperials

The most famous of Gaia's children were born next—the Titans and Titanesses. Twelve in total, Gaia gave birth to six sons and six daughters. These children, being the youngest, naturally were spoiled and given their own individual identities in myths, much more so than their brothers in Tartarus.

FACTS

Although we have encountered several deities so far, they weren't actually considered to be "gods" and "goddesses." They all held power but as the personification of an element or division of the universe. It is the Titans and Titanesses that would become known as the first line of gods and goddesses.

Let's first introduce the Titans:

- **Coeus:** Not much is known about Coeus except that he becomes the father of Leto, who becomes the mother of Apollo and Artemis.
- **Crius:** Again, he seems to be left out of most myths, but he does become the father of Astraeus, Pallas, and Perses.
- **Cronus:** The youngest of the Titans, Cronus has his very own action-packed myth. We'll get to him in just a moment.
- **Hyperion:** He is the first god of the sun, but later sires Helios, who is more commonly known to be the Sun.
- **Iapetus:** This Titan is best known for fathering the champion of mankind, Prometheus, as well as Epimetheus, Menoetius, and Atlas.
- **Oceanus:** The eldest of the Titans, Oceanus is the god of the rivers.

Now the Titanesses:

- **Mnemosyne:** Also referred to as Memory, she later gives birth to the Muses.
- **Phoebe:** She is considered the first goddess of the moon, and also the mother of Leto.
- **Rhea:** A mother-deity or earth goddess, Rhea will later give birth to the Olympians.
- **Tethys:** Tethys is known as the first goddess of the sea. She later gives birth to numerous children, including 3,000 (!) daughters—the Oceanids.
- **Theia:** This Titaness is best known for giving birth to Helios, Selene, and Eos.
- **Themis:** Also considered a mother-deity or earth goddess, Themis is the mother of Prometheus, the Hours, and the Fates.

Uranus Loses a Limb

We've established that Uranus was afraid of the Hecatoncheires and the Cyclopes and imprisoned them in Tartarus because of this fear. Well, he certainly didn't favor the Titans either. In fact, he downright hated them. And the feeling was mutual.

Uranus loved his position as ruler of the universe and was not willing to give up that ultimate power—and he viewed his children as threats to that power. Therefore, he also decided to get the Titans out of the way. However, instead of imprisoning them with their other siblings, Uranus got a bit more creative with the punishment of the Titans. This time, with each birth, he shoved the child back into the womb of Gaia. All twelve were returned to the womb just after being born. Uranus was pleased with himself and was able to relax knowing that his power was no longer threatened.

As you can imagine (well, probably not!), Gaia wasn't all too pleased with her situation. Being forced to endure physical discomfort, if not utter pain, is horrible in itself, but don't forget that she was also a mother. As a mother, it pained her even more to see the punishments inflicted upon her children. She eventually got fed up with Uranus's treatment of his family and decided to take action.

Gaia made a sharp sickle out of either iron or flint (the myths vary, but you can be sure it was sharp!). She then voiced her complaints to her children. She suggested they rise up and punish Uranus for his mistreatment of the whole family. The Titans and Titanesses were afraid of their father and refused their mother's request. Gaia, however, did not give up. She continued with her complaints and mutinous pep talk until one boldly came forward and offered to help take revenge upon Uranus. Cronus was the youngest of the Titans. Gaia smiled down upon this favored child and told him her plan.

Cronus lie in waiting that night, armed with the sickle. Uranus finally came and embraced Gaia in love. Cronus, wasting no time, grabbed his father's genitals and sliced them off with the sickle. The severed organ was thrown from the heavens into the sea.

SSENTIALS Some myths state that the attack on Uranus actually caused the birth of Aphrodite, the goddess of love. Legend has it that the discarded organ hit the sea, causing a great white foam. Aphrodite was born of this foam and emerged from the sea fully grown.

After this incident, Uranus seems to drop out of the picture as far as the myths are concerned. He was no longer worshipped or honored with sacrifice, and held no power.

Cronus Crowned as Ruler

With the success of Cronus, the Titans, Titanesses, Cyclopes, and Hecatoncheires were all freed. Cronus took his place as ruler of the universe and married Rhea, his sister. You'd think that after all of this, Cronus would be a fair and benevolent ruler. But power got the best of him, just as it had done his father.

No sooner had the Hecatoncheires and the Cyclopes been freed, they were once again imprisoned in Tartarus, this time by Cronus. He felt the same fear of these giants as did his father. Apparently, he did not seem to fear the Titans, and they were allowed to keep their freedom. At this point, these Titans and Titanesses paired off in marriages:

- Themis married Iapetus
- Phoebe married Coeus
- Theia married Hyperion
- Tethys married Oceanus
- and, of course, Rhea married Cronus

Like Father, Like Son

Cronus was just as power hungry, if not more so, as his father. Because of this, he did not make for a very good ruler. But the similarities between he and his father don't stop there. Cronus was also a horrible father. Apparently, Cronus was aware of a prophecy stating that one of his children would overthrow his power. Just like dear old dad, Cronus wouldn't hear of the possibility of his power being threatened. So he devised a scheme to put his own children out of commission.

He remembered that it was actually his mother's doing that ultimately brought about the ruin of his father. But he also realized that that probably wouldn't have come to pass had not Gaia been so burdened by the children in her womb. Therefore, he decided to place the burden on himself rather than risk placing it on the mother.

Once a year for five years, Rhea gave birth to a child. As soon as it was out of her womb, it was in the mouth of Cronus. You see, his grand scheme consisted of his swallowing each newborn child, therefore literally taking the burden upon himself. Don't worry, he didn't chew them up, but rather swallowed them whole.

Naturally, as a mother, Rhea was overcome with grief and rage. She simply couldn't stand to have her children permanently taken away from her so soon after birth. This is where Cronus's plan backfired. He underestimated a mother's love and natural instincts toward her children, which became the driving force behind Rhea's own scheme of revenge.

When she conceived her sixth child, she asked her parents for help. They sent her to the island of Crete. There she gave birth to her youngest, Zeus. Rhea returned to Cronus following the birth, but left Zeus behind. She substituted a large stone wrapped in swaddling clothes for the baby Zeus and offered it to Cronus. Wasting no time, Cronus immediately swallowed what he thought was his sixth child.

Zeus's Childhood

Zeus had been left in the ultimate care of Gaia, but for practical purposes, left in the care of the Curetes (minor gods) and the Nymphs (nature goddesses). The Curetes would mimic the rituals of the Cretan youths by performing dances and clashing their weapons together. These loud dances and the sounds from the clashing weapons hid the cries of the baby Zeus so his father would not discover him.

His safety being taken care of, he still needed nourishment like any other baby. One nymph in particular was responsible for feeding Zeus, and so Amalthea suckled Zeus through his younger years. Some myths say that Amalthea was a she-goat and talk of the extreme gratitude Zeus felt toward her. To show his appreciation, when Amalthea died, Zeus used her skin to create a shield that he carried with him into battle. As his last gift, Zeus turns Amalthea into a constellation otherwise known as Capricorn.

Zeus was well cared for and grew into adulthood with no obstacles. A strong and healthy young man, Zeus felt he was ready to fulfill his prophecy and overthrow his father. He left the island of Crete and went to visit his cousin, Metis, who was an Oceanid, the daughter of Tethys and Oceanus. She was well known for her wisdom and offered to help Zeus in his quest. She advised him to become a servant of Cronus and then to place an elixir in his drink. Zeus did as he was told. The elixir caused Cronus to vomit and out came Zeus's brothers and sisters, all still whole and unharmed.

War with the Titans

Now that Zeus had rescued his siblings, he had the beginnings of an army with which to challenge the power of Cronus. There was no question that Zeus would be the leader of this army.

Cronus wasn't so lucky in family loyalty though. Not all the Titans decided to join in the war. None of the Titanesses participated, and Oceanus, Cronus's brother, also refused to fight. Helios, son of Hyperion, also refused to take part in the war. And Prometheus and Epimetheus, sons of Iapetus, blatantly refused to pledge loyalty to Cronus, and in fact eventually sided with Zeus's army. The remaining Titans decided that Atlas, son of Iapetus, would be the one to lead them into battle.

ESSENTIALS Prometheus pledged loyalty to Zeus, not because he was necessarily in favor of the Olympians, but because he possessed the gift of prophecy. He knew what was coming and used this knowledge to offer advice to the Titans. When the Titans disregarded him, Prometheus joined the Olympians; he wanted to be on the right side of things when all was said and done.

The Titans under Atlas set up command at Mount Othrys, and the children of Cronus, under Zeus, set up command at Mount Olympus. With sides having been chosen and central command areas in place, thus began the war with the Titans.

This war was far from some petty skirmish. As you know, the Titans were awesome creatures and possessed considerable strength. And the children of Cronus were just as strong and cunning. The two sides met on the battlefield every day for ten years, going back and forth with victories and losses. Even after ten years, the war was still no closer to being decidedly won. However, Gaia interceded and offered advice to Zeus.

According to Gaia, if Zeus would free the Cyclopes and Hecatoncheires from Tartarus, he would find in them very powerful allies. Zeus wasted no time and immediately went down into the depths of the Underworld and faced Campe, a monster appointed by Cronus to guard the giants. Zeus had little difficulty in slaying Campe and successfully freed his uncles. Just as Gaia had predicted, the Hecatoncheires and the Cyclopes were so angry with Cronus that they didn't hesitate to join forces with Zeus.

This addition to Zeus's army was the turning point of the war. The Cyclopes not only offered their strength, but also built grand weapons for the sons of Cronus. Among these were lightning, thunder, earthquake, a trident, and a helmet of invisibility. The Hecatoncheires were no small addition either. They continuously threw great boulders at the Titans' fort causing it to weaken.

With such extreme power backing him, Zeus decided to lay siege on Mount Othrys. But mere strength would not win him the war, so Zeus took his time and devised a plan that would leave the army of Cronus no choice but to surrender. Using the Helmet of Invisibility, Zeus's brother walked into the camp unnoticed and stole all of Cronus's weapons. Next, the other brother of Zeus distracted Cronus with the trident while Zeus fired off shots of lightning bolts. Meanwhile, the Cyclopes and Hecatoncheires were occupying the rest of the Titans with rains of boulders. The plan was successful and the end of the war that almost destroyed the universe was finally over.

First Acts as Supreme Ruler

First and foremost, Zeus had to dispose of his enemies. The army of Cronus was sent down to Tartarus to be imprisoned for eternity where the Hecatoncheires stood guard to ensure no chance of escape.

One enemy did escape imprisonment in Tartarus, but only to find himself on the receiving end of an even greater punishment—Atlas. Because Atlas was the commander of the opposing army, Zeus felt a special punishment was needed. Atlas was sentenced to hold the weight of the sky and heavens upon his shoulders for eternity.

Just as Zeus was harsh with his punishments of his enemies, he was very giving in his rewards of his allies. Because the Titanesses did not participate in the war, Zeus allowed them to retain their power and positions in the heavens. He also restored the powers of any immortal who supported him and had been shunned by Cronus. And of course, his brothers and sisters would be granted their own rights and powers, but we'll get to that in the next chapter when we introduce the Olympians.

CHAPTER 5

Introducing the Olympians

You've made it through the chaotic creation of the universe, the various schemes for revenge and power, and a ten-year-long war. Whew! But your journey has not been in vain. You have now reached the gates of the famed Mount Olympus. You've certainly earned this backstage pass. Are you courageous enough to step inside and meet the gods and goddesses face to face?

The Original Six

As you know, Cronus lost his power after being overthrown by his very own children. However, this struggle for power did not continue. Instead the children of Cronus united, dividing reign among them. A supreme ruler was needed, however, and all agreed Zeus would best rule over them. The decision was unanimous and final.

These original six Olympian gods and goddesses included:

- Zeus
- Poseidon
- Hades

- Hera
- Hestia
- Demeter

The Brothers

After the fall of Cronus, the three brothers divided the dominions between them. The three divisions were made fairly—each god drew lots. The realms up for grabs were the heavens, the seas, and the land of the dead. It was agreed upon that earth and Mount Olympus would remain as joint domain without one god in particular having control.

As luck would have it, Zeus drew the heavens. This made him the ruler of the gods as well as of the heavens. Zeus, often helmeted, is normally depicted as wielding one of his thunderbolts and wearing the aegis. He is also often accompanied by an eagle, which symbolically serves as his attendant.

 SSENTIALS

Some myths say that Poseidon created the horse or at the very least tamed them. Regardless, he was known to many as the god of horses, and was said to give away horses as gifts to those he favored. And his great chariot was always drawn by horses or monstrous variations of the horse.

Poseidon drew the realm of the seas. Myths often describe Poseidon as a rather violent god, associating him with savage sea storms and earthquakes. He is depicted as being tall with a long flowing beard, normally wielding his trident (which is, if you remember, one of the weapons made by the Cyclopes during the ten-year war). Although the best guess might be fish, horses and bulls are most often associated with Poseidon. Good luck figuring that one out. What do horses and bulls have to do with the sea?

Last, but certainly not least, is Hades, who drew the land of the dead—otherwise known as the Underworld. The Underworld is not representative of Hell, nor is Hades considered in any way evil or satanic. The myths describe Hades as a loner, rather uninterested in the world of the living. He is often depicted holding a key, signifying his "jailer" status. He, like his brother, is also associated with horses, and in some myths is even said to have created the horse.

The Sisters

Though the sisters of Zeus were left out of drawing lots, they certainly held their own when it came to wielding power. And it is recognized that the order of the universe would not be complete without the domains of these three goddesses.

Hera is often considered the greatest of all Greek goddesses. She is, after all, not only the sister but also the wife of Zeus (but we'll get into that in the next chapter), which makes her the queen of the Heavens. She is described as very jealous and vindictive, with a quick temper and fearsome passion. As the first lawful wife, she is the protector of wives. She is also considered to be the goddess of marriage and childbirth. She is depicted as a queen often is: tall, stately, and wielding a scepter. Her bird is the peacock.

Hestia isn't very well known in mythology. Little is recorded of her, though she is considered to be the goddess of the hearth and the home. She is thought to have been worshipped in every household of the ancients and was held as quite sacred. Though no description is given of her, she is closely associated with the countenance of virginity and is not associated with any animal.

Demeter, whose name means "Mother Earth," is an (surprise!) earth goddess, though not to be confused with Gaia, the actual Earth. Demeter holds the power of fertility and agriculture. Whereas her sister Hestia never left Mount Olympus, Demeter rarely stayed there. She preferred to spend her time on earth, close to the soil. She is depicted as sitting down with either a serpent or torches. Her bird is the crane and her emblems are the poppy, narcissus, and an ear of corn.

A Dozen Distinguished Deities

Now that you have been introduced to the original six Olympians, it only makes sense to get the rest of the introductions out of the way. There are twelve great Olympians in all, each playing a respected role in the order of the universe. Now, without further ado, the remaining great Olympians:

Ares

The least favored of all the Olympians was Ares, god of war. And no wonder. He lived for battle and bloodshed, deriving great pleasure from destruction. But still, he was one of the "Greats" and therefore, held high rank.

Ares is described as always wearing a helmet and armor, and carrying a spear, sword, and shield. Though he was the war god, he was not always victorious. In fact, he was defeated in battle several times throughout the myths. He is associated with the dog and the vulture.

Athena

As the goddess of wisdom, Athena was held in high regard by all, mortal and immortal alike. She was also the goddess of war, crafts, and skills. Unlike Ares, however, Athena was not bloodthirsty. She would rather have peace than war. Even so, during those times that she was in battle, she proved herself to be an invincible strategist, dominating the field.

Athena is depicted as wearing a full suit of armor, a helmet, and an aegis. She wields a spear and a shield that has a picture of the Gorgon's head painted on it. She is associated with the owl (which symbolizes wisdom), and an owl is often seen perched on her shoulder.

Artemis

Being goddess of the hunt, Artemis was little interested in anything else. She roamed the mountainsides with a band of nymphs, hunting animals and, at times, even men. But don't think her bad. She was also the protector of children, wild animals, and the weak. Legend has it that her arrows could cause sudden death without pain, but if one were to get on her bad side, Artemis was said to have been quite vindictive and vengeful.

FACTS

Artemis and Apollo would not have been born if Hera had her way. But their mother, Leto, was able to escape Hera and give birth, first to Artemis. Though an infant, Artemis was said to have helped her mother through nine days of intensive labor to give birth to Apollo. Because their mother had suffered so much for them, Artemis and Apollo would continuously protect and indulge her throughout the myths.

Artemis is most often depicted carrying her weapon of choice—a bow and arrows. Some myths even describe her as a girl-child—a virgin with eternal youth—as tame as the wild animals she hunted and protected. As all wild animals are within her domain, she is not associated with one in particular.

Apollo

Apollo was the twin of Artemis. He was considered the god of archery, as well as of music and poetry. While his sister lived only for the hunt, Apollo was a versatile god and enjoyed a great many things. He was at times a shepherd or cowherd, at other times a great musician not to be seen without his lyre or cithara. He was also involved in prophecy and medicine.

With his hand in so many arts, there isn't a "usual" depiction of him. However, he is invariably described as an ideal beauty—truly tall, dark, and handsome. Apollo is associated with several different creatures, including the wolf, deer, dolphin, crow, vulture, and swan, and is also associated with the laurel plant.

Hermes

Hermes was the god of commerce and flight (formally). Informally, he was best known as the messenger of the gods. He brought luck to people, guided travelers and merchants, and became the patron deity of rogues and thieves. Hermes was quite the active god, known for his agility and athleticism.

In keeping with his messenger status, Hermes is normally described as wearing a winged hat and winged sandals—speedy delivery indeed! He is also sometimes seen carrying either a golden herald's wand or a staff with two serpents' heads. To get a good picture of Hermes in your head, imagine that one little boy you've encountered at least once in your life who is terribly mischievous, but so cute and with such a kind heart (although it may seem deeply hidden at times) that you simply have to adore him—this is Hermes.

Aphrodite

Nearly everyone has heard of Aphrodite—the goddess of love. (Or perhaps you know her as Venus, which is the Roman name.) Some myths view her as a flaky and ridiculous character, while others describe her as a generous and benevolent goddess, due just as much reverence as the other Olympians. Regardless of her character, Aphrodite is always viewed as passionate. That was her duty after all—to make love.

Needless to say, Aphrodite is depicted as being a great beauty, with a sweet and seductive smile. The myths revolving around her almost always involve a love affair, either with Aphrodite as one of the participants or with the goddess intervening in the lives of others. She is associated with the dove, and her plants are the rose and myrtle.

Hephaestus

Believe it or not, the goddess of love had a husband—Hephaestus. Now, you probably think that this god must have been the most beautiful and passionate god around if he was lucky enough to capture the one and only goddess of love. Unfortunately, no, he wasn't. In fact, he was thrown out of heaven at his birth because of his ugliness and deformities. (If your curiosity is piqued, see Chapter 15 for complete details on the marriage of Aphrodite and Hephaestus.)

ESSENTIALS   Some myths state that Hephaestus was born healthy and without any deformities at all. He was tossed from the heavens by Zeus when he took Hera's side in an argument against Zeus. He fell for an entire day and then landed on an island. This myth attributes Hephaestus's lameness to this fall and the not-so-gentle landing.

Hephaestus was the god of fire, smithing, craftsmanship, and metalworking. He built the great homes of the gods and goddesses, made armor for those he favored, and could pretty much build anything that was asked of him. He was most often depicted as being lame and not so handsome. Instead of being associated with animals, Hephaestus is associated with volcanoes, which were thought to be his workshops.

Dionysus

Better known as the party god, Dionysus was the god of the vine, wine, and revelry. Whereas most of the Olympians kept their distance and snubbed the mortals, Dionysus mingled with his mortal followers. His religious festivals turned into rites of ecstasy—everyone had a good time.

Dionysus is depicted as being a lover of peace. He felt his greatest gift to bestow upon his loyal followers was that of wine: to be able to relieve a person of the burdens of the day—if only for a while. This isn't to say that he was never cruel—he was after all still a god. And those who opposed him were often met by the wrath of a god. Dionysus isn't associated with an animal or a plant (except of course the vine); he is most often associated with dance, music, wine, madness, and sex.

FACTS

You may have noticed that there are supposed to be twelve great Olympians, but that you have been introduced to fourteen in this chapter. No, you didn't count wrong. Dionysus is said to have taken the place of Hestia, who eventually fades out of mythology. Hades is the other deity often not counted. His world was the Underworld, and he rarely visited Mount Olympus. Therefore, most do not consider him one of the great Olympian gods.

Mount Olympus

The home of the Olympian gods and goddesses deserves a little recognition, wouldn't you say? However, the descriptions of this place are rather vague in ancient mythology. Some myths state that it was indeed a mountain higher than any other mountain on earth. It had several peaks, each the residence of a different deity with Zeus residing on its topmost peak. Other myths refer to Mount Olympus as part of the heavens and not on earth at all.

Regardless of its exact location, Mount Olympus was a magnificent dwelling, clearly fit for the gods. Beyond the entranceway of clouds were several luxurious palaces and halls, supposedly built by Hephaestus, where the gods and goddesses lived and held parties.

For the most part, life on Mount Olympus was an easy and peaceful one. The gods and goddesses would lounge around feasting on ambrosia and drinking nectar while listening to music and watching dances being performed for their enjoyment. Mount Olympus was untouched by the various natural disasters and inconveniences we have on earth. There were no thundershowers, snow, rough winds, earthquakes, hailstorms, or tornadoes. The atmosphere was at peace, making the inhabitants peaceful (most of the time anyway).

Mount Olympus wasn't only the residence of the gods and goddesses, but also their command center, so to speak. This is where trials were held, laws were created, and important decisions were made.

Law and Order Under the Olympians

As ruler of gods and men, it was Zeus's duty to bring ultimate order to the universe. An order of sorts had already been established, but it was only basic in its form. Zeus felt this should be taken further and detailed more precisely.

Taking matters into his own hands, he made love to his aunt, Thetis, who was the goddess of eternal order. Their union produced six daughters who became the personifications of those very principles needed to complete the ultimate order he desired. The daughters included:

- **Eirene:** The personification of peace
- **Eunomia:** The personification of law and order
- **Dike:** The personification of justice
- **Atropos:** One of the Fates and responsible for cutting the thread of life
- **Clotho:** One of the Fates and responsible for spinning the thread of life
- **Lachesis:** One of the Fates and responsible for determining the length of the thread of life

With order now established in the universe, it was now Zeus's job to maintain it and he was fully capable of this duty. Zeus was known to be a fair but strict leader. He firmly believed in the idea of justice and carried out punishments to uphold that idea.

As supreme ruler, Zeus did not allow his emotions or biases to get in the way of a ruling. If he felt he could not make a judgment impartially, he would either bring the matter before a council of other deities to help him determine the ruling, or find another way (such as a contest) to determine the final decision. For instance, Zeus's brother Poseidon had a tendency to fight for land and often started battles with other gods and goddesses. Zeus sometimes felt as though he could not make an impartial ruling in the favor of either his own brother or, say, his daughter. Who would want to make that choice? So he would instead either bring the matter before the council or create a contest in which the winner would rightfully claim the land. However, in some cases, Zeus thought it best that not one party was favored over the other. To handle these situations, he used compromise to settle the matter.

ALERT

If you are a mortal woman (or even a goddess for that matter), look out for Zeus! Though he most often thought through things quite extensively before performing any action, women were his weakness and he would allow his lust to control his actions.

Some myths say that even though Zeus was the supreme ruler, he did not have complete control. Remember the Fates he fathered? These three women are often considered to be superior to even the greatest of the gods. Therefore, Zeus himself was subject to them.

Mutiny on Mount Olympus

One would think that the beauty, peacefulness, and splendor of Mount Olympus would be enough to keep the peace. You've seen that in mythological times law and order have been set, justice most often prevails, and the universe is ruled with intelligence instead of with sheer force. But with all these grand notions of utopia, there was still a rebellious attitude working within the society of deities that would become a threat to the power of Zeus.

A Mob Is Assembled

A rebellion of some sort is almost always expected in any society, and the great gods and goddesses of Mount Olympus were no exception. The rebellion began with three key figures: Athena, Hera, and Poseidon. (However, several myths ultimately credit Hera as the mastermind behind the scheme.) These three each felt he or she could rule better than Zeus, and perhaps begrudged having to answer to him. Regardless of their personal reasons, they banded together to rally the other gods and goddesses against Zeus—all except for Hestia.

The group worked together to quickly chain Zeus to his bed while he lay sleeping. Setting his weapons out of reach, they congratulated each other on a successful and easy rebellion. However, the celebration soon took a turn for the worse. Now that Zeus had no power, who would take his place?

The gods and goddesses began to argue, each convinced that he or she would be best placed as supreme ruler. None of the powerful deities were willing to back down. The argument continued for a long while, and did not taper off. If anything, it only grew more heated as the frustration level rose.

While the deities were preoccupied with their claims to power, a sea deity named Thetis came to Zeus's rescue. She ventured down to Tartarus and appealed to Briareus (one of the Hecatoncheires) for help, who consented and unchained Zeus. The deities dared not challenge an angry Zeus face to face and quickly backed down. Reclaiming his position as supreme ruler, Zeus forced all Olympians to vow that they would never again challenge his power.

Hera's Punishment

Zeus, as lord of justice (and also probably as an act of revenge), was moved to punish Hera for her insubordination. And such disloyalty called for no small punishment. Therefore, Zeus decided to suspend Hera from the heavens. He attached chains to her wrists, which held her over the edges of the heavens, and anvils to her feet to weigh her down. She was eventually released and never again incited another rebellion.

ESSENTIALS This punishment of Hera is certainly recorded in mythology, however some myths argue a different reason behind the need for her punishment, asserting that Zeus actually punished her in this manner because of her relentless and overzealous persecution of his son, Heracles.

War with the Giants

As the rulers of the universe, it's no surprise that the power of the Olympians was challenged. However, it wasn't only for power that they were threatened. Gaia (Mother Earth) was terribly upset at having her children, the Titans, imprisoned in Tartarus. She therefore rallied the Giants to avenge her children.

The Giants were a very powerful race. They had a basic human form, but their legs were the bodies of serpents. Depicted as having wild, thick hair and beards, and of great stature, they certainly weren't the prettiest creatures around; rather, they instilled fear in everything that crossed their paths.

If the Olympians were ever to have an enemy who could match their power and strength, it was the Giants. The Giants could not be killed by an immortal alone. Instead, an immortal and a mortal had to slay a Giant simultaneously in order to kill it. Some myths say a plant existed that made the Giants immune to the attacks of mortals. Luckily, Zeus caught wind of this and had the plant removed from the earth before the Giants could get hold of it.

Let the Battle Begin!

The Giants initiated battle by bombarding the heavens with boulders and flaming trees, which certainly caught the Olympians attention. They quickly buckled down for war, making a valiant effort to fight the Giants. But since the Giants could not be killed, the Olympians were struggling to simply keep their hold.

Bringing Down the Big Boys

An oracle had warned the Olympians that they would never be able to win the war without the help of a mortal. Zeus, therefore, sent Athena down to earth to recruit Heracles, the son of Zeus, born of a mortal woman. With Heracles' entrance to the war, things started looking up for the Olympians. Athena and Heracles joined forces to bring down the first victim of the war, one of the Giants' leaders, Alcyoneus. Athena attacked and Heracles shot him with a poisoned arrow. Alcyoneus was a special case, however, and he didn't die right away. He was granted immortality for as long as he stood on his native soil. Therefore, Athena—with all her great wisdom—advised Heracles to drag the Giant outside of the bounds of his land. Heracles did as he was told and Alcyoneus died on the spot.

The next to fall was Alcyoneus's co-leader, Porphyrion. Porphyrion attacked Hera, meaning to kill her, but instead Zeus filled him with lust for her, turning his desire to kill into a need for love. With Hera as the decoy, Zeus and Heracles positioned themselves. Zeus hurled a thunderbolt at him, while Heracles simultaneously shot him with an arrow, at which point Porphyrion dropped dead. Hera remained unharmed.

Some myths state that Zeus had an ulterior motive when filling Porphyrion with lust for Hera. (As you will see in the next chapter, deceit and revenge play a big role in the marriage of Zeus and Hera.) It is said that Zeus used the Giant to test the virtue of Hera. When Hera withdrew from the Giant's advances, Zeus then killed him.

The war was pretty much a sure shot for the Olympians after the fall of the two leaders. But the Giants did not give up easily. It was only through the combined efforts of all the Olympians that the war was ended.

The Scariest Monster of All

Gaia was rather upset at hearing the news of the Giants' defeat. Her sons were still locked up in Tartarus and it was beginning to look like they would forever remain there. But Gaia had one last item up her sleeve. She gave birth to a monster—half man, half animal, *all* horrifying.

Typhon had a hundred serpentine heads, each equipped with a flickering tongue and eyes that shot flames. Each of the heads also spoke in a different voice, sometimes that of a human, sometimes that of a god, sometimes that of a beast, and sometimes that of something sent straight from Hell. He had wings and his body was encircled with snakes. And just to make matters worse, this guy was huge! Spreading his arms, one arm reached all the way to the west, and the other reached all the way to the east.

Run Away! Run Away!

At the sight of Typhon's advance toward Olympus, the gods and goddesses fled. Not only did they flee, but they also transformed into various animals to disguise themselves. Aphrodite and Ares turned into fish, Apollo transformed into a bird, Hephaestus became an ox, Dionysus turned into a goat, and Hermes changed into an ibis. Only Zeus stood his ground against the fearsome enemy (although some myths claim Athena stayed as well).

Zeus's first reaction to Typhon was to use his almighty weapon—the thunderbolt. Hurling thunderbolts in constant succession so that the entire earth began to quake, Zeus was able to push Typhon back a little. Thinking the monster was wounded, Zeus grabbed his sickle and left his fort, descending upon Typhon. However, Typhon wasn't quite as weak as Zeus thought, and the fight that ensued was quite fierce. Eventually, Typhon wrestled the sickle away and used it to cut the tendons in Zeus's arms and legs, leaving Zeus on the ground, helpless. Typhon placed the tendons under the protection of Delphyne, a dragon. He then carried Zeus off to a cave.

But not all was lost. Hermes and Pan joined forces to trick Delphyne. While the dragon was preoccupied, they stole the tendons and restored them to Zeus. Regaining his strength, Zeus wasted no time in returning to Olympus and arming himself with thunderbolts. He then went in search of Typhon.

No Rest for the Weary

Eventually, Zeus caught up with Typhon and showed him no mercy. Though Typhon did his best to withstand the rain of thunderbolts upon him, he simply was no match for them. So he fled in hopes of finding harbor and renewing his strength. He came upon the Fates who advised him to eat the food of the mortals in order to be healed. Typhon trusted their advice and did as he was told. But the food of mortal men only served to weaken him more.

Zeus once again caught up to Typhon and relentlessly showered him with more thunderbolts. Typhon tried hurling mountain peaks back at Zeus, but he used the thunderbolts to deflect them. The battle continued on, becoming quite bloody, until finally Typhon fled once more. But this time he didn't get away. According to one myth, Zeus picked up an island from the sea and flung it at Typhon. The island crushed the monster, trapping him. The myth states that because Typhon was immortal, he still resides beneath the island and the volcanic eruptions are merely the fire breath of the monster.

Another myth says that Zeus set Typhon on fire with the thunderbolts, seized the monster, and flung him down into Tartarus. There he is imprisoned with the Titans. Many say that Typhon is the cause of all dangerous winds, and that is where the word "typhoon" came from

ALERT

The horror does not die with Typhon's defeat! Before he was overcome by Zeus, Typhon fathered several monstrous children: the Chimaera (a fire-breathing monster with the head of a lion, the body of a goat, and the tail of a snake),the Lernaean Hydra (a large snake with several heads), the Nemean Lion (a monstrous lion with an impenetrable skin), Orthros (a two-headed dog), and the Sphinx (a monster with a woman's head and a lion's body).

Zeus was once again victorious in battle. Following this, no one would deny him the right as ruler of gods and men. Thus the Olympians came to rule the universe until the end of time.

This Is Just the Beginning

You have now been introduced to the great Olympian gods and goddesses. But if anything, this brief introduction should only serve to raise your curiosity about these magnificent and powerful deities. The great Olympians have managed to ward off all threats to their power, and will rule the universe for the rest of time.

The Olympian gods and goddesses reoccur throughout the ancient Greek myths, making them the dominant cast of characters in Greek mythology. They each have their own stories in which they star, but quite often their stories intermingle, creating interaction not only among the deities but also with mortals and the happenings of the world as well.

If you are to become familiar with the spectacular stories of classical mythology, it is imperative that you get to know these "Greats." The brief introductions offered here only serve to get you started. In the following chapters, you will get to know these gods and goddesses better by viewing their characters through the stories in which they participate.

CHAPTER 6

A Marriage Made in the Heavens

Surely you've heard the phrase "a match made in heaven." Well, the marriage of Zeus and Hera is literally that; however, their marriage doesn't quite live up to the bliss that famed phrase implies. This chapter will give you a sneak peek at the trials and tribulations suffered by these two great Olympians in their bond of matrimony.

The Seventh Lover

Although best known of Zeus's wives, Hera was not the first (and she probably wished she hadn't been the last). Zeus was quite the lusty young buck and his conquests caused more than a little bit of a stir. He was a god who knew what he wanted, and took what he wanted with very little regard for others.

Number One

Zeus's first marriage was to Metis. If you recall, she was the wise one who advised Zeus to give Cronus an elixir to make him throw up his children, thus releasing Zeus's brothers and sisters. According to the myths, Metis wasn't willing to succumb to Zeus at first. In fact, she tried to escape him several times by taking on different forms as a disguise. In the end, the constant flight being rather tiresome, Metis gave in to Zeus. The two conceived a daughter who would become Athena. Although Metis was pregnant, she did not give birth in the traditional sense. See Chapter 11 for the rather unusual birth of Athena.

If you think divorces are messy today, just be grateful you weren't an ancient deity! The dissolution of the marriage between Zeus and Metis was a quite a bit different than the divorces of today. Zeus put an end to their marriage by swallowing his wife.

Number Two

Following Metis, Zeus married Themis, one of the original Titanesses and the goddess of eternal order. Working very closely with and acting as advisor to Zeus, Themis was a prime candidate for his lust. They produced several children together including the Moirai (the Fates): Atropus, Clotho, and Lachesis; and the Horae (the Hours): Eunomia (Discipline), Dike (Justice), and Eirene (Peace). As you recall, Zeus finally brought complete order to the universe by fathering these children. The end to this marriage isn't quite as extreme; Zeus simply leaves Themis for another woman.

Number Three

Bachelorette number three wasn't a bachelorette at all. Eurynome, a daughter of Oceanus and Tethys, was married to Ophion, a Titan. Not only was she married, but she was also the sister of Zeus's first wife, Metis. But of course, that didn't stop Zeus from wanting her and as you know, Zeus usually got what he wanted. He and Eurynome produced the three Graces (Charities): Aglaia, Euphrosyne, and Thalia. These three daughters were often depicted as the personification of grace, beauty, friendship, and artistic inspiration.

Number Four

Zeus's next lover was none other than his very own sister, Demeter. As you recall from the last chapter, Demeter is an earth goddess. Much like the royal lines of the recent past, the ancients felt it was important to keep the godly blood pure and therefore inbreeding was common practice.

Not much is recorded about their love affair. (It must not have met the steamy standards of the affairs of the gods!) However, we do know that of their union a daughter was produced—Persephone, Queen of the Underworld.

Number Five

Zeus's next conquest was Mnemosyne (Memory), a Titaness. This pair made love for nine consecutive nights, which led to Mnemosyne giving birth to the nine Muses: Calliope, Clio, Erato, Euterpe, Melpomene, Polyhymnia, Terpsichore, Thalia, and Urania. (The Muses and their functions will be discussed in greater detail in Chapter 17.) It isn't stated why this apparently compatible couple split up, but their love affair did indeed come to an end and Zeus moved on to his next target.

Number Six

Following Mnemosyne was Leto, the daughter of the Titans Coeus and Phoebe. As you have probably guessed, this union also produced children. But these weren't just any children. Leto gave birth to the famed twins Apollo and Artemis, who later took their places among the great Olympian gods.

Again, it isn't noted why Zeus did not stay with Leto, but following this affair, he suddenly decided it was time to settle down. His next conquest would be his permanent wife (which doesn't necessarily imply faithfulness on Zeus's part!).

"Lucky" Number Seven

Zeus set his sights on his other sister, Hera. He thought that only she matched him in power well enough to become his permanent wife. By now, Zeus was so used to getting what he wanted that it never occurred to him that he couldn't have Hera. But Hera, by nature a jealous person, wasn't too keen on Zeus's advances for she knew about his past loves. Therefore, Zeus had to come up with a scheme to trick Hera into becoming his wife.

Zeus noticed Hera walking in the woods one day. He cleverly disguised himself as a cuckoo and then created a great rainstorm. In the guise of the cuckoo, he played upon Hera's sympathy. She took the poor drenched bird and clutched it to her body, folded in the protective covering of her dress. Zeus transformed back into his own body and violated the unsuspecting Hera. Dishonored and shamed by the violation, Hera consented to be his wife.

FACTS

Some myths state that this wasn't the first time Zeus and Hera had been together. They had secret rendezvous several times before, even prior to the war with the Titans. This may serve to explain Hera's jealousy and resentment toward Zeus's other lovers.

A Grand Wedding

The marriage between the ruler of the gods and his bride was certainly a grand affair. Although Zeus (as well as other characters of mythology) had been married before, this was to be the first formal and lawful wedding ceremony.

The myths vary on the location of the divine marriage ceremony:

- The *Iliad* places the ceremony on the peak of Mount Ida in Phrygia.
- Other sources say the marriage took place in Euboea, which is supposedly where the deities came to rest after returning from the island of Crete.
- Probably the most famous location is that of the Garden of the Hesperides near an eternal spring that gushed forth with ambrosia. (Because it doesn't make sense that a spring would gush forth food, ambrosia is probably referring to the nectar of the gods.)

QUESTIONS?

What is ambrosia?

Ambrosia is the food of the gods (nectar was the drink of the gods). It is said that whoever tastes of the ambrosia will become immortal. Ambrosia is often a general term for food, and not a specific type, although some myths do describe ambrosia as an edible flowerlike plant.

The wedding itself was a huge party, with all the gods and goddesses in attendance. Yes, even Hades left his dark realm of the Underworld to see his brother and sister wedded. It is said that the tradition of bringing gifts to the newlywed couple began here. But of course, the gifts of gods were a bit more elaborate and mystical than the ones we give today. For example, Gaia's wedding gift to Hera was a tree of golden apples. The tree was planted in the Garden of the Hesperides and protected by the nymphs.

This first ceremony became the standard for sacred marriage throughout Greece. Festivals were held in honor of the sanctity of marriage and to commemorate the union of Zeus and Hera. It became tradition in Athens for the brides to be given apples and pomegranates, which were favorites of Hera. All throughout Greece, a statue of Hera dressed as a bride would often be wheeled through the town prior to the wedding ceremony. Sometimes the statue's path would lead to the marital bed. Also, the month attributed to Hera became the traditional time for weddings to take place. Hera herself became known as the patron deity of wives.

The Children of Zeus and Hera

It is rumored that the wedding night of Zeus and Hera lasted for 300 years! Even for such an extended honeymoon, the couple had only three children—together, that is.

Ares

Ares was their only son. As you know from the previous chapter, Ares would grow to become the god of war and take his place among the great gods of Olympus. As one of the greats, an entire chapter has been dedicated to him (Chapter 10), so we won't riddle you with the details of his life quite yet.

Eileithyia

No less exceptional in her own right was the daughter Eileithyia (who some myths infer was born out of wedlock). Eileithyia is often referred to as the goddess of childbirth. Hera sometimes took advantage of her daughter's important role, with Eileithyia rarely questioning her mother's wishes. For instance, in a fit of jealousy, Hera wanted to prevent Leto from giving birth to Zeus's children. She therefore tried to prevent Eileithyia from going to the side of Leto. Eileithyia, though wanting to do her mother's bidding, was bribed by other goddesses to Leto's bedside, thus allowing the birth to take place.

Another instance involved the birth of Heracles. Again, Hera's jealousy was at full force. She told her daughter to sit outside the room of Heracles' mother (Alcmene, a mortal lover of Zeus) at the time of birth, keeping arms, legs, and fingers crossed. This caused the birth of Heracles to be postponed for several days.

FACTS

The successful birth of Heracles is credited to the servants attending Alcmene during childbirth. Together, they devised a scheme to trick Eileithyia into moving out of position in order to break the spell. Though the child had not been born, the attending women cried out exclamations of his birth. Eileithyia, shocked that her spell did not work, got up and went to see the child. Having uncrossed her limbs, the spell was broken and Alcmene was able to give birth.

Hebe

As the sister of Ares and Eileithyia, Hebe took on less prominence, but certainly did not lack in terms of her beauty. This child was the personification of youth and was therefore forever young and beautiful. She served as a maid to the divine household. Hebe is often depicted serving nectar (the drink of the gods). She also drew baths, harnessed horses, and basically took care of household chores.

One myth states that Hebe was released of her duties of serving the gods when she accidentally tripped and fell down at an important festival. The fall in itself was forgivable, but in doing so she indecently exposed herself to all the guests, which was unforgivable. Even so, she was still popular (perhaps even more so after the fall!) and would later become the gift-bride of Heracles once he was admitted into the heavens.

A Fourth Child

Hera gave birth to a fourth child, Hephaestus, who would later become one of the great Olympian gods. However, the myths surrounding his birth vary a bit. Some say that he was also the child of Zeus. But the more popular myth—made known by Hesiod—was that Hera conceived Hephaestus without the aid of Zeus or any other man. If you're wondering what it's like to be the child conceived of only one parent, check out Chapter 15, which gives a full account of the life of Hephaestus.

Zeus's Love Affairs

As you've seen, Zeus was quite prolific before his marriage to Hera, but if you are thinking marriage settled him, think again. If anything, his love affairs became even more frequent and heated. His "I get what I want" attitude is prominently shown throughout his string of many lovers. After reading this section, you will be able to see why Hera is proclaimed the most jealous and vengeful of all Olympian deities. And who can blame her?

Aegina

Aegina was the daughter of the river god Asopus. Zeus took a liking to this young girl and transformed himself into an eagle to steal her away. Asopus, furious, searched all over Greece trying to find his daughter. Zeus, however, put an end to this hunt by striking at Asopus with bolts of lightning. Zeus carried Aegina off to an isolated island and there she conceived a son, Aeacus. After Aeacus was born, Aegina left the island, but begged Zeus that it become populated. He granted her this wish and the island later held her name.

ESSENTIALS

Aeacus followed in his father's footsteps. Although he was not a god, he ruled over the island of Aegina. He was known to be a just and fair ruler. He took justice so seriously that he banished his own sons from the island when they murdered his other son even though this left him heirless.

Alcmene

Alcmene was a mortal woman—and married. Though married, she refused to consummate the marriage until her husband, Amphitryon, completed an act of revenge for her. Zeus disguised himself as her husband, returning successfully from his mission. Alcmene accepted Zeus into her bed believing it to be her husband. One myth states that Zeus ordered the god of the sun to take a few days off, thus allowing the night of lovemaking to last longer.

Needless to say, her husband wasn't all too happy to return to a wife who claimed to have already slept with him. But because it had been Zeus, there really wasn't much a mortal could do about it. The coupling with Zeus led to the birth of the famed hero Heracles.

Callisto

The myths vary on the true identity of Callisto. Some say she was a wood nymph, some say she was the daughter of the king of Arcadia, while still others say she was the daughter of the king of Thebes. Regardless, she was definitely an attendant of Artemis. She took a vow of chastity, as was the requirement of all attendants of Artemis. However, Zeus fell in love with her and, well, we know how that goes . . .

Because she vowed to remain a virgin and chose to avoid the company of all men, Zeus had to disguise himself as Artemis to get close to her. The plan worked and Zeus was able to get his way. She was pregnant with her son Arcas when she was discovered by Artemis. Because she had had sex, and therefore broken her vow, nothing less than death was her punishment.

Danae

Danae was the daughter of the king of Argos. According to a prophecy, Danae's son would rise up and kill her father. Knowing this, her father imprisoned Danae in a tower with bronze doors to keep her away from all men. But then, Zeus wasn't a man, he was a god. Zeus was able to reach her by transforming himself into a shower of golden rain. As always, Zeus got what he wanted and the result was a son, Perseus. If you are curious about whether or not the prophecy came true, read about Perseus in Chapter 19.

Electra

Electra was the daughter of Atlas. There are several myths surrounding her, yet none describe Zeus's seduction of her. Even though there isn't a juicy story to go along with their love affair, it was an important one. Due to the union, Electra produced a son, Dardanus. Dardanus would grow to become the founder of the royal house of Troy.

Europa

Europa was the daughter of the king of Phoenicia. Zeus looked down from the heavens one day and noticed Europa playing on the beach and was immediately transfixed by her beauty. For this lovely lady, Zeus transformed himself into a glamorous white bull and presented himself to the maiden.

Initially, Europa was frightened of the creature, but Zeus laid himself at her feet. A little more at ease, Europa began to pet him, then climbed upon his back. Zeus carried her into the ocean and swam to the island of Crete. There he changed back to his true form and made love to Europa beneath a tree on the shore. The tree from then on would always be evergreen. Europa bore Zeus three sons: Minos, Sarpedon, and Rhadamanthys.

Ganymede

No one it seems is safe from the lust and love of Zeus, not even males. Ganymede was a son of the royal Trojan family. He was considered in some myths to be the most beautiful of all mortals—men and women alike. Because of his great beauty, he was stolen from his home and brought to Mount Olympus where he became a cupbearer for the gods, particularly Zeus.

The myths vary in describing the kidnapping of Ganymede. Some say that Zeus himself stole the boy. Another says that Zeus's favorite eagle was given the mission. Still others proclaim Zeus ordered one of the lesser gods to carry out the task. Regardless of how he was taken, Zeus compensated the boy's father by giving him a pair of magnificent horses.

Io

Io was a virgin priestess of Hera's. (Yes, this is dangerous ground to tread, but Zeus wants what he wants!) Zeus knew he had to avoid Hera at all costs, so he lured Io to meet him at a specified place in the woods. He then covered the area with a great thick cloud, which served to conceal their affair. When they finished, he turned Io into a white heifer and tried to pass her off as ordinary. Unfortunately for Io, Hera didn't buy into it. But we'll get into Hera's reaction to all this in a moment. First, let's continue with Zeus's lovers.

Leda

Leda was the daughter of the king of Aetolia. Zeus once again had to transform himself in order to get his way—this time into a swan. (Well, we have to at least give him credit for creativity!) Zeus was successful in his scheme, and Leda was with child (or children, for there is talk of twins) following the coupling. There are disputes about which of Leda's children were actually Zeus's. She bore several, including Helen, Castor, Polydeuces, Clytemnestra, Phoebe, Timandra, and Philonoe. Most commonly, though, Polydeuces and Helen are known as the children of Zeus.

Maia

Maia was the eldest daughter of Atlas. She was also the most beautiful. Zeus, of course, took notice of her. To avoid Hera, Zeus would sneak away from his sleeping wife at night to go visit Maia. She bore him the son Hermes, who as you know, would become one of the great Olympians. For some reason, Maia was one of the few lucky lovers of Zeus who never suffered the wrath of Hera.

Semele

Semele was a mortal woman with whom Zeus fell in love. He came to her disguised as a mortal man, but confided in her that he was indeed the ruler of the gods. Unlike some of his other lovers, Semele did not try to escape the advances of Zeus. They enjoyed a brief love affair, which caused Semele to conceive a son who would later be Dionysus. Zeus promised to give Semele anything she wanted. Taking advantage of this, Semele asked Zeus to show her his true form. Of course, a god's splendor is too much for a mere mortal, and therefore when he came to Semele in his true form, she immediately burst into flames.

Taygete

Taygete was yet another daughter of Atlas. It seems as though these poor young maidens simply cannot escape the eye of Zeus. Of course, he felt he had to have her, leaving her with very little choice in the matter. However, some myths state that Zeus came to Taygete only when she was unconscious. Zeus's visits resulted in the birth of Lacedaemon.

FACTS

Atlas had seven daughters by the Oceanid Pleione: Taygete, Electra, Alcyone, Celaeno, Merope, Maia, and Asterope. These divine daughters are known collectively as the Pleiades.

Many More

You should now have a pretty good idea of the various trysts of Zeus. Although there are quite a few mentioned here, these are certainly not all. Zeus had numerous love affairs during his marriage to Hera. As the ruler of the gods and men, clearly the women of the world were pretty accessible to him.

But don't think for a moment that Hera just stood by and watched. Even though she was a goddess, she felt the same emotions mortals do—with jealousy quite often taking front stage. Hera is known throughout mythology to be a very jealous and vengeful goddess. In the next section, you will see how Hera's wrath prevailed upon several of Zeus's lovers.

The Wrath of Hera

Although it was Zeus's infidelity that caused such pain to Hera, she had a tendency to take it out on his lovers instead of him. Granted, most of the lovers tried every trick in the book to escape Zeus's advances, but even so, Hera felt that the lovers were to blame and deserved punishment.

That Pesky Fly

Probably one of the best-known stories of Hera's wrath is that of her revenge on Io. If you remember, Io was the lover of Zeus who was later turned into a white heifer. Well, Hera wasn't to be fooled. She played along with Zeus's claims that the heifer was an ordinary cow and asked if she could have it as a present. Zeus, hands tied in the matter, consented and handed Io over to Hera. Hera placed the heifer under the protection and guard of Argus, a monster with a hundred eyes.

Zeus felt bad for Io and sent Hermes to release her. Hermes succeeded in slaying Argus and setting Io free. But this wasn't to be the end. Hera found out what happened and sent a gadfly to torment the heifer. The gadfly followed Io around, continuously stinging her. Io had nothing to do but wander the lands tortured by the tormenting fly. Eventually, Io was returned to her true form, after begging the forgiveness of Hera.

Persecution of Mother and Son

Another famous story surrounding Hera's wrath is that of Alcmene and Heracles. As you know, Hera persuaded her daughter Eileithyia to complicate matters during Alcmene's pregnancy with Zeus's child. This didn't pan out exactly as she had hoped, so her wrath became even greater, this time toward Alcmene's son Heracles rather than to Alcmene herself.

Poor Heracles, initially an innocent in the matter, he was continuously persecuted by Hera for the better part of his life. She did everything in her power to punish Heracles, including making him a slave, sending serpents to kill him, and driving him to madness (which caused him to kill his own wife and children). Even throughout all of this, Heracles was able to hold his own, so Hera's anger was never truly avenged. (Chapter 19 gives a greater account of the life of Heracles.)

 **ESSENTIALS**

Even though Hera spent a good deal of her time trying to make the life of Heracles a living hell, the hatred wasn't everlasting. When Heracles died, he descended to Mount Olympus where he reconciled with Hera. To show good faith, Hera even gave her daughter as a bride to him.

A Lover's Spat

Hera and Zeus once got into a heated debate over whether the man or the woman derived the most pleasure from sex. Zeus claimed that women had greater pleasure, and Hera claimed that it was the man who had all the enjoyment. As the debate was going nowhere, they decided to call in a consultant—Tiresias.

Why Tiresias? Tiresias had lived as both man and woman, and therefore was an appropriate judge. As a child, Tiresias came upon two snakes mating. He took a stick and beat the coupling pair, killing the female. At once, he was transformed into a woman. He lived as a woman for seven years until by chance he came upon another pair of snakes mating. This time he killed the male snake, and was transformed back into a man.

When asked to settle the debate, Tiresias was adamant in his answer that women derive more pleasure from the act of making love—so much more so in fact that a woman derives nine times the amount of enjoyment than that of a man. Hera was so furious with this answer that she immediately struck Tiresias blind.

CHAPTER 7
Sovereign of the Sea

O ften considered second in command to Zeus, Poseidon was the powerful god of the sea, garnering more fear than respect. Poseidon was like a bully in the schoolyard—but much more dangerous. He had control of the seas and the ability to create earthquakes. He was a god best avoided if at all possible. In this chapter, you will get to know Poseidon and the many myths that surround him.

The Power of Poseidon

As you know, when the domains were divided by drawing lots, Poseidon drew the seas. However, his power extended beyond the sea to include both lakes and freshwater springs as well. Some myths say he also controlled the rivers, though the rivers had their own, lesser deities.

Poseidon is often known as the "earth shaker" as he also had the power to create earthquakes. Using his trident, he could generate savage sea storms, force the waves as high as he desired, summon sea monsters, and cause landslides and floods. He answered to no one except Zeus, and even Zeus could not always reign him in before severe damage was done. It is no wonder he was feared by all, especially seafarers.

FIGURE 7-1:
Sea monster,
from 15th- or
16th-century
woodcuts

But even with the power of the seas at his fingertips, Poseidon was not satisfied. He felt he deserved more, and his greed took him so far as to challenge the power of Zeus. If you remember, he was one of the original three Olympians who built up the conspiracy against the ruler of the gods. That of course failed, and Poseidon was left once again subordinate to Zeus. Even so, he felt that he could heighten his standing by gaining the most patron cities.

Poseidon also had the power to shapeshift. Like most of the gods and goddesses, Poseidon could transform himself into any animal or mortal he chose. He took advantage of this power quite often, making it difficult for those who tried to escape him or simply avoid him for that matter. Poseidon may very well have been standing face to face with you without detection!

The Fight for City Patronage

Each city in the ancient world had a particular god or goddess whom its citizens honored. This isn't to say that these people could not pray to other deities, but that they held the highest regard for one in particular. Often temples would be built in the honored one's name, which became the town's primary place of worship. Statues were also erected in his or her honor. Sacrifices, though still conducted on a personal level, became a town event. Poseidon recognized the power in this system and did what he could to gain the favor of as many cities as possible.

At Odds with Athena

Poseidon's best-known fight for a city was with Athena over the city of Athens. You know that Athena was the goddess of wisdom, but did you know that Poseidon was considered to be the least clever of the Olympian gods? This alone caused a jealously that made Poseidon want to fight with Athena, although it was rumored that Poseidon harbored other bones to pick with Athena. Whereas Poseidon was the god of the sea, Athena brought the art of shipbuilding to mortals. Therefore, she was to blame for bringing man to the seas, which had otherwise been reserved only for the god and his creations.

Remember, too, that Poseidon was credited with creating the horse, a beautiful and wild beast. Athena rained on this parade as well when she brought the bridle to mortals. This enabled men to tame Poseidon's creation and use it for their own purposes. There was quite a bit of animosity between the two deities, and this only heightened when they both decided to lay claim on the city of Athens.

Some myths state that Poseidon actually had possession of the city before Athena even noticed it. He shoved his trident into the ground at Acropolis and created a spring. But then, Athena came along and planted an olive tree, demanding that the city be hers. Poseidon, hotheaded as always, immediately challenged Athena to fight, but Zeus interceded. However, Zeus didn't feel he could reach a fair decision, so he took the argument before others.

One myth states that Zeus allowed the people of Athens to decide which of the two gifts of the deities was more useful, thus naming the one to be honored. The people decided that the olive tree was more useful than a salt-water spring, so Athena took possession of the city.

Another myth states that Zeus took the argument before the other Olympian gods. The gods voted for Poseidon, and the goddesses voted for Athena. Because Zeus did not vote, this left Poseidon one vote shy of a tie, and Athena claimed the city.

SSENTIALS

Although Poseidon lost out as the patron deity of Athens, he was still honored there. But because he flooded their land, the inhabitants withheld their admiration for quite a while. It was Zeus's intervention, in the end, that reconciled the people of Athens with Poseidon.

Yet another myth states that Zeus took the matter to Cecrops and Cranaus, early kings of Attica. Cecrops was biased toward Athena and maintained that he witnessed her claim of the city to precede that of Poseidon. Therefore, the arbitrators ruled in Athena's favor.

All the myths agree that Athena won the city, and this is where the name Athens comes from. Since Poseidon was, after all, the first to claim the city, in retaliation he caused a great flood to drown out the city's countryside.

Never Give Up

Poseidon wasn't a god who gave up easily. He continued to challenge the gods and goddesses for city patronage. Several disputes took place, with Poseidon more often that not being the loser. The following list highlights some of the more popular conflicts:

- He challenged Dionysus for the island of Naxos and lost.
- Poseidon wanted Delphi, but had to go up against Apollo, who beat him out.
- He and Athena went head to head again for Troezen. You guessed it, Poseidon lost out.
- Poseidon even dared to challenge Zeus for Aegina. Zeus, of course, was the winner.
- Poseidon took on the Queen of the Heavens for the city of Argos, but Hera won.

FACTS

When Poseidon challenged Hera for Argos, Zeus did not feel he could reasonably decide between his brother and his wife, and therefore appointed Phoroneus to act as judge. (Phoroneus was credited with dividing men and women into cities in the first place.) With Phoroneus's ruling, Poseidon took a different approach this time in retaliation—he dried up all the water sources of the countryside.

In Need of a Queen

Amphitrite was the daughter of Nereus (the Old Man of the Sea) and Doris (a daughter of Oceanus). She was part of a circle of deities called the Nereids, who were goddesses or nymphs of the sea, said to be the personification of the waves. Some myths say their number reached one hundred, while others claim there to have been only fifty. Regardless, Amphitrite stood apart from her many sisters in one respect; she was the lead of the chorus.

One day, Amphitrite and her sisters were dancing and singing on the island of Naxos. Poseidon happened to notice her and was immediately awestruck. He fell in love and carried her off to be his bride. Or so one story goes. Other myths argue that Amphitrite did not give in so easily.

Hide and Seek

Though Poseidon was the ruler of the seas, Amphitrite wasn't all too impressed. After all, her own father was the Old Man of the Sea, a marine deity in power long before Poseidon came to rule. But Poseidon claimed to love her, and wasn't used to being told no. Amphitrite wanted nothing to do with Poseidon and tried to hide from him by escaping to the extreme depths of the ocean, but to no avail. Poseidon had many subjects within the seas and could always locate her. This myth says that a band of dolphins basically took her prisoner and handed her over to Poseidon. She finally conceded to be his wife.

ESSENTIALS

Several sea deities existed before Poseidon's time, and most of them were peaceful deities. However, when the realms were divided and Poseidon became ruler of the seas, he replaced these older deities and assumed several of their characteristics—all but the peacefulness that is. Imagine the ancients' dismay of having to go from calm to chaos under Poseidon's violent rule.

Yet another myth explains that Amphitrite tried to hide from Poseidon under the protection of Atlas. But again Poseidon sent his subjects to find her. A dolphin located her and after pleading Poseidon's case, persuaded her to go to him. In this myth, Amphitrite marries Poseidon of her own free will. Poseidon was so grateful to the dolphin that he turned the creature into a constellation.

Amphitrite's Children

Amphitrite bore Poseidon three children: Benthesicyme, Rhode, and Triton. The myths do not recognize anything exceptional about

Benthesicyme aside from being a child of Poseidon. Rhode is a bit better known. Apollo was in love with her and named the island of Rhodes for her. However, she became the wife of Helios and bore him seven sons and one daughter. Triton, however, was even better known. This son was given the honor of being Poseidon's herald. He was half man, half fish. He also possessed the power to calm the seas at will. (To read more about Triton, see Chapter 17.)

The Paternal Poseidon

Much like his brother Zeus, Poseidon took on many lovers. But unlike Zeus, Poseidon's wife wasn't vindictive and jealous. In fact, not much is noted in the myths of Amphitrite even taking notice. (Though it is rumored that she did take notice of Scylla, and in a fit of jealousy, turned her into a monstrous creature.) But his lovers can't be denied, for he fathered many children by them. Poseidon had affairs with both mortals and immortals alike. The following list of lovers is not complete but includes his better-known conquests.

Aethra

Aegeus, ruler of Athens, was unable to have children by his wife so he went to seek the advice of an oracle. Receiving advice he didn't understand, he then went to the king of Troezen. The king got Aegeus drunk and sent his daughter, Aethra, to his bedchamber. She made love with Aegeus that night, but also left his bedside that same night to make a sacrifice. During her leave, Poseidon approached her. This pair also made love. (Some myths say she was actually raped by Poseidon and that the whole thing was a setup by Athena.)

On this night a child was conceived—whether fathered by Aegeus or Poseidon, we can't be sure. But the common belief is that the child was Poseidon's, although Aegeus claimed the child, the hero Theseus, as his own. (See Chapter 19 for further details of the life of Theseus.)

The oracle that Aegeus didn't understand warned him not to open his wine flask until he reached the highest point in Athens. The king of Troezen understood all too well what the oracle meant. After hearing these words, he wasted no time in getting Aegeus drunk and sending Aethra to his bed.

Amymone

Amymone was one of the fifty daughters of King Danaus. She, along with her sisters, was sent by her father to find water in the land of Argos. Poseidon had dried up the land so locating water was an impossible task. After walking for miles and miles, Amymone became tired and decided to rest. Left alone, she was approached by a satyr. (Another myth states that Amymone accidentally hit the satyr with a spear in pursuit of a deer.) The satyr attempted to rape the girl, but Poseidon interceded, chasing away the satyr with his trident.

Being the hero, Poseidon felt he deserved a reward and courted Amymone for himself. After making love to her, Poseidon used his trident to create a spring so Amymone could bring water back to her family. However, some myths state that he did not create the spring intentionally but rather accidentally struck a rock while aiming blows from his trident at the satyr. Regardless, Amymone succeeded in her goal of finding water, and Poseidon succeeded in adding another lover to his list.

Amymone and Poseidon produced a son from this union: Nauplius, who would become known as a hero to the seafaring community due to his extensive knowledge of the seas and astronomy. He also founded the town of Nauplia, a famous naval port near Argos.

Demeter

Another of Poseidon's conquests was the pursuit of his own sister, Demeter, who could not be bothered by the advances of her brother. So she transformed herself into a mare to escape him. But Poseidon wasn't to be put off. He transformed himself into a stallion and mated with her in a pasture, both in the form of horses.

Together they produced Desponia, a nymph, and Arion, a wild horse. Desponia was worshipped alongside her mother in Arcadia. The people of Arcadia built statues to the mother and daughter in the form of women with mares' heads. Arion was a famous winged horse who could also speak. Some myths say that his right feet were those of a human.

Iphimedia

Iphimedia was a married woman, but unhappily so. Her husband, Aloeus, was also her uncle and a son of Poseidon. Iphimedia was in love with Poseidon and made a habit of walking along the edge of the sea. She would often sit down and scoop up the water, allowing it to flow over her breasts, which allured Poseidon enough to succumb to her advances. The union of Iphimedia and Poseidon produced two sons: the Giants Ephialtes and Otus.

ESSENTIALS

Some myths argue that Iphimedia wasn't the biological mother of Ephialtes and Otus. Rather, they state that these two Giants were the sons of Gaia (as were the other Giants). Even so, these myths still credit Iphimedia for raising the two and acting as their nursemaid.

Medusa

As you remember, Medusa was a Gorgon, who had snakes for hair and a stare that could turn anyone to stone. However, some myths say that she wasn't always the hideous creature that we conjure up today. These myths reveal that she was once a very beautiful woman, and her beauty caught Poseidon's eye.

While Medusa was in one of Athena's temples, Poseidon took the opportunity to approach her. They made love in the temple, which was simply unacceptable to the virgin goddess Athena. As a punishment, Athena turned Medusa into the horrifying creature she is best known to be. However, this still didn't seem to appease Athena, for she also helped Perseus to slay Medusa.

Perseus cut off Medusa's head and from the blood of this severed head sprang the children of her union with Poseidon: Chrysaor and Pegasus. Chrysaor means "the man with the golden sword," and he was in fact born wielding a golden sword. He would grow to marry Callirhoe (an Oceanid) and father two children: Geryon (a Giant with three heads) and Echidna.

SSENTIALS If you remember, Echidna was a horrible beast: half woman, half serpent. Not all myths agree that she was born of Chrysaor and Callirhoe. According to Hesiod, she was the daughter of Phorcys and Ceto. Some myths even state that she was the daughter of Gaia and Tartarus. Regardless of her origin, all agree that she was one horrifying creature!

The second son, Pegasus, was a winged horse, who would later play a role in several myths. He flew around wild and free until tamed, according to differing myths, by either Athena or Bellerophon. At the end of his days, he was changed into a constellation.

Theophane

Theophane was a very beautiful young girl with several suitors. She too caught the eye of the sea god. Poseidon wanted nothing to do with competition with the other suitors so, in typical fashion, he stole the girl and removed her to an island.

In hot pursuit, the suitors followed this beauty. They eventually found her location, but before they could reach her, Poseidon turned Theophane and the rest of the inhabitants of the island into sheep. To keep an eye on the happenings of the island, Poseidon transformed himself into a ram. When the suitors reached the island and found nothing but a big flock of sheep, they decided to have a feast. When Poseidon saw what was going on, he changed the sheep into wolves and . . . well . . . the suitors were no more.

Poseidon wasted no time in mating with Theophane. Because they both held the shape of sheep, their child was born a ram. But this wasn't just any ram. This child of the sea god (who was never given a name) had a fleece of gold and grew up being able to speak and fly.

Thoosa

Thoosa was the daughter of Phorcys (a son of Gaia). Her love affair with Poseidon is rather unremarkable but did produce offspring: the Cyclops Polyphemus. Understand that this was not a Cyclops of the original race. Rather this was one a different breed of violent and savage creatures. He loved most the taste of raw flesh, if that tells you anything of his character, of both beast and man alike. One of our heroes, Odysseus, will come up against this beast in Chapter 19.

Poseidon and the Trojans

Though we won't go into detail about the Trojan War until Chapter 20, an overview of Poseidon wouldn't be complete without mentioning his relationship with the Trojans, as this is a myth that helped to bring this god to fame.

Poseidon and Apollo were forced to help Laomedon, the king of Troy, build walls around his city as punishment for participating in the uprising against Zeus. They were to be compensated for this great work, yet when it came time to pay up Laomedon refused, leaving both gods angry. After all, this had been no easy task and took a full year to complete. Apollo sent a great plague to the city and was satisfied with this punishment. Poseidon sent a great sea monster to harass the city, but this still wasn't enough to avenge him.

This is why when the Trojans went into battle later on, Poseidon took sides with the Greeks despite being ordered not to by Zeus. But he wasn't always supportive of the Greeks. Earlier, when the Greeks had wanted to build a wall around their fleet of ships, Poseidon implored the gods to deny them for fear that this wall would outshine the glory of the wall he had built. Poseidon was also known to have harassed Greek captains during their sea voyages.

ESSENTIALS
Surprisingly, Poseidon came to the aid of Athena in yet another attack on the Greeks. One of the Greeks had committed the act of rape in one of Athena's temples. They were punished, but the offender was killed at the hands of Poseidon.

To put it simply, Poseidon made it hard for everyone during the Trojan War because of his anger and bitterness. He was a god to hold grudges for as long as it took to get revenge. Selfish and disloyal, Poseidon would switch sides without notice as long as it benefited his cause. He was a very powerful god indeed, but a god not to be trusted.

On the Rare Flip Side

We've established that Poseidon was a rather harsh god, always ready to fight, not so clever, and unable to be trusted. But, believe it or not, Poseidon was capable of acts of kindness through his own free will:

• Poseidon allowed the twin brothers Castor and Pollux a bit of his own power—the ability to calm the seas. He also named these two as protectors of sailors, thus giving away a little bit of his own glory.
• When Ino and her son Melicertes threw themselves into the sea, Poseidon took pity on them and changed them into sea deities.
• He was also known to have given away his precious creation—the horse—as a gift to those he favored. This act of kindness is witnessed throughout many myths.

See, Poseidon wasn't all bad. Even though he continually strove to be admired and exalted for his power, he seemed to only succeed in instilling fear in the ancients. Therefore, they quite often prayed to him, not out of respect but out of fear.

CHAPTER 8
The Dark Prince

The Underworld was a place where all souls (or shades as they are often called) go after death. The Underworld had many divisions, some good, some not so good. Death was just as complicated as life in the ancient world. In this chapter you will take a tour through the realm of the dead, but more importantly, you will get to meet Hades, the Lord of the Underworld.

A Private God

As you know, Hades drew the realm of the dead when the brothers were dividing the domains among them. You may think he got the short end of the stick, but this realm suited him very well. Hades was a private god, somber and grim, who enjoyed solitude. Although often described by the ancients as being cold, Hades was never associated with evil. He was simply the lord of the dead. He performed his duties with an unrelenting sense of responsibility and completed them in a very efficient manner. Therefore, he allowed no room for pity—nor any type of emotion for that matter—to interfere with his work.

As you know, Hades was one of the original six Olympians. But because he didn't socialize with them, and rarely visited Mount Olympus, he was basically kicked out of the top twelve. This suited Hades just fine, though, as he had no desire to take part in the divine counsel. Still, Hades' powers were in no way diminished, for the Underworld was a realm touched by no other god. He had complete control; even Zeus steered clear of his ruling.

The Abduction of Persephone

Though Hades was quite the private god and rarely left his realm to visit the land of the living, he was recorded to have visited at least one time. It was during this visit that he came across the beautiful Persephone, the daughter of Demeter and Zeus.

As legend has it, Persephone was picking flowers on a plain in Sicily, accompanied by nymphs when Hades took notice of her. He was so immediately overwhelmed by her beauty that he didn't bother to take the time to court her, but instead simply abducted her against her will and took her back down to the Underworld.

Here, Persephone was held as a prisoner. As you can imagine, her mother was quite upset at the sudden disappearance of her daughter and traveled the world searching for Persephone. (The travels of Demeter will be explained in greater detail in Chapter 9.) It was because of Demeter's great sorrow that Zeus would not allow a marriage to take place between Hades and Persephone.

ESSENTIALS Even though Zeus did not allow the marriage to take place, some myths say that he was partly responsible for the abduction of Persephone in the first place. According to these myths, Hades did not kidnap Persephone right away. He was in love with her for a while before Zeus helped him devise a plan to steal the girl away in secret.

Eventually, Zeus sent Hermes to reason with and persuade Hades to give Persephone her freedom. Hades couldn't stand the thought of giving up Persephone, but the message sent by Hermes was to be interpreted as a direct order from Zeus. Hades had little choice but to let the girl go. However, he found a loophole.

As a rule, anyone who ate food within the kingdom of the Underworld could not return to the land of the living. While he pretended to comply with Zeus's orders and give Persephone her freedom, he also tricked her into eating a seed of a pomegranate. Because Persephone ate while still in the Underworld, she lawfully belonged there.

Even Zeus could not deny this rule. However, because Demeter was so distraught and Hades had disobeyed Zeus in a sense, Zeus worked out a compromise. Persephone was ordered to live with Hades in the Underworld for four months of the year, and to live with her mother on earth for the remaining eight months. (Some myths show the number of months to be divided evenly, six and six.)

Persephone became the wife of Hades and thus the Queen of the Underworld and eventually became resolved toward her duties as wife and queen. Some myths claim that in time she reciprocated Hades' love.

The House of Hades

Now that you know the rulers of the dead, it only makes sense to describe their domain, the Land of the Dead. As stated before, the Underworld had different divisions. It helps if you can think of the Underworld as a prison with different cell blocks. One cell block is for the exceptional (normally heroes), another cell block is for the common folk, and a third is for the very bad, those in need of punishment. But there is more to the Underworld than these "cell blocks," as we will soon see.

SSENTIALS   Some people mistakenly refer to the Underworld as Hades. Hades is the name of the god, not the place. The Underworld goes by several names: The Land of the Dead, the Nether Regions, the House of Hades, and the Infernal Regions, to name a few. While these are all acceptable names, it is considered bad form to refer to the Underworld as Hades.

Geography of the Underworld

Some myths situate the Underworld at the very edge of the living, just past the ocean's shoreline. Later and more common myths situate the Underworld beneath the earth. There are also said to be many various entries into the Land of the Dead, mostly through caves or lakes.

Several rivers surround the Land of the Dead. These rivers include:

- Acheron: the River of Woe
- Cocytus: the River of Wailing
- Lethe: the River of Forgetfulness
- Pyriphlegethon: the River of Fire
- Styx: the River of Hate

Entering the Underworld

It is said that when a person dies, Hermes comes to collect the shadow (or soul) of that person to lead him or her into the Underworld. One must also cross one or more rivers. In order to do this, one had to employ the services of Charon, the ferryman of the dead. He required payment of a coin to gain passage on his ferry. However, he only steers the boat. The shadow must do the work of rowing. If one could not pay the fee, he or she was sentenced to wander the shoreline for a hundred years before gaining admittance to the boat.

FIGURE 8-1:
Charon, from *The Last Judgement,* by Michaelangelo, Sistene Chapel

Even after surviving the treatment of Charon, one still has to pass Cerberus, the dog of Hades, before entering the gates of the Underworld. Cerberus isn't just any dog. Some myths say that he had three heads, while others say he had fifty. Regardless, he loved to eat raw flesh—certainly not man's best friend. But Cerberus seemed to get along fine with shadows entering the Underworld. His targets were those who tried to escape and living mortals trying to enter.

Traveling along the Dividing Road, the shadow comes to a fork in the road, where he is met by the Judges. The Judges decide which path the shadow is to take, thus deciding in which area of the Underworld the shadow will forever reside.

It became a custom for the ancients to place a coin beneath the tongues of their loved ones after death. This enabled them to pay Charon and cross into the realm of the dead. Those who were not properly buried, or not buried at all, could not gain admittance and would wander the shores for a hundred years.

The Cell Blocks

There were three main areas of the Underworld in which the shadows were sentenced to reside. Though it is often the Judges of the Dead who determine which path the shadows take, sometimes the gods intervene and make the ultimate choice, although Hades himself does not. He is simply the innkeeper of the Netherworld. He appoints others to do the work for him.

Elysium

Elysium (or sometimes known as the Elysian Fields) was an island for the blessed. This is where the very good, most often heroes, were sent following their death. Elysium was a paradise of sorts, where men and women enjoyed a comfortable life in death. Games were held, music was played, and good times were had by all. The fields are always green and the sun always shines.

Some myths, however, do not make much of a distinction between the splendor of Elysium and that of the Asphodel Fields. Or, rather, that those who were sent to Elysium could not determine the difference. Because all shadows were merely shadows of the former self, none could really grasp what was going on around them, and determining their specific place was nigh impossible. Even so, this was considered the best "cell" of the three.

Asphodel Fields

More often than not, a shadow was sent to the Asphodel Fields, a place of limbo. It was neither good nor bad—just kind of stuck in the middle. A final resting place for most commoners, Asphodel Fields held more than Elysium and Tartarus combined.

Here, the shadows normally mimicked the activities from their former lives. Memories weren't a part of this area; therefore, a shadow usually existed and acted very much like a machine with no individuality. A very neutral place, with no redeeming or negative qualities, the Asphodel Fields was a place of monotony and with very little variety or socialization. Even so, it was still a much better place to be than Tartarus.

Tartarus

Tartarus is said to be located beneath the Underworld. It was so far beneath the earth, in fact, that it is said that the distance between Tartarus and the earth is the same distance between the earth and the heavens. A dark and dismal place, Tartarus was feared by all, even the gods and goddesses. It was here that the very wicked were sent to suffer eternal punishment.

The following are a list of crimes punishable by imprisonment in Tartarus: murdering for adultery, keeping one's wealth all to oneself, treason, raping one's own daughter, and committing fraud and persuading others to do the same, to name but a few.

The punishments in Tartarus were rumored to be quite severe. Those most often mentioned as the inflictors of punishments were known as the Erinyes. They each held whips and snakes and used these to torment the prisoners. Sometimes food and drink would be placed before the starving and suffering shadows, and the Erinyes would ensure that the food would stay just slightly out of reach.

The Judges and the Judged

You are probably curious as to who the Judges of the Dead were. You'd be more than a little curious if you were an ancient, for these were the beings who decided your destiny in the Underworld. Though the Judges were an important symbol of the Underworld, the truth of the matter is that they most often sent a shadow to the Asphodel Fields without much consideration. The gods were responsible for ultimately deciding if someone was wicked enough to send to Tartarus or if someone was brave and good enough to be sent to Elysium. So really, these Judges were more for form than practice. Regardless, it's good to know whom you'd be dealing with.

Aeacus

Aeacus was the son of Zeus and Aegina and at one point during his life was considered to be the most pious of all the Greeks. If you remember, Aegina left her son on a deserted island, which Zeus then populated to keep the boy company. He grew to become the ruler of the island, called Aegina after his mother.

He fathered three sons: Peleus, Telamon, and Phocus. When Phocus grew into a great athlete adored by all, the two older brothers became very jealous, so envious in fact that they murdered him. Aeacus discovered this truth and banished his two remaining sons from the island, leaving him heirless.

This act of supreme justice as well as his undeniable uprightness and piety convinced Zeus to honor him upon his death. And this is how Aeacus became a Judge of the Dead. As an added honor, Aeacus was given the responsibility of being the keeper of the keys of the Underworld.

Minos

Minos was another son of Zeus, born of Europa. He was a king of Crete, and much like his father, ruled with justice and equity. It is said that his laws were so well executed and written that they stayed in force for approximately 1,000 years.

However, Minos wasn't quite the ultimate good guy. He fought with Poseidon, had numerous adulterous affairs (some of which caused the women to die), and banished his own brother out of jealousy. Regardless of these not-so-great deeds, he was still renowned for his amazing leadership and dedication to justice. So he, too, was made into a Judge of the Dead following his death. It is also rumored that among the Judges, he was the one given the power of final decision.

FACTS

The fight between Poseidon and Minos was a result of Minos's refusal to sacrifice a bull that was sent to him by Poseidon specifically for that purpose. As an act of revenge, Poseidon caused the wife of Minos to fall in love with that very bull. The two mated, which resulted in the birth of the Minotaur.

Rhadamanthys

Yet another son of Zeus, Rhadamanthys was also the brother of Minos. Some myths say that Rhadamanthys ruled Crete before Minos came to power. He was the ruler to establish a code of laws that became so popular they found their way into Sparta as well. Apparently, he lost his position as ruler of Crete when he and Minos got into a dispute over the affections of a young boy. Minos was the stronger of the two and drove his brother off the island.

Rhadamanthys found his way to the Aegean Islands where his popularity as a great ruler preceded him. Needless to say, he ruled over the islands until his death.

He was also made into one of the Judges of the Dead. However, some myths say that he had a different responsibility as Judge, which was to settle all disputes amongst the shadows. Other myths state that he participated in punishing those imprisoned in Tartarus, or was the immediate ruler of Tartarus.

Escaping Death

Although the typical term in the Underworld was eternity, a lucky few did manage to escape. Most of these had not yet died and therefore hadn't gone through the burial proceedings. Instead, they went down into the Underworld of their own free will—and with a purpose.

Heracles

Heracles' descent into the realm of the dead was one of his twelve labors, set upon him by Eurystheus. However, the descent itself wasn't the only requirement, for he was also given the task of capturing and returning to the land of the living with Hades' dog Cerberus. Not an easy task by any means.

However, Heracles succeeded in reaching the Underworld, guided by Hermes and protected by Athena. He beat Charon until the ferryman agreed to take him across the river. There he met with Hades. A fight ensued during which Hades was wounded and had to be rushed to Mount Olympus to be healed. Heracles captured Cerberus, using no weapons, and left the Underworld as easily as he had come.

FACTS

This trip wasn't Heracles' only visit to the Underworld. When he turned over Cerberus to Eurystheus as completion of his task, Eurystheus was so afraid he hid in a giant jar. Heracles then returned Cerberus to his master in the House of Hades.

Orpheus

Orpheus lost his beloved wife to a snake bite. He tried to live without her but was in such despair that he went into the Underworld to try to retrieve her. Orpheus was a very gifted musician and it was only because of this skill that he was able to reach the Queen of the Underworld. He was able to charm all the monsters, and even Hades, with his lyre.

Persephone took pity on him and allowed him to take his wife back to the land of the living on one condition—that he not look back. The pair made their way back unharmed, but just before reaching the other side, Orpheus was overwhelmed with the desire to look back and make sure his wife was still with him. He did so, and his wife was pulled back into the Nether Regions while Orpheus had to return to the living alone.

Aeneas

Aeneas was visited in the land of the living by his father's ghost, but needed further guidance. He therefore set out to visit his father's shadow in the Underworld. Knowing he would not succeed in this mission alone, he sought out the prophetess Sibyl, and she agreed to help him.

She advised him to first pick the talismanic Golden Bough from the nearby woods, which the Queen of the Underworld held sacred. Aeneas did as he was told and Sibyl took him as far as the River Styx. Here, Charon noticed the Golden Bough and deemed this present to Persephone worthy enough of a free ride across the river. Aeneas found his father in Elysium and was able to consult with him. Successful in his mission, he was also successful in his return to the land of the living.

Theseus

Theseus's descent into the Underworld wasn't his idea. He, unlike the others who journeyed there, had no great personal mission; rather, he went along to help his friend Pirithous kidnap Persephone. You see, Theseus had decided he wanted to marry Helen so Pirithous helped him kidnap her. Then Pirithous decided he wanted to marry Persephone, so Theseus was obligated to return the favor.

They struggled and fought their way through the obstacles of the Underworld and finally reached the Hades' palace. Upon arrival, the two simply stated that they were going to take Persephone. Hades, not about to let this happen (after all he went through enough to get her for himself!), invited the two men to take a seat. They did so and found themselves stuck in the Chairs of Oblivion. There they stayed put for years.

However, during Heracles' visit to the Underworld, he came across the two men. Theseus was allowed to be rescued by Heracles, since he was only along for the ride. Pirithous, however, was not allowed to be freed and remained in the Underworld forever.

Sisyphus

Sisyphus is considered to be the cleverest of mortal men. He did after all cheat death. During his time in the land of the living, Sisyphus committed many crimes against the gods, especially Zeus. In anger and retaliation, Zeus sent Death after Sisyphus, but Sisyphus outwitted Death and held him prisoner. While Death was held prisoner, no one could die. Ares finally intervened and Death was freed and overtook Sisyphus.

Thus Sisyphus reaches the Underworld in the traditional way, through death. But before he died, he told his wife to deny him burial rights. Therefore, in the Underworld he was denied passage across the River Styx, as he could not pay the fee. Pleading to Persephone to be granted three days in the land of the living to punish his wife for her neglect, he was allowed temporary freedom. As a result, Sisyphus was one of the lucky few to break the rules and escape the Underworld.

Sisyphus, as you probably guessed, did not return to the Underworld as he had promised Persephone, nor did he punish his wife. He lived to a ripe old age in complete defiance of the gods. However, since he was a mortal, he again returned to the Underworld, where he was immediately sent to Tartarus to suffer extreme torture for eternity.

The Underworld Spawns Religious Rites

As you can see, unless you were favored by the gods and sent after death to Elysium, the afterlife did not hold much promise. Simple mortals didn't have much to look forward to in death.

It was out of this bleakness that several religious rites and cults came into existence. For instance, several new faiths centered around individual deities (such as Demeter or Dionysus). Supposedly, these deities would give to those of the greatest faith the secrets of the Underworld—including a map of the Underworld labeled with which rivers and springs to avoid and which ones to drink from—thus ensuring their residence in Elysium. With this newfound hope of a greater afterlife, many became very pious and devoted to their religion and own deity.

CHAPTER 9

Home Is Where the Heart Is

T he last two original Olympians are the goddess of the hearth and the goddess of the harvest and fertility. As they stand for the virtues of the home, these two seem somewhat more placid than the others. This isn't to say that they are boring or have minimal power. They are just as important as their siblings, although they represent a softer side of godliness.

Demeter's Sphere of Influence

Demeter was the goddess of fertility, harvest, and grain. As an earth goddess, Demeter preferred to spend most of her time next to the soil; therefore her time spent on Mount Olympus was minimal. This isn't to say she didn't make her presence known there though. Unlike Hades, she was still very much involved in the happenings in the home of the Olympian deities and would often participate in councils or tribunals. But her presence was best felt on the earth. This is why she, more than any other Olympian deity, could claim to rule the earth. As her domain, the earth was her home.

Demeter was a very popular goddess throughout all of ancient Greece. Some attribute her popularity to the fact that she was among the people most often, traveling from countryside to countryside. Others say that her popularity came about because of the necessity of her blessing. Because she was the goddess of the harvest and grain, the ancients relied heavily upon her to provide them with the food they needed to survive. It was only natural that they held her in high esteem.

On the other hand, her popularity could have very well stemmed from the simple fact that she was a kind and generous goddess. Just as Poseidon was feared rather than respected by most, Demeter was respected rather than feared. Of course, she was still a goddess and deserved the reverence paid to any deity, for she did in fact hold the power of destruction just as she held the power of creation.

An Act of Sacrilege

Although Demeter was kind as a general rule, do not forget that the deities felt emotion just as humans did. On a dime, her kindness could change into cruelty should she be threatened or crossed. As you will soon see, when Demeter lost her daughter, she allowed her emotion to take control, which resulted in hard times for the human race. Another example of Demeter's uncharacteristic cruelness was experienced by a young and foolish lad, Erysichthon.

Erysichthon was the son of the king of Dotion. He had an idea to build a great hall in which to hold feasts, but he needed timber in order to do so.

Having no respect for the gods, he entered a sacred oak grove belonging to Demeter and planned to chop down enough trees to build his banquet hall.

As he began cutting, the trees spilled blood from the wounds. A passerby warned him not to proceed, but Erysichthon defied the man and beheaded him. As he continued his task, the tree spirits cried out in despair and called upon Demeter.

We see throughout classical mythology that the gods and goddesses often had great tolerance and the capacity to forgive even their worst enemy. But blatant sacrilege was simply not excusable and usually resulted in death. Death wasn't the worst part though; it was the way the person died that was chilling. The death was usually creative and sometimes involved irony, but almost always involved great suffering.

Demeter came to Erysichthon disguised as a priestess. She first begged him to stop his axing, but when he paid her no heed, she ordered him to withdraw from the grove. Laughing at the audacity of the priestess, Erysichthon threatened her with the ax. Demeter backed down and told him to carry on because he was going to need the dining hall.

Demeter was appalled by this blatant act of sacrilege. This was certainly something she could not allow herself to overlook. She then called upon Peina (Hunger) to plague Erysichthon for the rest of his days. Peina was glad to be of assistance to Demeter and immediately went in search of the foolish boy.

Possessed with Perpetual Hunger

As promised, Peina plagued Erysichthon, causing him to have a continuous desire to eat, a need that could never be quelled. Erysichthon ate everything in sight, to no avail. Within just a few days, he had spent his entire fortune on food, though he still was not appeased.

Finally, he was left as a beggar, possessing nothing but a daughter. His daughter sold herself into slavery to help provide provisions for her father's never-ending hunger. Eventually, Erysichthon was left with absolutely nothing. At this point, he began to eat his own legs. But being perpetually hungry, even this had no impact. He eventually went insane, devoured all his flesh, and died.

As you can see, even Demeter was a goddess not to be crossed. Gentle as a flower for the most part, she did possess a nasty side that shone through from time to time, when the occasion called for it.

The Love Affairs of Demeter

Demeter never married. But that didn't mean she was a virgin goddess like her sister Hestia. Perhaps she simply never found the "right" one. Even so, she wasn't beyond looking, for she racked up a few lovers.

Her first lover was none other than the lustful Zeus. The union of Demeter and Zeus produced a daughter Persephone and a son Iacchus. As you know, Persephone became the Queen of the Underworld. Iacchus was a minor deity who played a major role in the Eleusinian Mysteries (this will be explained in further detail in just a moment).

FACTS

Persephone wasn't born with this name. She was originally called Kore, which means "maiden" or "virgin" and describes her life before the abduction by Hades. Persephone is sometimes translated to mean "destroyer," which could correspond with her role as Queen of the Underworld.

Another of Demeter's love affairs was inspired by her attendance at a wedding. There she met the bride's brother Iasion and instantly fell in love. Theirs was a heated affair in which they made love in a fallow field. But Zeus found out about the affair and in a fit of jealousy struck the mortal Iasion with a thunderbolt. Some myths say this attack killed him on the spot while other say that it simply crippled him for life.

From this tryst in the thrice-plowed field, Demeter conceived two sons: Plutus and Philomelus. Plutus, meaning "wealth," became the protector of the abundance of harvest. Some myths say that Zeus blinded Plutus to ensure that he would not unevenly distribute the wealth among the people. Philomelus was a farmer and content to simply work the land. He had no need or want for riches. The myths state that Philomelus invented the concept of having two oxen pull a cart. He was eventually turned into the constellation of the Ploughman.

It is rumored that Demeter was also smitten with a young nymph, Macris, who was placed in charge of the baby Dionysus. Macris and her father raised and cared for the young god. But Hera eventually found out about the hidden child and in a fit of jealousy (as Dionysus was a son of Zeus by another woman), she drove Macris from her homeland. Macris took refuge in a cave on a small island. To help the poor young nymph, Demeter taught the people there how to plant and harvest corn. It is never stated that Demeter and Macris had a love affair, but it is whispered that Demeter was quite taken with her.

Wandering the Countryside

The most popular myth starring Demeter is one she shares with her daughter Persephone. As you recall from the previous chapter, Persephone was abducted by Hades. When Demeter discovered her daughter missing, she acted as any mother would, overwhelmingly distraught, so much so that she cared for nothing but finding her daughter. All duties and responsibilities as goddess of fertility and harvest were set aside in light of the tragedy.

When Persephone was abducted, she let out a terrific cry, which reached her mother's ears. Demeter immediately dropped what she was doing and left to help her daughter. However, when she reached the area from which the voice came, she couldn't find Persephone anywhere. Embarking on a frantic search, Demeter wandered the whole of the earth for nine days and nine nights with a great torch in hand. During this time, she did not eat, drink, bathe, or sleep.

On the tenth day, she came across Hecate (a minor deity) who knew of the abduction but did not know who had taken her. However, Hecate led Demeter to Helios (the Sun god) who, due to his omniscient view of the world, had witnessed the kidnapping. Helios told Demeter the story and tried to reassure the mother that the daughter was in good hands with Hades.

Demeter was beside herself with fury, pain, and sadness. She abandoned Mount Olympus along with her duties as an Olympian goddess. This act of desertion left the world blanketed with a plague of drought and famine. The earth was now sterile, the existing plants and crops died, and new crops refused to grow.

Travels as Told by Homer

Demeter was determined to hide on earth until her daughter was returned to her, and so she began to wander the countryside. Sometimes she was met with great hospitality; other times she was ridiculed. For instance, when she was received into the house of Misme, she was offered a drink, as was the custom of hospitality. However, when she drank rather quickly (being very thirsty), the son of Misme made fun of her. Furious with this blatant disregard for the rules of hospitality, Demeter threw her drink on the boy, turning him into a lizard.

Weary with pain, she transformed herself into the form of an old woman while in Eleusis. There she stopped beside a well to take a rest from her troubles. A daughter of King Celeus came upon the old woman and invited her to take refreshment in the king's house. Demeter, pleased with this act of kindness, agreed, and followed the girl home.

Here she was met with great acts of hospitality, not only by the king's daughter but by the queen as well. Demeter was impressed with this household and with one woman in particular, Iambe, who was the daughter of Pan and a servant in the house of Celeus. A jovial sort, Iambe was the only person who could make Demeter smile.

Demeter became a servant in the house of Celeus along with Iambe. Gaining the queen's trust rather quickly, Demeter became the wet nurse for Prince Demophon, and she found in Demophon a comfort only a child could give. She decided to give the boy the gift of immortality. To do this, Demeter fed him ambrosia and set him in the fire at night in order to burn away his mortality. But she was discovered doing so by the queen who interfered with a scream. Demeter, angry with this interruption, threw the child down.

Transformed back into her true form, Demeter ordered this royal house to build a temple to her. She also taught them the proper religious rites to perform in order to honor her. This practice later became known as the Eleusinian Mysteries.

Never interrupt a goddess while she is in the middle of casting a spell! Some myths say that when Demeter was interrupted by the queen, she dropped the baby into the fire and he was immediately burnt up. Let this be a lesson learned.

A Necessary Compromise

As Demeter had neglected her duties for nearly an entire year, Zeus realized that if he did not interfere, soon the human race would be wiped out due to starvation. Putting forth the effort, Zeus finally found his sister.

However, she would not listen to reason and simply demanded that her daughter be restored to her. Zeus knew he had no other choice than to appease his sister, therefore he ordered Hades to return Persephone. As you know from the previous chapter, Hades agreed to comply but first tricked Persephone into eating in the Underworld.

And so the compromise was reached to have Persephone spend part of the year with her mother on earth and part of the year with Hades in the Underworld. The ancients believed that it was due to this divided time that the seasons were created. During Persephone's stay in the Underworld, we have the winter months when vegetation dies and crops will not grow. While she is with her mother, the earth is sown and the crops are harvested.

Eleusinian Mysteries

The Eleusinian Mysteries were religious rites held in honor of Demeter and Persephone and were the most sacred of ritual celebrations in all of ancient Greece. If you recall, Eleusis was the city in which Demeter stayed during the better portion of her time of mourning. Here a temple was built in her honor, and here the Eleusinian Mysteries were observed. It is said that Demeter herself established this cult and taught the people to worship her accordingly.

Because it was a secret cult, it was considered a mystery religion. Only those formally initiated were allowed to participate, and not a word was to be spoken of the happenings taking place during these rituals. There were even stipulations regarding those who could be initiated. For instance, a pledge could not have shed blood at any point during his or her lifetime. Women and slaves were not forbidden to participate, as was often the case.

FACTS

The mystery religions included the Dionysian cults, the Orphic cults, the Cabiri cults, and of course the Eleusinian Mysteries. They were quite popular and even supported by the city and state governments. However, the spread of Christianity had a negative impact on these faiths, and was a key component in the death of mystery religions.

It seems as though the initiated took their pledge of secrecy very seriously and were careful to honor it. They did such a good job of keeping their mouths shut that today, scholars scratch their heads when it comes to the exact nature and happenings of the Eleusinian Mysteries.

Hestia Honored

Though she is introduced last, Hestia was the eldest of the original Olympian deities. But in keeping with the old adage "Save the best for last," her introduction has been saved for the end. As you will see, Hestia was considered the most compassionate, most virtuous, and most generous of all the Olympian deities. A goddess to the utmost degree, she was regarded as pure goodness.

Hestia was the goddess of the hearth. This may not sound like much, but she was responsible for the very foundation of all that characterized the home. In essence, she was a family goddess, and every household worshipped her. Like a great guardian, she watched over and protected the home, all members of the family, and the happenings around the house.

ESSENTIALS

The hearth represented the epicenter of the family. Because the ancients obviously did not have electric and gas heat like we do today, the hearth was one of the most important places in the home. As the location of the cooking fire, it was continuously maintained. The family gathered around it to receive warmth, but it also served as a common setting in which to spend time with each other.

Though the primary focus was on the home, she also became the protector and goddess of communities. By extending her powers outward, she reached the city halls, civic gatherings, and communal properties. To put it simply, she was the goddess of all the ideals of togetherness.

She had very few temples built specifically in her honor (aside from those of the Vestal Virgins), but none were needed. Hestia was satisfied with the home itself being used as a temple in which the inhabitants worshipped her on a regular basis. When she became idealized as the protector of the community, public hearths also became sacred to her.

As a goddess who was regarded as the central force upholding the ideals of togetherness, her inspiration and impression spread to the home of the gods and goddesses. Therefore, she eventually represented the hearth of Mount Olympus. She spent all her time there, never leaving to traipse about the earth like her siblings. Even Hades left his home more than Hestia did.

Hestia is very rarely mentioned in the myths, and she doesn't have a myth of her own. Some believe that this is due to the fact that she never visited the earth and did not intermingle with mankind. But others believe that the reason she does not star in myths is because she was a chaste goddess, and it is sacrilegious to gossip about her. Therefore, she simply wasn't spoken of frequently.

The Vestal Virgins

Though the goddess of the hearth did not require the typical temples to honor her, there was one temple erected for her that some consider to be the most famous temple of all deities: the Temple of Vesta. Located in Rome, this temple was kept by priestesses collectively called the Vestal Virgins.

The temple was actually built in the name of Vesta, who was the Roman equivalent of Hestia (hence the name Vestal Virgins). Six priestesses invariably served at any one time. They were chosen from the best families of Rome and had to have two living parents as well as a nice countenance and no physical deformities. Entering training between the ages of six and ten, these girls were given the mark of distinction at a very young age. The Vestal Virgins were a very important part of the Roman culture, and for a child to be chosen was a great honor to not only the child, but also to the child's family.

Becoming a Vestal Virgin

When chosen, a young girl would be required to take a vow of chastity and promise to belong to the temple for a period of thirty years. The training itself took a period of ten years, following which the girls went into service for ten years. During this time, they were responsible for maintaining the Vestal Fire and sprinkling it with holy water every day. To let the fire go out was thought to bring bad luck to Rome. Being such an important task, the punishment was severe—a beating by rods. After the period of service was concluded, the virgin then spent another ten years training vestal students.

FACTS

The initiation of a child into the service of the goddess included a ceremony in which she was escorted to the Temple of Vesta. Here she was met by other Vestal Virgins, who dressed her in white clothing and cut her hair.

Following her thirty years of service to the temple, the woman was then allowed to become a private citizen. She could then marry and bear children if she so chose. However, most who served as Vestal Virgins decided to continue serving the goddess for the rest of their lives. It was, after all, the only life they had ever known.

Those women who served the goddess were treated in a different fashion than the common women of the city. Because they were not bound to any man and therefore were not under the power of a man, they had some of the same rights as a man. For instance, they could participate in court trials and create wills to bequeath their belongings to anyone they chose.

Breaking the Vow of Chastity

The greatest crime these women could commit was to break the vow of chastity. To do so was not only betraying the goddess, but the city of Rome as well, since the city's well-being depended on their trustworthiness. Breaking this vow was simply unacceptable, and deemed more severe even than allowing the Vestal Fire to extinguish. The Romans therefore came up with a punishment to match the severity of the crime.

If a Vestal Virgin broke her vow of chastity, she would be punished by being buried alive. As if this wasn't bad enough, there was an entire ceremony that went along with the burial.

The woman would first be wrapped in thin strips of cloth, and then covered with thick linens. This would stifle the cries and pleas coming from the poor woman. She was placed on a stretcher that was normally used to carry the dead and carried through town in a ceremonial procession. A priest would say his prayers above the burial site and the girl would be stripped of the heavy linens.

She was lowered into the vault and placed on a bed. The vault, which had been prepared earlier, contained a day's worth of water, food, and light. The vault was shut and the grave filled in. They were careful to smooth the earth at the surface so no one would be able to tell that the area marked a gravesite.

Because she was buried without the proper burial rituals performed, it was thought that she would never be able to reach the Land of the Dead. This sacrifice was meant to appease the deities so no harm would befall Rome.

Hestia's Unsuitable Suitors

Hestia was like Athena in that she loved peace. But while Athena would participate in war if need be, Hestia absolutely refused to become part of any dispute regardless of its severity. It was due partly to this strong belief in peace that Hestia, though essentially goddess of the home and family, did not marry and have a family of her own. But this isn't to say that she didn't have suitors.

Her brother Poseidon and Apollo, the god of music, courted her—or at least wanted to. But rivalry sparked between the two gods, creating a heated argument that had the potential to turn into a small war. Hestia, not wanting war to take place and certainly not wanting to be the catalyst for war, refused them both. But as you know, a woman's word in ancient times wasn't always enough to make things happen. Therefore, she needed Zeus to intervene.

Hestia swore an oath to remain chaste forever, and Zeus favored this, thereby granting her permission to remain a virgin and offering her his protection. It is because Hestia was a virgin goddess and upheld this honor to the highest degree that she required the Vestal Virgins to remain chaste as well.

But not everyone respected Hestia's vow of chastity. During a Dionysiac festival, Priapus, son of Aphrodite and Dionysus, saw Hestia (Vesta) and immediately fell in love with her, or rather fell in lust with her. When Hestia fell asleep that night, Priapus attempted to violate her. He was on the verge of reaching his goal, when an ass brayed very loudly, waking the goddess. Hestia, aware of the danger, screamed and Priapus ran away. From then on, asses were adorned with flowers during the Feast of Vesta.

ESSENTIALS

Priapus, a god of gardens and symbol of fertility, was rumored to be a less-than-handsome guy. Some myths claim he was so ugly his own mother wanted nothing to do with him. He is described as having a gnarled and severely deformed body, though what was most amazing was the enormous size of his genitals.

Chapter 10

The Art of War

After reading about Demeter and Hestia, you probably have a warm, fuzzy feeling, secure in the goodness of the deities. Don't get too comfortable. To shake things up a bit, we are now going to visit the opposite end of the spectrum. Just as Hestia was an advocate for peace, Ares was an advocate for war. As the god of war, he lived for bloodshed and battle. If you find any pleasure in violence as entertainment, you will love this chapter—and this god.

A Detestable Deity

Ares was the son of Zeus and Hera, so he was born as a child to be respected. But that all changed as he grew older and developed a personality and identity of his own. Even though he was one of the twelve great Olympian gods, not many could bring themselves to like him, not even his own parents.

Ares was a god who cared for nothing but battle; bloodshed was the ultimate goal. He didn't bother with ideals of justice, nor even the strategic challenges of war. He simply wanted to heighten the terror and destruction that normally accompanies war. Most storytellers associate him with the very spirit of war, lacking morality, principles, and decency.

Indeed, Ares even looked the part of a great warrior. He was always seen wearing armor and a helmet, and carrying a shield and either a sword or spear (or sometimes even both weapons). Ares also had the war cry down pat. He would emit a horrible cry right before or during battle, which would instill a deep fear in the hearts of the enemy. He was a manly man, muscle-bound and tall enough to tower over mortals. To look at him, one would think he was the ultimate warrior, fearless and brutal.

However, there was one quality that kept this violent god in check. He lacked cleverness and wisdom. Ares didn't bother with thinking things through very well, and it's quite possible he didn't have the capability to do so. He lived for the moment of bloodshed, but if it came down to the need for strategy or policy, he was nowhere to be found; he was your typical not-so-bright schoolyard bully—strong and scary, but easily outwitted.

Living Among the Wild

Ares lived in Thrace, which was a non-Greek land located north of the Aegean Sea and southwest of the Black Sea. The people of Thrace didn't speak Greek, but they had another language that was quite appealing to Ares: they spoke of war.

The Thracians were divided into tribes, each of which had a warlord as chief. They were a rowdy people, occupying their time by becoming intoxicated and picking fights. Not only were they somewhat savage, but they also had skill. They often wielded heavy swords and were quite ferocious in battle. This was the ideal place for Ares to dwell—among bloodthirsty, war-loving bullies. Besides, being despised by mortals and immortals alike, he did not feel at home anywhere else (though it probably didn't bother him all too much to be disliked).

Battles were sometimes held between the tribes of Thrace in order to acquire prisoners of war. The Thracians would sell these prisoners as slaves to Greek traders. It is said that during shortages of war captives, the Thracians would even go so far as to sell their own children into slavery.

On the War Path

Ares wasn't a complete loner. Myths often depict him as being accompanied by at least one, or sometimes even all, of the following:

- Deimos: the personification of fear.
- Enyo: the goddess of the battle.
- Eris: the personification of discord.
- Phobos: the personification of terror.

These four beings are often seen as attendants of Ares as he prepared to go into battle. While Ares would create a fog of fury that would cause the two enemy sides to become filled with desire for battle, these other four would work to instill a terror and sense of discord in the men, which would serve to make the battle even more bloody and desperate.

God of War in Love

Though Ares was generally hated by most, this didn't keep him from having several love affairs. Perhaps he was a kinder god when in the throes of love. Or perhaps he was found attractive because he possessed that "bad boy" image. Who knows? The fact remains that for whatever reason, Ares was rather successful in acquiring lovers.

Loving Aphrodite

The most popular of these affairs was his tryst with Aphrodite, goddess of love; as they say, opposites attract. She was the one Olympian deity who cared for Ares. Their love affair was a torrid one and rather scandalous, but we will get into the details of that in Chapter 15. For right now, all you need to know is that together they produced four children (though some say five).

To be loved by the goddess of love wasn't always a good thing. Quite often jealousies arose against the object of her affections, and murder, resulting from these jealousies, sometimes followed.

Deimos and Phobos, as you know, were the personifications of fear and terror, but they were also the sons of Aphrodite by Ares. These two delighted in accompanying their father on battle excursions. Harmonia was the daughter of the divine couple. She would later be given in marriage to Cadmus, king of Thebes. Anteros was also born of Aphrodite and Ares. He would grow to become the god of passion, and sometimes called the god of tenderness. Some myths say that Eros (god of love) was also their child, though other myths place his birth during creation.

Aerope

Ares also fell in love with a young, mortal woman named Aerope. Not much was known about their love affair aside from the fact that they produced a son together. Sadly, the birth of a god's son was too much for this young woman to bear and she died during childbirth. However, the child was saved, for Ares made sure the child was able to suckle at his mother's breast.

Aglaurus

Aglaurus was a name shared by mother and daughter. However, it was only the daughter Ares was in love with. Her father was Cecrops, a king of Athens. From the union of Aglaurus and Ares, a daughter was born, Alcippe. The rape of Alcippe by Poseidon would be the reason for Ares being put on trial for murder (we will get to that in a moment).

Chryse

The union of Ares and Chryse produced a son, Phlegyas. One account of Phlegyas tells the story of his attempt to avenge his daughter who was violated by Apollo. When Phlegyas learned of the rape, he set fire to Apollo's temple at Delphi. Apollo, not willing to stand for this type of sacrilege, shot and killed Phlegyas. But that wasn't all. Apollo sent Phlegyas to the Underworld where he suffered the torture of having a huge boulder hung over his head that could fall at any moment.

Cyrene

Cyrene, a nymph, was the daughter of the king of Lapithae. Her affair with Ares produced a son named Diomedes. Diomedes would become the king of the Bistones in Thrace. He was best known for his savage mares, four in total, which he fed a daily meal of human flesh. He will show up later in a myth of Heracles.

Demonice

Yet another affair gave Ares children. By Demonice, Ares had four offspring: Evenus, Molus, Pylus, and Thestius. Evenus later becomes the king of Aetolia and has a river named after him. Molus met an untimely death when he tried to rape a nymph and was beheaded. Pylus was not well known, and Thestius became a king in Aetolia.

Harpinna

Harpinna was the daughter of the river god Asopus. The union of Ares and Harpinna produced a son named Oenomaus. Oenomaus grew up to become a king of Pisa. He also founded a city, which he named for his mother, Harpinna. (Some myths claim that Sterope, one of the

Pleiades, and not Harpinna was the mother of Oenomaus, but Ares is still the father.)

Otrere

Otrere was Queen of the Amazons. Together with Ares, she produced a daughter, Penthesilea, who took her mother's place as Queen of the Amazons. However, she was slain by Achilles while in battle. When Achilles looked upon her after stripping her of her armor, he fell in love with the dead beauty and was saddened by the loss.

QUESTIONS?

Who is Achilles?
Achilles was the son of Peleus, king of Phthia, and Thetis, a sea goddess. Achilles was considered to be the greatest Greek warrior of the Trojan War, earning this title by slaying the greatest Trojan warrior, Hector.

Protogenia

Protogenia was the daughter of Calydon and Aeolia. Calydon, a great hero, was held in such high regard that a country in Aetolia was named for him. Aeolia herself was a famed heroine. Though the bloodlines called for another hero in the family, Protogenia bore a rather ordinary child by Ares, Oxylus.

Pyrene

The union of Ares and Pyrene produced a son, Cycnus, who inherited his father's bloodlust, and ambushed and murdered travelers on religious pilgrimages to Delphi. He used the skulls of these victims to build a temple to honor his father. He is most famous for battling Heracles. However, Cycnus didn't stand long against the hero Heracles, who was aided by Athena. Angry because of the death of his son, Ares tried to take revenge on Heracles. However, Zeus intervened using his thunderbolts and the death of Cycnus was never avenged.

Amazon Warriors

It has been briefly stated that Ares mated with an Amazon queen and from that union produced another Amazon queen. Therefore, Ares was quite important to the entire race, not just those individuals looking for help in battle. The myths surrounding these women were quite popular in ancient times, and so we will spend a bit more time on these children of Ares.

The Amazons were an entire race of women warriors. They kept apart from the rest of society, and stood as their own nation of sorts. They had their own laws, their own means of providing food and shelter, and their own government, ruled by a queen. They relied on no one and considered themselves entirely self-sufficient.

No one is quite sure about the location of the Amazon's kingdom. Some say they lived in Thrace, others say the Caucasus. Still others argue that their dwellings were on the plains of Scythia. Some even swear they lived in Themiscyra. Regardless of where their actual homes were, they were well known to all the ancient people, and their myths became a popular subject of entertainment.

Though the Amazon race is considered to be completely mythological, it may have had a basis in real life. In Scythia there were male shamans (spiritual leaders) who dressed up as women and fought as men. It is possible that the stories of these man–woman warriors were told by travelers who had passed through Scythia. And from there, imagination and elaboration take over.

The Men and Children

The Amazons could not stand to be in the presence of a man. The exception to this was if the man was a servant and was performing the most menial task. Of course, they also needed men to preserve their race. So often Amazon women would mate with a stranger to get pregnant, normally a traveler or foreigner. They certainly didn't want the man sticking around for the birth. There was no such thing as a father for the Amazon children.

If a male child was born, the tribe disposed of him, although the method for this is under debate. Some stories say they were made lame and were left to die, or if they got lucky a passerby would take pity on the child. Others say the children were blinded and discarded. Yet others say the male babies were outright killed and thought of no more. And lastly, it is rumored that the luckiest of the male children would be kept and raised to be slaves of the tribe.

Though they weren't treated poorly like the male children, the female children were also mutilated a bit at birth. The Amazon women were warriors, don't forget, and relied heavily on their bows and spears to provide food to protection. Therefore, the female children had their right breasts removed at birth so they would not get in the way of their shooting abilities.

Warrior Princesses

The Amazons followed in the footsteps of Ares and revered war. War was their passion and their talent. Not only did they worship the god Ares, as the father of their tribe, but they also worshipped Artemis. Since she was a virgin goddess and represented the female strength, they held her in very high regard.

Several famed Greek heroes appear in myths with the Amazons. Among these brave souls were Heracles, Bellerophon, and Theseus. The Amazons were also featured in the Trojan War. They came to the aid of the Trojans and their queen, Penthesilea, who lost her life at the hands of Achilles.

Superwomen

The Amazon women were depicted like male warriors of the time. Normally seen riding horseback, the Amazons had armor made of animal skin and always carried either a bow or spear. They were viewed as possessing the strength of a man, savage as a wild animal but especially dangerous since they possessed reason and cunning.

FACTS

The Amazons were a favored subject in Greek art. Most often, art depicting the Amazon race centered around the Amazonomachy. The Amazonomachy was the battle between the Greeks and the Amazons and is illustrated in all mediums of art and in architectural carvings in Athens.

The myths of the Amazons entertained men and women alike, but in different ways. As ancient Greece was essentially a man's world in which women had few rights, the Amazon women stood as a symbol of freedom and strength and were mostly admired on a personal level by the housewives of the time, if a little hesitantly. The men, on the other hand, were in awe of them. Most weren't sure whether they should be admiring or afraid. The thought of a woman possessing the same, if not greater, strength of a man and having no use for men whatsoever was a little frightening. But just as the horrors of war are frightening, they are also fascinating at the same time. And it was in this light that the men of ancient times held the Amazon race.

Battles with Athena

As you know, Ares was the god of war and Athena, the goddess of war. So how can there be two deities representing the same faction? In entirely different ways. Ares loved the bloodshed and destruction that war brought. Athena would much rather have had peace, and stood for the justice and ideals the battles upheld. Because of their differences of opinion, these two deities often warred with one another.

The animosity between Athena and Ares showed itself on the battlefield during the Trojan War. Ares joined the Trojan forces, while Athena fought with the Greeks. During one of the many battles, Ares was fighting alongside Hector (the best of the Trojan warriors) when he came face to face with Diomedes (not the son of Ares, but a different one). This Diomedes was King of Aetolia and held in very high regard as a magnificent warrior among the Greeks.

Of course, being on opposite sides during the war, Ares and Diomedes welcomed combat with each other. But as Ares attacked, he caught Athena's attention. Athena used the Helmet of Invisibility (which belonged to Hades) to intervene and set Ares' spear off course. This allowed Diomedes to get in a blow, which wounded Ares. The wound was bad enough that Ares was forced to leave the battlefield and return to Mount Olympus where Zeus took care of the injury.

Athena and Ares also went head to head during the dispute of the gods. Amidst all the confusion and arguments, Ares attacked Athena with his spear. Either his aim was off or he wasn't clever enough to aim it elsewhere, for the spear hit Athena's aegis, which was magic. The spear didn't hurt Athena at all, but instead made her angry.

Athena, who had quite an aim, picked up a stone and hurled it at Ares. Stunned from the blow, Ares collapsed to the ground. Aphrodite saw what happened and tried to help Ares escape the battlefield. But Athena, apparently still quite angry, attacked Aphrodite and struck her the old-fashioned way—using her bare fist.

Tried for Murder

It shouldn't surprise you that Ares, in light of his hunger for blood and destruction, was placed on trial for murder. In this story, justice seems to have prevailed. But you can decide for yourself whether he should have been found guilty or not.

Halirrhothius was the son of Poseidon and a nymph, Euryte. He came across Alcippe (one of Ares' daughters) near a spring in Asclepius, which was in Athens. He lusted after her and succeeded in ravishing her against her will.

When Ares learned of the ill treatment of his daughter, he was livid. And of course, Ares being Ares thought nothing of killing Halirrhothius to avenge his daughter's violation. (Some versions of the story state that Ares actually saw the act of violence upon his daughter, and killed Halirrhothius in a rage of blind fury right then and there.) But now, Poseidon was pulled into the disaster. Being very protective of all his children, Poseidon wasn't willing to let the matter drop. Therefore, he took Ares to court for murder.

Some myths tell an entirely different story regarding the death of Halirrhothius. In these versions, a dispute began when Attica was allotted to Athena instead of Poseidon. Halirrhothius was sent to cut down the sacred olive trees of Athena. But an accident occurred in which the ax flew out of his hands and cut off his own head.

The trial was held on the hill at whose foot the murder had been committed. The tribunal of gods gathered there and listened to the accounts by both the defendant and the prosecutor. After deliberation, the tribunal acquitted Ares of the charge.

This hill later became known as Areopagus, which means "hill of Ares." Here court was held for several years (during the time of democratic Athens), dedicated to cases of homicide. There were approximately 250 members, and for quite a while the legal decisions of this court were final.

Ares Imprisoned

As you recall, the two Giants Otus and Ephialtes (sons of Poseidon) were said to wreak havoc among the gods and goddesses. One of their finest exploits involved the imprisonment of Ares.

Though still in their childhood, the two Giants were of great strength and size. They set out to capture Ares because they held him responsible for the death of Adonis, a beautiful young boy for whom Aphrodite felt great love. Some myths say her love was romantic and passionate, while others say her love for the boy was that of a mother for her son. Regardless, Ares was none too pleased with the attention Adonis was getting from his lover.

While Adonis was hunting on Mount Lebanon, Ares found his opportunity to do away with the boy who was reaping all of Aphrodite's affection. Ares transformed himself into a wild boar and gored Adonis to death. Not a very pretty picture, but a result of a deity's extreme jealousy nonetheless

ESSENTIALS

The death of Adonis was fitting in that it tied in with his birth. Adonis was a child of incest. His grandfather was tricked into impregnating his mother. When he discovered what had happened he tried to kill her. However, she was changed into a tree by the gods to escape death. Adonis was born when a wild boar charged the tree, splitting it in two, allowing Adonis to emerge.

Some myths say that Otus and Ephialtes were upset by the death of Adonis because he was entrusted to their care by Aphrodite. Or perhaps, they simply favored the boy as most did. Or it is possible they simply used this as an excuse to inflict punishment on one of the Olympian gods. Whatever the reason, the two Giants set out to capture Ares.

They were successful in their quest and bound Ares with chains. Not seen as adequate punishment, the two imprisoned Ares, still bound, in a bronze cauldron (some say a gigantic jar) and left him there. Ares suffered misery for thirteen long months before being released. But it wasn't the Giants who released him but rather the Giants' stepmother Eriboea who is credited with Ares' escape. She tipped off Hermes to the location of Ares. Hermes, using his cunning ability of stealth, was able to cleverly bypass the two Giants and release Ares. Hermes got there just in time, too, because Ares was very near death by then.

Although his imprisonment was a traumatic experience, Ares still did not learn a lesson from it. Once he recovered psychologically and physically, Ares recaptured his bloodthirstiness and returned to his warring ways.

CHAPTER 11

The Peaceful Warrior

This chapter is going to introduce you to Athena, goddess of war and wisdom. Unlike Ares, Athena would rather have had peace, much preferring to use reason and intelligence to settle a dispute. But if war were needed, she was the one to have on your side. Skilled in strategy and warfare, Athena was able to outwit even the god of war.

The Birth of Athena

Though you already know Athena was the biological daughter of Zeus and Metis, what you don't know is that Metis didn't physically give birth to Athena. Granted, you haven't received the delivery room stories of the all the other gods, but the story of Athena's birth is just too good to pass up.

When the love affair between Zeus and Metis resulted in a pregnancy, Gaia came forward and warned Zeus that if Metis had a daughter, she would then have a son. The son would grow to become even greater in strength than Zeus and take over the kingdom of the heavens. Zeus, all too aware of a son's ability to take away his father's power, decided to prevent this birth.

Zeus's solution to the problem? Swallow the mother.

ESSENTIALS   Some myths say that Metis tried to escape from Zeus by transforming herself into a fly. But this didn't fool Zeus. He simply swallowed the fly instead.

However, when it came time for Metis to give birth, Zeus was struck motionless by a piercing pain in his head. Crying out in suffering, he ordered Hephaestus to use his ax to split open Zeus's head to relieve him of the pressure and pain. Hephaestus did as he was told. As soon as the ax split the skull, the daughter of Zeus emerged fully clad in armor. Instead of a baby's wail, the world was met by an adult's war cry.

To get an idea of the vigor of this young goddess, check out this story. According to legend, Athena, in her younger years, had a friend by the name of Pallas. Pallas was the beautiful daughter of Triton, a sea deity. The two girls often practiced warfare with one another. One day they quarreled as young friends will do from time to time. The quarrel was nothing exceptional, but Pallas tried to strike Athena. Zeus, being overprotective of his daughter, interfered and deflected the blow. Naturally, Athena wasn't going to stand there and be attacked, so she struck at Pallas. However, Pallas was frightened of Zeus and neglected to defend herself. The blow killed young Pallas.

Athena was deeply sorry for the death of her young friend, and erected a statue in her honor. The statue took its place next to Zeus on Mount Olympus, but fell to the earth in what would later become the city of Troy.

The Almighty Athena

Athena inherited her mother's wisdom and her father's sense of justice. These two features combined made for a brilliant and merciful goddess. Those in need of aid, especially heroes and soldiers, would call upon Athena's protection. Under her care, characters such as Heracles and Odysseus were able to complete their missions unharmed.

But her realm of protection did not limit itself to people. She was also considered the protector of several cities, including Athens and Argos, and was credited by some with the law and order of civilization. Being wise and just, Athena sat on many councils and took part in her fair share of tribunals. In fact, it is said that she was the one to create the tradition of trial by jury in Athens.

A Goddess Who Has It All

As if wisdom and war weren't enough, Athena was also the patron goddess of several other matters: goddess of the arts, including literature, poetry, music, and philosophy. Her very being inspired poetry, and several wrote of her gray eyes and her stately presence.

In contrast to the at-times cold hand of intelligence and reason, Athena showed her warmer side by becoming the patron of spinners and weavers. It is said that she invented weaving and other domestic crafts performed by the women of ancient Greece. Just as men were able to relate to her in terms of war and strategy, she enabled the women to feel that same closeness through their own activities.

But it wasn't just the men who participated in battle who knew and respected Athena. She gained the favor of all men in reciprocating the respect due to them for the hard work they endured. Not afraid of hard work herself, she also became the patron of metalworkers, carpenters, and the majority of skilled workers.

Well, Almost Has It All

Though she could relate to almost every person on earth in one way or another, she was unable to relate to those bearing the weight of motherhood. Nor did she ever know what it was to be caught up in the throes of passionate love. Athena was a virgin goddess, and had no desire to be otherwise. This isn't to say she didn't feel emotion, for the goddess certainly was compassionate. But she simply would not allow a passionate love to interfere with her sound judgment, as it seemed to do with nearly every other deity. She did of course enjoy the company of men, but in a fashion of camaraderie only.

Athenian Cult

As you can imagine, several shrines and temples were built to honor Athena. Nearly everyone had a reason to worship her. And of course, being a protector of several cities, several elaborate sanctuaries were devoted to her alone, the two most popular being the Parthenon and Eerectheum, both of which were located atop the acropolis in Athens.

The Parthenon

The Parthenon is one of the best-known temples of ancient Greece, partially due to the fact that remains of the temple are still standing today. It has become a hot spot for tourists and a hot topic for those studying architecture.

FACTS

Parthenon means "chamber of the virgin." Though the temple was built in Athena's honor, it also illustrates other deities even though they are not worshipped here. There are several carvings of scenes taken from Greek mythology such as the war between the gods and the Giants.

The Parthenon was built to house a 35-foot high statue of Athena, made of ivory and gold. This immense temple, though built to honor the goddess Athena, also served to glorify Athens as a whole. Of course, the religious Athenians still honored and worshipped the deities in the Parthenon, but on the whole, it was more for show. Looking at the Parthenon, no one could question the grandeur and wealth of Athens.

The Parthenon was certainly a sight to see. Expensive and elaborate, the temple was quite a display. Even so, it simply did not serve the practical purposes that many of the other temples did. In fact, the traditional rituals and sacrifices were made to the older cult statue of Athena, which was housed in the Erectheum.

Erectheum

The Erectheum was smaller than the Parthenon and situated nearby. This temple, though not nearly as grand and luxurious as the Parthenon, served a more practical purpose. It was here that the olivewood statue of Athena was placed, the statue that served as part of the Panathenaea festivals.

During midsummer, those wishing to pay tribute to the goddess Athena would gather together on what was thought to be Athena's birthday. Athletic and musical competitions took place, but the greatest event was the dressing of the wooden statue. Every year, a select group of women made a new woolen gown for the statue. During the festival, a great show was made of taking this gown through the city and draping it over the statue in the Erectheum. Yet another festival involving this statue took place every four years and was called the Great Panathenaea. During this celebration, the statue would be carried to the sea and washed.

Athena the Inventor

With such a versatile mind and an array of abilities, Athena was revered for many things and her duties kept her quite busy. However, she did manage to find time to throw in a few inventions here and there. She was fond of mankind and took pleasure in giving the race gifts every once in a while; her inventions were almost always in favor of the human race.

Athena's natural sense toward practicality was illustrated in her toolmaking: the plow, the yoke, and the bridle were all gifts to make life easier and more efficient for the ancients. On a culinary note, she is also credited with introducing olive oil.

Athena is also thought to have overseen the building of the first ship, the Argo. Some argue that this wasn't the first ship, but allow that it was the largest ship to have ever been built. (This was the ship used by Jason and the Argonauts during his quest for the Golden Fleece.)

Yet other credits to Athena's name were the introductions of the war chariot, the flute, the trumpet, and the science of mathematics. The list goes on, and the ancients were quite grateful to Athena for her generous presents.

An Adventurer's Best Friend

Several myths starring Athena are those that feature some great hero or adventurer trying to overcome an obstacle or trial. With her favorable traits of intelligence and skill, Athena was naturally the deity called upon. If she felt the request was justified, she would come to the aid of the distressed adventurer. The following are a few of the most popular cases in which Athena became a saving grace.

Diomedes

As you know from the previous chapter, Diomedes was a famed hero of the Trojan War. However, his successes cannot be noted without giving credit to Athena. As one of the lucky few under her protection, Diomedes made a name for himself as a great warrior.

During the Trojan War, Diomedes fought on the side of the Greeks. He was responsible for wounding Ares during battle and driving him from the field. Aphrodite was also wounded while trying to help Ares from the field. (Some myths say that Diomedes wounded her, but others credit the wound to Athena.) But during that very same day, he also managed to wound Aeneas (son of the Trojan prince Anchises and an excellent fighter) and also to kill the Trojan prince Pandarus—a war's worth of work completed in one day—and all thanks to Athena's aid. It is all but stated that if Athena hadn't been there to offer her aid, Diomedes would not have survived the war. But her assistance didn't stop with the battles. At the end of the war, Athena also offered her protection to Diomedes to ensure a safe and speedy voyage home.

When accepting the aid of one deity, be aware that you may be inciting the anger of another. Because Diomedes was helped by Athena in driving Ares from the battlefield, Aphrodite vowed to get her revenge and succeeded in making the wife of Diomedes commit adultery against him.

Heracles

Heracles took on what is known as the Twelve Labors. (You will get the full story behind these tasks in Chapter 19.) These labors were seemingly impossible tasks to complete. And indeed, no mortal man would have been able to accomplish even a one without the aid of an immortal. Luckily for Heracles, he not only had the advantage of being the son of an immortal, but was also able to obtain Athena's aid as well. Unluckily, he had the wrath of Hera pitted against his every move. So, this makes for quite a suspenseful story.

Of course, you don't want the story ruined. So, for the moment, just know that Athena proclaimed herself the protectoress of Heracles during his entire mission. She came to his aid several times by offering guidance, always keeping him a step ahead of the game. Without a doubt, Heracles would never have made it as far as he did without the help of the goddess of wisdom.

Jason

Jason is famous for his quest for the Golden Fleece. Again, this is a story that will be fully explained in Chapter 19. But just to give you a rundown, Jason goes on a quest in order to reclaim a throne that is rightfully his. The Golden Fleece belonged to a great flying ram, son of Poseidon and Theophane. Obviously, the task was near impossible and never meant to be completed.

Though the task in itself was a great challenge, Jason had to overcome several other challenges along the way. This is where Athena comes in. She provided him with the bravery and spirit to take on these obstacles. Of course, with Athena on his side, it is inevitable that he would overcome these obstacles. But for the rest of the story, you'll just have to keep reading.

FACTS

Athena wasn't the only deity Jason had rooting for him. Both Hera and Aphrodite played a role in helping Jason during his quest. In fact, it was Hera who implored the other two goddesses to offer their assistance.

Perseus

Perseus, one of the great heroes you will read more about in Chapter 19, accepted a mission from King Polydectes to retrieve the head of the Gorgon Medusa, a hideous and dangerous sight with hair of snakes and a stare that could turn both mortals and immortals to stone. To obtain the head of this creature was considered an impossible task. But nothing was impossible with the goddess Athena on your side.

Athena had her own reasons for wanting to see Perseus succeed. To put it simply, she hated Medusa. So when Athena learned of this quest, she gave Perseus a bronze shield and offered her guidance. Perseus readily accepted this help. Athena was able to point him in the right direction the whole way.

When he finally reached the home of the horror, Athena advised him on what to do. Using his shield, he did not have to look directly at Medusa and was able to use the mirror image to decapitate her.

Since without Athena, Perseus would never have been successful, he gave his thanks by mounting the head of Medusa on Athena's shield. This shield becomes a symbol of the goddess and thereafter she is rarely depicted without it.

ESSENTIALS

Some myths state that Perseus didn't have to use the shield at all. He simply kept his eyes shut and trusted Athena to guide his sword, knowing that her hatred of Medusa would not fail him. In this way, Perseus was merely the pawn and not actually the murderer.

FIGURE 11-1:
The Gorgon Medusa, from a 6th-century B.C. vase

Odysseus

The great Odysseus was a favorite of Athena. In fact, she had a respect for him that most deities do not have for mere mortals. Odysseus possessed intelligence, cunning, and a sense of justice that reminded Athena of herself. She showed her appreciation of this pious man by aiding him throughout both the Trojan War and his journey home, which was quite a task, considering his journey took ten years to complete.

As you can imagine, if a journey takes ten years, it might have been riddled with obstacles. Indeed it was. Odysseus was confronted with many complications; however, he remained pious and Athena remained his protector. You may be wondering how so powerful a goddess could not have seen Odysseus quickly and safely home as she did Diomedes. Well, unfortunately, Odysseus was on Poseidon's bad side. Not a good place to be when you have to cross the seas during your journey home. (To get all the good juicy details, see Chapter 19.)

Highlights of Athena in Myth

As the goddess of wisdom, war, and skill, Athena played a role in many myths. Sometimes she was singled out as a main character, whereas other times she remained in the background until needed. She was a popular deity among the ancients, and one way the storytellers were able to show their respect was to add her as a character to some of their most popular stories. The following are a few of the instances in which Athena appeared in the myths, seemingly as an afterthought, but important nonetheless:

- Athena, along with Hermes, purified the Danaides of the murder of their husbands.
- She strikes Marsyas for playing a double flute she had cursed and thrown away.
- Athena casts the deciding vote during the trial of Orestes for murdering his mother.
- The goddess bestowed several punishments on Ajax because he continually offended her.
- Athena competes in a competition of beauty with Hera and Aphrodite.
- She was going to make one of her favored mortals, Tydeus, immortal, but changed her mind when she witnessed him eating the brains of his enemy.

It isn't difficult to find myths in which Athena plays a role. If this wise goddess interests you, check out the reading resources appendix to find more reading material. Athena is a character you won't be disappointed in.

CHAPTER 12
The Thrill of the Hunt

As the daughter of Zeus, Artemis took her place among the twelve great Olympian deities as the goddess of archery and hunting. She was the elder twin sister of Apollo and was a self-proclaimed virgin goddess. Artemis was usually depicted as an untamed, young girl, roaming the mountainsides and uncultivated lands and perpetually on the hunt.

Lady of the Wild

As the daughter of Zeus and Leto, Artemis was one of the many to suffer the jealous fury of Hera. When it came time for Leto to give birth, she had a difficult time finding someone to shelter her for all were afraid of Hera's wrath. However, she finally went to her sister Asteria on the island of Ortygia and was able to find refuge there. Here Leto gave birth first to Artemis and, immediately following, Artemis was strong enough to help her mother give birth to Apollo.

This aid in her mother's childbirth of Apollo led Artemis to later be regarded as a goddess of childbirth. She took on the responsibility of watching over mothers in labor. Legend has it that those who died in childbirth were actually killed by the arrows of Artemis.

Zeus favored his daughter, and told her to ask for anything she wanted. Artemis at the young age of three asked to be given a bow and arrows, all the mountains on earth as her home, and eternal virginity. Zeus granted her all she wanted and more. Along with these gifts, he also gave her thirty cities.

Hera, of course, was jealous of the attention granted to a child of Zeus not of her womb. So she tormented the young girl by insulting her, spilling her arrows, and striking her. Perhaps it is due to this treatment as a child that Artemis grew to become very strong-willed and unyielding in the punishment of those who offended her.

Aside from Hera's torment, Artemis had a rather happy existence. She roamed the mountainsides in the company of her nymphs, dividing her time between hunting and punishing those who offended her.

Strangely enough, the goddess of the hunt was also the protector of all wild animals. Though she killed animals, she did not want to see them suffer. It is said that her arrows provided a clean and painless death (when she wanted them to). As a predator, Artemis kept the animal population in check and, therefore, the numbers were kept low enough that starvation and overpopulation weren't a plague to the animal kingdom. But on the less practical side of things, it should be noted that

Artemis simply enjoyed the challenge of the hunt. The mountains were her playground and hunting her favorite game. Homer gives her the name "Lady of Wild Animals."

An Overprotective Daughter

Artemis could be at times harsh, and sometimes even downright cruel, but one of her greatest qualities was her complete and unreserved devotion to her mother. Both she and Apollo recognized the difficulty their mother had in bringing them into the world, and respected none other above her. Throughout the myths Artemis and Apollo join forces to either protect their mother or seek revenge on her offenders.

Torturing Tityus

Hera, filled with jealousy and recognizing that she was unable to prevent the birth of the divine twins, still wanted to get her revenge on Leto. Therefore, while the twins were away from their mother, Hera filled the Giant Tityus with overwhelming lust for Leto. The Giant, acting on his desires, tried to rape Leto, but Leto called out to her children who did not hesitate to come to their mother's aid. The two shot their arrows at the Giant and killed him before he had violated their mother. (Some myths say that Apollo wasn't present and the death of Tityus was credited to Artemis alone.)

After his death, Tityus was sent to Tartarus. He was secured to the ground, covering several acres (the myths vary from two to nine acres). His punishment was for a pair of vultures to be sent every day to feed on his liver, which grew back at night. Tityus had his hands tied and was unable to fend off the birds.

ESSENTIALS During Leto's pregnancy, Hera sent the great Python to pursue Leto. Though Leto managed to escape and bear the children in safety, Apollo never forgot this. He strangled Python shortly after his birth to avenge his mother.

Niobe Speaks Hastily

Niobe was the wife of Amphion, a son of Zeus. She bore him six daughters and six sons. (Some myths disagree with this number and claim that she actually bore seven daughters and seven sons. Some even claim she gave birth to ten daughters and ten sons.) As a proud mother of so many children, Niobe made the mistake of bragging about them during the feast day of Leto. But she went too far. Obviously not thinking of the consequences, Niobe said that her children were better than the twins of Leto, and that she was superior to Leto for having twelve children whereas Leto had only two.

Leto was furious and offended by the audacity of this woman and called upon her children to exact revenge. Happy to oblige their mother, the twins murdered all of Niobe's children with their arrows. Artemis killed the six daughters, and Apollo killed the six sons. Some myths say that not all the children were killed; two were spared, one girl and one boy.

According to the *Iliad*, the children were not buried right away but remained unburied for ten days. Finally, the gods buried the children themselves on the eleventh day. Niobe was so grief-stricken that she could not keep from continuously crying. The gods took pity on her and turned her into a block of marble. But even so, she still could not stop weeping. So, from this block of marble flows a stream, which is said to be Niobe's never-ending tears.

Artemis Takes Offense

As an Olympian deity, Artemis was no doubt due the same respect paid to each of the other eleven deities. However, it seems she was often forgotten and sometimes blatantly ignored, which Artemis found quite irksome. And, as you will see, those who offended her were punished without mercy.

Actaeon

Actaeon was the grandson of Apollo. He grew up to become a great hunter, trained either by his father or the centaur Chiron. Actaeon came across Artemis while she was bathing in a spring. Though he did not try to advance on her or even disturb her in any way, Artemis was furious at having been seen naked. She was afraid Actaeon would brag about the scene, and so took steps to prevent it.

Actaeon, being a hunter, naturally had his hunting dogs with him. Artemis turned the poor man into a deer, and his very own dogs devoured him on the spot. The hounds had no idea they had just eaten their master and went howling through the forest in search of him. Eventually, Chiron had to create a statue in the image of Actaeon in order to pacify the dogs.

Not all who suffered the wrath of Artemis were necessarily guilty of doing anything wrong as you have just witnessed in the story of Actaeon. When Artemis is involved, one should do his best to stay out of the wrong place at the wrong time.

Admetus

Admetus was the king of Pheres. He fell in love with Alcestis, the daughter of the king of Iolcos. However, the king would not consent to their marriage. The king sent a proclamation out that stated that no man could marry his daughter unless that man had a chariot that was drawn by a wild boar and a lion yoked together. Luckily for Admetus, he was favored by Apollo who fulfilled this requirement for his friend.

Admetus won the hand of Alcestis. However, he forgot to offer the due sacrifice to Artemis on his wedding day. Furious with this omission, Artemis planned her revenge. Admetus and Alcestis found the bridal chamber to be filled with snakes on their wedding night. Only Apollo was capable of soothing his sister's anger, and he did so on behalf of Admetus, so this was the extent of his punishment.

Agamemnon

Agamemnon, the commander in chief of the Greek forces during the Trojan War, was already on Artemis's bad side due to family history. Even in knowing this, he made the mistake of offending her.

Before heading off to Troy, Agamemnon set off on a hunt and returned successfully with a mighty stag. Feeling proud, he mistakenly commented that his hunting ability equaled that of Artemis. Other myths say he flat out boasted to be a better hunter than Artemis. Obviously, in either case this called Artemis to action.

As punishment, Artemis would not allow the winds to blow, which meant the entire fleet of Agamemnon could not proceed to Troy. The only way to have the winds released was for Agamemnon to sacrifice his eldest daughter, Iphigenia, to Artemis.

Agamemnon sent for his daughter and indeed sacrificed her to Artemis. Some myths reveal that the killing did take place, whereas others say that Artemis switched Iphigenia with a deer at the last minute and took the girl off to Tauris where she became a priestess in Artemis's temple.

Oeneus

Oeneus was the king of Calydon and was normally a very pious man who took care to honor the deities appropriately. However, one year he must have been preoccupied, for he forgot to honor Artemis in the sacrifices at the end of the harvest. As you know, Artemis didn't like to be left out.

As punishment, Artemis sent a monstrous boar to ravish the city of Calydon and its surrounding fields. The boar did his share of damage, killing several of the men who had banded to dispose of the beast, and was finally killed by Oeneus's son Meleager.

FACTS

The Calydonian Boar Hunt was a famous event in which several heroes and princes of the age took part. Included in the hunting party were characters such as Jason, Theseus, Atalanta, Castor, Polydeuces, and Peleus. The event was so highly rated by the ancients that it stands next to the Trojan War and the quest for the Golden Fleece in all-time favorite events.

Protecting Her Virginity

Artemis was the third of the virgin goddesses, the other two being Hestia and Athena. As you know, Artemis was granted the right to remain a virgin forever by her father Zeus. However, remaining so wasn't as simple as just saying the words. In fact in some cases, she had to fight to maintain her right, at times resorting to violence in order to protect her virginity.

The Giant Otus declared his love for Artemis. As if this weren't enough to incite Artemis's anger, the Giant went a step further and tried to violate her. At the same time Otus's brother tried to violate Hera. Though unsuccessful, just attempting this was enough to motivate Artemis to kill them.

As the brothers were out hunting, Artemis transformed herself into a deer. She waited for the brothers to position themselves opposite each other and then ran between them. They each threw a spear meaning to kill the deer, but Artemis dodged the attacks and the spears hit the two Giants, killing them both.

Because Artemis was so adamant in her virginity, she also required this quality in all of her attendants; none in the presence of Artemis should ever desire the love of a man. As you will see, even an unwanted union with a man (or god for that matter) was unacceptable.

Callisto was one of Artemis's dedicated attendants, and as such she had vowed to remain chaste forever. However, Zeus had his eye on the young maiden and as you know, not much stood in the way of Zeus's love interests. One myth states that Callisto was so committed to Artemis that she not only vowed chastity but also shunned all contact with men. This made things difficult for Zeus.

In order to get close to Callisto, Zeus disguised himself as Artemis. Accepting Artemis into her presence, Callisto was shocked to find herself face to face with Zeus. Zeus violated the girl and left her be.

Unfortunately, Callisto became pregnant from this unwanted union. One day when Artemis and her attendants were bathing in a spring, Callisto was forced to undress as to join the party. Artemis discovered the pregnancy and in her anger, changed Callisto into a bear. Artemis shot and killed the bear, though she may have been persuaded to do so by the jealous Hera. Regardless, the young girl died because of Zeus's lust.

Zeus felt bad for the death and changed Callisto into the constellation of the Great Bear.

What happened to Callisto's baby?
Zeus did not want his child destroyed, so he sent Hermes to rescue the child from Callisto's womb immediately following her death. The child was a son who was named Arcas and he grew up to become the king of Arcadia.

The Many Deaths of Orion

Although Artemis didn't care much for the company of men, Orion was an exception since he was an excellent hunter. Artemis considered him a friend, and the two were said to have gone on hunting expeditions together in Crete on several occasions. There are several myths surrounding the death of Orion. But in all accounts, Artemis plays a major role:

Myth #1: Orion fell in love with Artemis and tried to rape her. Artemis called up from the ground a giant scorpion. The scorpion stung Orion several times, killing him.

Myth #2: Orion boasted that he would kill all the animals on earth and so Artemis killed him with her arrows.

Myth #3: Artemis was so taken with Orion that she actually considered marrying him. Apollo became jealous and, while hunting with Artemis in Crete, he saw Orion swimming in the sea at a great distance. He challenged Artemis to a shooting contest with Orion as the target. Artemis accepted the challenge and shot her arrow at Orion's head, not realizing it was her beloved. Of course, Artemis never misses.

Myth #4: Orion tried to rape Opis, one of Artemis's attendants. Artemis shot and killed him.

Myth #5: Orion was in love with Eos (Dawn) and made her his mistress. Again, Artemis shot and killed him.

Though there are several different tales of his death, all agree that Orion was turned into a constellation following his death, which is how we recognize the name today.

Wild But Loyal

As you can see, Artemis was quite the complicated character. Perhaps you are going back and forth between admiration and fear of this young but ferocious goddess. Surely, this is how many of the ancients felt as well. However, you cannot debate that Artemis wasn't genuine. She loved her mother so she protected her and punished her offenders. She had rights as a goddess to be honored and when a person disregarded this, that person deserved to be punished. Her love of the hunt was heightened by her respect of the very animals she hunted.

As an independent goddess, Artemis knew what she wanted and what she needed, and she managed to get both on her own. She was free-spirited and nature-bound. Her depictions in ancient art seem to suit her well: a young girl dressed in a short tunic carrying a bow and arrows, and as wild as the countryside she roamed—the tomboy of the Olympian deities.

In the next chapter, you will meet her twin brother, Apollo. In many ways, he was much like his sister, though by the same token, he is very different—as twins often are. One thing remained steady though, and that was the devotion brother and sister felt for one another. You have already seen how loyal they both were to their mother; well, they were no less loyal toward each other.

For instance, Apollo fell in love with the mortal Coronis. The two shared a great love affair, which left Coronis pregnant with Apollo's child. However, while she was pregnant, she was unfaithful to Apollo and married a mortal man. Apollo was devastated. Artemis, taking vengeance on her brother's behalf, shot and killed Coronis. Apollo's child was taken from his mother's body and reared by the centaur Chiron.

ESSENTIALS

Coronis, in an attempt to explain her infidelity, claimed that she was afraid the immortal Apollo would grow tired of her when she aged and her beauty faded. Because she did not want to be left alone, she joined up with Ischys instead. Regardless of her reasons, the deed was done and she paid dearly for it.

Apollo showed his love for his sister as well. But we won't get into his stories quite yet. Just know that the divine twins were often seen together throughout classical mythology, whether it be fighting side by side or simply enjoying a challenging hunt together. If you have found Artemis to be an interesting character, you are sure to love her brother.

Chapter 13

The Master Marksman

You've met the sister; now it's time to meet the brother. Artemis was the wild child; Apollo was the cultivated child. Apollo took great pleasure in a variety of activities including archery, music, healing, and prophecy. He took the time to master his hobbies, causing him to be considered as the embodiment of all the highest ideals of the ancient Greek world.

Tall, Dark, and Handsome

Not only is he smart, not only is he good-hearted, not only is he a god—but he is also tall, dark, and handsome! Apollo has it all, ladies. (Gentlemen, just remember nice guys finish last.) Apollo was often depicted as the ideal beauty: tall in stature, with a muscular build, the charm of youth, and long hair, slightly curling. Even with all of these attractive qualities, the young god was rather unlucky in love and suffered rejection several times, as you will soon see. However, this isn't to say he was always rejected. He certainly had a fair amount of notches on his bedpost.

Aside from his physical qualities, Apollo possessed great skill—several skills to be exact. Commonly known as the god of archery, Apollo didn't let his talents rest there. He also became the god of fine arts, music, religious purity, prophecy, medicine, and eloquence. Quite a lot for one deity to handle, wouldn't you say? But Apollo's success in these areas was all of his own doing. He appreciated the arts and therefore learned them thoroughly. An interest in medicine grabbed his attention so he became a master. Though several deities held the power of prophecy, Apollo focused on it intently, making himself the principal prophetic deity. And his insistence on religious purity came from his personal experiences.

Whereas his sister was associated with all wild animals, Apollo had a few select ones of his own. Most often he was associated with the wolf, which is rather ironic considering he was a shepherd and in charge of protecting the flocks from wolves. He was also connected to deer and several species of birds, including the crow, vulture, swan, and kite.

ESSENTIALS

Apollo was also the protector of shepherds. As a shepherd himself, Apollo was originally in charge of the herds of cattle that grazed the rural areas. However, as you will soon see, he gave up this duty in favor of obtaining musical instruments.

Granted, Apollo was an admirable deity, one to be respected and appreciated but as with all deities, he could also be rather harsh. You saw in the last chapter how he did not hesitate to commit murder in defense of his mother's honor. He was also known to send plagues to cities that defied him. Not quite as quick to lay down punishments as his sister, Apollo still would allow no one to deny his power.

God of Music

A talented musician he was, and several myths show off Apollo's artistic gifts. Even the Olympian deities recognized his musical ability and any opportunity to lounge around Mount Olympus listening to Apollo play his lyre was eagerly taken.

One myth involving Apollo's musical genius was the story of Marsyas. Marsyas was a satyr from Phrygia. He came upon a flute that Athena had cast away and began playing. He decided that the flute produced the loveliest sound he had ever heard and was willing to bet that the flute's music was sweeter than even Apollo's. He was so sure of its success that he outright challenged Apollo to a musical contest.

FACTS

Athena invented this first flute, but threw it away because she played it at a banquet of the deities and Aphrodite and Hera made fun of the way her cheeks puffed out. In fact, they laughed so hard that Athena was compelled to check it out herself. She looked at her reflection in a stream and was disgusted by the way playing the flute distorted her face. In anger she cursed the flute and cast it away.

Angry at the audacity of this satyr, Apollo accepted the challenge. The ground rules were set, the judges were chosen to be the Muses, and they determined that the winner would be able to do as he chose with the loser. Apollo was to play the lyre, and Marsyas was to play the flute.

During the first trial, both competitors played equally well. The Muses declared a draw, but this only served to drive on Apollo's competitiveness. In consequence, Apollo challenged Marsyas to play his instrument upside down. If you are familiar with these instruments, you know this is possible with a lyre, but certainly not with a flute. Obviously, Marsyas lost the challenge.

Apollo, victorious, chose a severe punishment for his competitor. He hung Marsyas to a pine tree and flayed him alive. Some myths say that the blood and tears (or possibly the tears of his friends) of the beaten satyr formed the river Marsyas. Other myths say that Apollo felt so bad for his treatment of the satyr that he broke his own lyre and then turned the satyr into a river.

The Playboy

As you can imagine a god of such talent, intelligence, and beauty was sure to attract a bit of attention. Apollo never married, but he did have several affairs. His charm was not wasted; he had several children by these affairs. The following are a few of the more popular instances of Apollo's success with the ladies:

- As you know, Apollo had a love affair with Coronis, who was killed for her disloyalty. However, she gave Apollo a son, Asclepius, who became known as the god of healing and medicine.
- Chione was visited by both Hermes and Apollo in the same night. She had a son for each union. To Apollo, she bore Philammon, who became known as a great minstrel.
- Apollo fell for Cyrene after witnessing her wrestling a lion. Together they produced two sons, Aristaeus and Idmon. Aristaeus was the inventor of bookkeeping, and Idmon became a famous prophet.
- Apollo had a tryst with Hecuba, the wife of King Priam. Their love affair produced a son, Troilus.
- Manto was given to Apollo as a prize. She perfected her prophetic abilities at Delphi and in the meantime gave Apollo a son, Mopsus. Mopsus grew up to become a famous prophet himself.
- Apollo's lover Phthia bore him three children: Dorus, Laodocus, and Polypoetes. Unfortunately, these three were killed by Aetolus to gain the country of Aetolia.
- Apollo's love affair with Rhoeo (who was also a lover of Zeus) produced a son, Anius. Anius became the king of Delos and was given the gift of prophecy.

- Thalia was one of the Muses; she bore Apollo the Corybantes. The Corybantes were the male followers of Cybele, a nature goddess.
- Urania was another Muse with whom Apollo had an affair. Their union produced two sons: Linus and Orpheus. Both grew up to be famous musicians.

Although this is a partial list, it is clear that Apollo favored the Muses, nymphs, and mortal women. All in all, pretty much what you would expect from Mr. Tall, Dark, and Handsome. Still, he experienced rejection too. . .

Unlucky in Love

As you have seen, Apollo did have a few flings, but that's all they were. Sadly, when Apollo was in search of love, he almost always came up empty-handed. Not all were impressed by the playboy's attempts at courtship, and Apollo was often left heartbroken and angry. The following are a few of the most popular stories of Apollo's love unanswered.

Cassandra

Cassandra was the daughter of King Priam of Troy and Hecuba. The myths state that she was the most beautiful of all the king's children. Many men admired her beauty and wished to court her, including Apollo. Apollo, however, had an advantage. He was, after all, a god and could undoubtedly offer her gifts no other could.

Cassandra wasn't interested in Apollo's advances. But unlike the typical god who would force her into compliance, Apollo agreed to bargain with her. He promised to teach her the art of prophecy if she would in turn promise to yield to his advances. The deal was made.

One myth states that Cassandra's parents had a great feast to celebrate the birth of their children (Cassandra had a twin sister) in one of Apollo's temples. However, when they left the temple, they forgot the children. As the children slept in the temple, serpents licked their ears and mouths and it was this act that gave them the gift of prophecy.

Apollo held up his end of the bargain, and Cassandra was given the gift of prophecy and taught how to use this gift to foretell the future. However, when it came time for Cassandra to pay up, she refused. Furious, Apollo spat in her mouth and condemned her to the fate of having the ability to prophesize, but never to be believed. Thereafter, several times (during the Trojan War especially) she tried and tried to convince others of the truth of her prophecies, but to no avail.

Daphne

The most famous story of Apollo's unrequited loves involved the beautiful mountain nymph Daphne. There are actually two stories concerning Apollo's great love for Daphne, but both have the same result.

In one version, Daphne was loved not only by Apollo, but also by Leucippus (the son of King Oenomaus). Daphne was interested in neither of her suitors. In order to get close to her, Leucippus disguised himself as a girl. This worked for a little while, until Apollo caught on to what was happening.

To get rid of the competition, Apollo persuaded Daphne's attending nymphs to bathe naked. When Leucippus refused to participate, the nymphs became suspicious. They stripped him naked and upon discovering his sex, killed him on the spot.

Even with the competition gone, Apollo still had no luck with Daphne. She fled from his advances and with no other alternative, turned herself into the laurel tree. Apollo held the laurel sacred from then on.

In the other version, Apollo fell in love with Daphne due to the intervention of Eros. As the story goes, Apollo had boasted that his own bow and arrows were superior to those of the god of love. Eros, determined to get his revenge, shot Apollo with one of his gold-tipped arrows, causing him to fall hopelessly in love with Daphne. But then he shot Daphne with one of his lead-tipped arrows, causing her to be resistant to any love.

Apollo chased after his love fervently. Daphne tried repeatedly to avoid him but to no avail. He pursued her all through the forests, until Daphne was left with no choice but to call upon her father's help. Her father, a river god named Peneus, came to the rescue and changed her into a laurel tree. Saddened by his loss, Apollo from thereafter decreed the laurel as his sacred plant.

A god in amorous pursuit can be a dangerous being. The deities rarely let anything get in the way of what they wanted (though there are a couple of instances in which mortals got the best of them). If you were a competing suitor, it was in your best interests to back down. If you were an attractive woman, it was best to try to keep out of sight.

Marpessa

Marpessa, the daughter of the river god Evenus and the granddaughter of Ares, caught Apollo's eye. Although Apollo fell in love with this "fair-ankled" girl (as Homer calls her), she was already engaged to Idas, a son of Poseidon. But that small obstacle didn't stop a god in love. Apollo abducted Marpessa and carried her away from Idas.

Devoted to his love, Idas pursued the god and dared to challenge him. (Idas was one of the few mortals who ever dared to challenge a deity.) The two came to blows, and Zeus had to intervene. Separating the fighters, he held each back while asking Marpessa to choose between them. Marpessa chose to marry Idas. She explained that she chose Idas because he too was mortal and she was afraid Apollo would grow tired of her as she aged and would end up deserting her.

Sinope

Sinope was another nymph whom Apollo adored. Several myths claim that Sinope was also adored by the ruler of the gods himself, and as you know, Zeus can be quite persistent in his amorous advances. Apollo himself was also quite persistent, though not always as successful as Zeus. Regardless, Sinope quickly learned that simply running or trying to avoid these two gods wasn't going to do her much good.

But she also learned that a god in amorous pursuit wasn't always as clever as he normally would be. So she decided to trick each of them in the same manner (though separately). She stopped running, pretending to have given up, and surrendered herself. However, she pleaded that in exchange for her surrender the god would grant her a wish. Overcome with love, each god fell for the trap and promised the young nymph anything she desired. Her wish? To be granted virginity for eternity.

Free Love

Although he was certainly a lover of the ladies, and loved by a few in return, Apollo did not limit his love affairs to women only. There are two famous stories of Apollo's love for young men. However, as these stories show, it seems as though being a young man and loved by Apollo was a recipe for tragedy.

Cyparissus

Cyparissus was the son of Telephus (Heracles' son) and lived on the island of Ceos. He was a very beautiful young man and loved by Apollo. Cyparissus's preferred companion was a sacred stag that had been tamed by nymphs (or some say Cyparissus himself tamed the beast). Day after day, Cyparissus could be seen leading the stag to graze and keeping it company throughout the better part of the day. Cyparissus was content with this peaceful existence, until one fated summer's day.

The stag was taking a nap in the shade to escape the noontime sun. Cyparissus, keeping himself busy while the stag rested, was throwing his spear about. Sadly, he inadvertently hit the sleeping stag with the spear, killing it.

Cyparissus was so grief-stricken, he wanted nothing more than to die himself. Apollo tried to comfort him, but nothing could soothe Cyparissus's heartache. He then asked the gods to be allowed to weep for all eternity. Taking pity on his love, Apollo changed Cyparissus into the cypress tree, and it was thereafter deemed a tree of sadness.

Hyacinthus

Hyacinthus was also a beautiful young man and loved by many. Both Apollo and Thamyris declared their love for the man at the same time. Hyacinthus, however, chose Apollo to be his companion.

QUESTIONS?

Who is Thamyris?
Thamyris was a beautiful musician, the son of Philammon and the grandson of Apollo. Some storytellers name him as the first man to fall in love with another man, crediting him as the first homosexual.

On one of their outings, Apollo and Hyacinthus played a game of discus throwing. Unfortunately, tragedy intervened. Differing accounts reveal what actually took place, the gentler version recounting that the discus hit a rock and rebounded, striking Hyacinthus in the head and instantly killing him. Other myths state that it was actually the intervention of Zephyrus (the west wind) that caused the discus to change direction and strike Hyacinthus's head. Apparently, Zephyrus was also in love with the young man, but since he favored Apollo, Zephyrus was overcome with jealousy and wanted to punish them both.

Regardless of how it happened, the outcome was the same: the young and beautiful Hyacinthus was killed. Apollo tried to revive the youth, but had to finally accept his passing. Terribly saddened, Apollo transformed the blood from the deadly wound into a flower and named it hyacinth to immortalize his friend's name.

A Mortal's Slave

Though it is more common for ancient myths to tell the story of mortals being punished by the gods, upon occasion the gods themselves were punished by their own. Two instances show how Apollo was handed down a punishment from Zeus. Zeus, as the god of justice, took his position very seriously and didn't show favoritism to the deities if they broke the law. Both of Apollo's punishments were to serve mortal men as a slave.

Apollo the Bricklayer

If you recall, early on there was a conspiracy against Zeus, headed by Hera, in which all the deities took part, except for Hestia. Apollo, of course, was one of the conspirators. Because of his participation, Zeus sentenced him, along with Poseidon, to work for King Laomedon building a great wall around the city of Troy.

The two gods worked as mortals for an entire year, laboring as bricklayers. At the end of their sentence, the construction of the walls was complete. The two gods approached the king and requested their wages, causing the king to laugh in their faces. He outright refused to pay the wages they had honestly earned. This infuriated the gods. However, Laomedon cut their ears off with a knife and threatened to bind Apollo's hands and feet and sell him into slavery. The gods left, planning their revenge. Poseidon sent a great sea monster to destroy the city and Apollo sent a plague to settle his anger.

A faithless king cannot be trusted! The king offered his own daughter as a sacrifice to the sea monster in order to save the city. But Heracles interfered. He promised to save the girl and kill the monster in return for the king's mares. A deal was made and Heracles kept his end, but in the end the king refused to give up the mares to Heracles.

Apollo the Herdsman

Apollo's second sentencing as a mortal's slave was due to a murder charge. Apollo's son, Asclepius, had become a famous healer; in fact he was known as the god of healing. The good physician had become so adept at his art that the death rate had been significantly lowered. Some myths even go so far as to say that Asclepius succeeded in bringing the dead back to life. This imposed upon Hades' line of business and Hades took the matter to Zeus. Zeus sided with Hades and struck Asclepius with a thunderbolt, killing him.

Apollo, outraged by the death of his son but unable to challenge Zeus directly, turned his anger toward the Cyclopes. If you remember, it was the Cyclopes who created the thunderbolts as weapons and gave them to Zeus. In retaliation, Apollo killed the Cyclopes. Zeus intended to throw Apollo in Tartarus for the murders, but Leto interceded on her son's behalf. Therefore, Zeus lessened the sentence to a year in the servitude of a mortal master, King Admetus of Pheres. (Some myths say that the sentence was nine years.) Apollo approached the king in mortal form and served him as a shepherd for the term of his sentencing.

However, the punishment backfired on Zeus. For one thing, Apollo enjoyed herding the cattle; he was after all the protector of shepherds. But to make his punishment even less severe was the fact that the king was very kind to Apollo. The king was known to be hospitable and an all-around good guy.

In return for the king's generosity, Apollo returned the favor several times over. He made all the cows give birth to twins. He helped the king to win the hand of the woman he loved. When Artemis was ready to inflict a severe punishment on Admetus for his neglect in paying her due respect, Apollo smoothed things over. He even granted the king the ability to substitute another mortal for himself when it came time for him to die. All in all, Apollo didn't fare all too badly in his punishment for killing the Cyclopes.

Delphi

A chapter about Apollo would not be complete without speaking of Delphi. Delphi was one of the most famous, and certainly one of the most influential, shrines of ancient Greece.

As you recall, Apollo went in pursuit of Python who had hunted his mother while she was pregnant with the twins. He caught up with Python at Delphi and killed her. However, Python was the daughter of Gaia, and some kind of honor was needed to appease her. Therefore, Apollo founded the musical and theatrical games of Delphi and named them the

Pythian Games. He also had to go to the Vale of Tempe in order to undergo purification to cleanse himself of the murder of Python.

It was here in Delphi that Apollo learned the art of prophecy. His tutor was Themis, a Titaness who was in possession of the oracle at Delphi. (Some myths disagree and state that Pan was the one to teach prophecy to Apollo.) Apollo then took over possession of the oracle of Delphi.

The oracle of Delphi became a hot spot for all those wishing to receive answers from the god Apollo. These oracles were delivered by Pythia, who was said to go into a trance and recite Apollo's answers to the questions posed. The oracle was so busy that the service of three Pythia at a time was often required.

FACTS

Answers given by the Pythia weren't always straightforward. For instance, King Croesus of Lydia asked the Pythia if he should invade Persian territory. The Pythia told him that if he did invade, a great empire would be destroyed. Only after the invasion and his defeat did he realize the great empire was his own.

Pilgrims traveled from all around to receive the oracle. However, the divination only took place nine days out of the year—the seventh day of each month, except for the three months in which Apollo left the sanctuary. As the demand far exceeded the supply, the pilgrims had to draw lots. Those who were chosen would undergo a purification ritual and ask their questions. Then the Pythia would utter an intelligible answer, a priest would write down the answer, and then hand it to the pilgrim.

Though a sketchy process, the oracle did not lose its popularity. In fact, it grew in popularity year after year. After the Romans defeated the Greeks, Delphi was ransacked by barbarians and ceased to function.

CHAPTER 14
Swift as the Wind

Now you will meet Hermes, the messenger of the gods and a very charming and likable god, though not always the most well behaved. He was rather mischievous and roguish, often playing tricks to demonstrate his cunning. But this isn't to say he was a bad guy. An interesting character, Hermes reminds one of that oh-so-cute little brother who always seems to get away with murder.

A Child's First Prank

If you remember, Zeus was enamored with one of the Pleiades, Maia. However, in order to see her, he had to sneak away from his sleeping wife. One of these nightly meetings produced a son, Hermes. But Hermes wasn't your average, run-of-the-mill baby.

Hermes was born at dawn on the fourth day of the month. By noon, Hermes was strong enough to escape his mother's sight and sneak out of the cave. As he was leaving, he saw a tortoise. He examined the shell and had a great idea. He killed the tortoise, fitted the shell with framework, and stretched seven strings of sheep gut across it. This was the first lyre ever built. He then taught himself to play the instrument and was quickly able to master it.

FACTS

Hermes was born in Arcadia where he at once became a very popular deity. The Arcadians believed that Hermes was the god of fertility for both humans and animals. Therefore, they held him responsible for keeping the animal kingdom populated.

His next few hours were spent exploring the countryside. In search of adventure, he came across the cattle of Apollo grazing in the pastures of the gods. Allowing his mischievous side to take over, Hermes stole fifty cattle. (Apollo was temporarily away from his herd at the time.) So that he wouldn't get caught, Hermes came up with a plan to cover his tracks. He tied brushwood to his feet, confusing the tracks he made. He also drove the cattle backward so the tracks were facing the wrong direction. In this manner, he managed to get the cattle away from the rest of the herd and to hide them in a faraway place.

But Hermes discovered that this act of thievery was witnessed by an old man named Battus, whom Hermes made promise not to tell. The old shepherd complied, but Hermes was not so trusting. After leaving the man, Hermes doubled back and disguised himself. He approached Battus as a stranger inquiring after any news of the missing cattle. He offered a hefty reward and Battus did not hesitate to tell all he knew. Furious that the man had broken his promise, Hermes turned him into a stone.

Reaching his destination, Hermes hid the cattle in a cave in Pylos. At a nearby river, he sacrificed two of the cows to the Olympian deities. He then burned the hooves and heads of the sacrificed cattle to get rid of the evidence. He also threw his brushwood sandals into the river. Satisfied that the cattle were safely hidden and that there weren't any witnesses to his act, Hermes crept back to his mother's cave by dusk. He dressed himself in the swaddling clothes he had shed before and lay down to sleep, looking the part of an innocent child.

By this time, Apollo had returned to his herd and discovered the fifty cows missing. He searched all over the world, and finally had to rely on his powers of divination to give him a clue. The omen led him to Hermes. Hermes, of course, proclaimed innocence and even claimed to not know what a cow was. Furious, Apollo searched the entire cave, but still came up empty-handed. He wasn't going to let the matter drop. Convinced of the young boy's guilt, he took Hermes before Zeus and accused him of thievery.

Again, Hermes feigned innocence, but Zeus saw through the lies. In fact, during his hearing before Zeus, Hermes stole a bow and arrows from Apollo. When Zeus ordered his son to lead Apollo to the cattle, Hermes did so willingly. (Zeus wasn't angry with his son; rather he was quite amused by his display of cunning.)

When the two reached the cave, Apollo questioned the absence of two of the herd. Hermes admitted to sacrificing the two to the Olympian deities, dividing the meat into twelve equal portions. Apollo wanted to know who Hermes thought the twelfth was, and Hermes, without hesitating, stated quite matter-of-factly that the twelfth god was himself.

While Apollo busied himself gathering the herd together, Hermes sat down and began playing his lyre. At once the god of music was enchanted. He wanted to know all about this new instrument and how such a thing could make such a beautiful sound. Hermes took advantage of Apollo's interest and offered to trade his lyre for Apollo's entire herd. Craving the beautiful music, Apollo readily agreed. To create peace, Hermes then gave back Apollo's bow and arrows. Apollo was amused by Hermes' skill; he didn't even know they had gone missing. The two became good friends.

Having given away his instrument, Hermes busied himself in making another. But instead of a lyre, he made a reed-pipe. After mastering this instrument, he positioned himself within hearing range of Apollo and began playing. Of course, Apollo was at once interested in this new instrument and followed the sound to the source. Once again impressed with Hermes' invention, Apollo asked what he could trade for the reed-pipe. The two settled on the exchange of Apollo's golden staff, which included the rights as the god of shepherds, for Hermes' reed-pipe.

ALERT

Be careful if you ever try to strike a deal with Hermes because he drives a hard bargain. In order to get the reed-pipe from Hermes, Apollo not only had to trade in his golden staff, but also had to grant Hermes the power of prophecy by reading pebbles.

The Messenger Boy

Hermes, though having made friends with Apollo, wasn't entirely in the clear for his mischievous acts during the first hours of his life. He was called before his father to be reprimanded. However, being the charming boy he was, Hermes was able to convince Zeus that he would never again commit a lie. But once again the cunning Hermes wanted something in return: to be Zeus's messenger.

Zeus agreed and gave his son a pair of golden, winged sandals, which allowed him to travel with the speed of the wind. He was also given a wide-brimmed hat and a herald's staff, which became the symbol of his position as a messenger of the gods.

As a messenger, Hermes was sent on several missions and was often entrusted with the welfare of the deities. Using his skill and cunning, Hermes was nearly always successful and he even managed to keep his promise to Zeus of not lying. The following are some of the more popular quests, though keep in mind there were many more:

- During Zeus's battle with Typhon, Zeus was left helpless when the monster stole his tendons. It was Hermes who stole back the tendons and replaced them in Zeus's body. This gave Zeus the strength to overcome the Typhon.

- After the Danaides (the fifty daughters of King Danaus) murdered their husbands, Zeus gave the orders to have them purified of these murders. Hermes and Athena were responsible for the purifications.

- When Io, Zeus's lover, was changed into a heifer, Hera sent Argus (a hundred-eyed monster) to keep watch over her. Zeus, wanting to help Io escape Hera, sent Hermes to kill Argus. Hermes did as he was told and helped Io to escape.

- After Zeus showed Ixion great hospitality and allowed him to sit at the table of the gods on Mount Olympus, Ixion tried to seduce Zeus's wife, Hera. This act was unacceptable and Zeus ordered Hermes to escort Ixion to Tartarus and chain him to a wheel, covered with serpents, which never stopped turning.

- Ares was captured by the Aloadae during their war with the Olympian gods and placed in a bronze jar. It was Hermes who rescued Ares, saving him from death in confinement.

- During Odysseus's long journey home, he was held up by Calypso for several years. She wanted him to become immortal and remain with her forever. Odysseus, however, wanted to go home. Zeus sent Hermes to convince Calypso to release Odysseus, which she did though it broke her heart.

- Upon Zeus's orders, Hermes led Aphrodite, Hera, and Athena to Paris. Paris was named the judge over the dispute between the three goddesses as to whom was the most beautiful.

- Zeus asked Hermes to accompany him to earth in order to test mankind. The two wandered the earth disguised as travelers. No one would offer hospitality to the two except for one couple, Baucis and Philemon, who were rewarded by the gods for their kindness.

- Zeus entrusted his son, Dionysus, into the care of Hermes who was ordered to keep Dionysus hidden from Hera.

- At Zeus's command, Hermes went to the Underworld to retrieve Persephone from Hades.

Though in the service of the gods as a messenger, Hermes wasn't treated as a true servant. The deities respected and trusted him. As you can see, he came to their aid quite often, and at least a couple of them owed their lives to him.

ESSENTIALS

Hermes wasn't always given pleasant tasks to complete. He once had to sell Heracles into slavery in order to purify him of committing murder.

Reconciling with Hera

As you know, Hera's wrath often fell upon the illegitimate children of Zeus. Her relentless persecution of Heracles is a prime example of this. Hermes, being the son of Zeus but not of Hera, was also in a dangerous position. But his standing in Hera's eyes only worsened due to the fact that as Zeus's messenger, Hermes was often put in charge of protecting the mistresses and illegitimate children of Zeus. This did not bode well for the young god. Fortunately for Hermes, though, he was blessed with cunning and cleverness and was able to use this to his advantage before Hera brought her wrath down upon him.

Hermes dressed himself in the swaddling clothes of a baby. (Still young, he could get away with this.) He then passed himself off as Ares, Hera's son. He positioned himself on Hera's lap asking to be fed. She complied with his wishes and suckled the child. Having finished, Hermes revealed his identity. Because Hera had suckled him, she was considered his foster mother. This forced Hera to treat him as her own son. In this way, Hermes escaped the harsh punishments normally inflicted upon Zeus's illegitimate children.

More Than a Mere Messenger

Hermes' duties went beyond just those of the deities' messenger. As the protector of travelers, Hermes was thought to have removed the stones from the roads. These stones were often collected and piled around pillars along the roads as mini-shrines dedicated to him. Later these shrines became more elaborate and resembled a phallus shape, as Hermes was also a fertility god. In fact, several pillars adorning cities in Greece were often carved to show only the god's face and genitals.

FACTS

The name Hermes is said to have come from the Greek word herma, meaning "pile of marker stones." This explains the small roadside shrines built to honor him in the form of a pile of stones.

Being quite athletic, Hermes became associated with athletes and games. He is credited with inventing the sports of boxing and wrestling, as well as gymnastics. Sports and games were held in his honor at Pheneus. Gymnasiums were built in his name and usually had statues and carvings of Hermes within. All of the gymnasiums and athletes of Greece were under his protection.

In addition to these sports, Hermes was also credited with several other inventions. For instance, it is said that he, along with the Fates, created the Greek alphabet. He also invented astronomy, weights and measures, and the musical scale, and some even say he invented numbers.

Hermes was responsible for guiding the shadows of the dead to the Underworld. As this was an important task normally undertaken only by Hades, this shows the trust and respect the other deities felt for him. He would escort the shadows from the upper world to the lower regions all the way to the River Styx, and from there the shadow would ferry across the river with Charon. It was Hermes who retrieved Persephone from the Underworld. It was also Hermes who escorted Eurydice back down to the Underworld just when she had almost gained her freedom.

As if all this wasn't enough, Hermes was also considered the god of eloquence and speech, of crops, of mining, and even of buried treasure. He was also the god of prudence and cunning, of sleep, of fraud, of perjury, and of theft.

A jack-of-all-trades, Hermes greatly resembled his half brother Apollo in his diverse talents. He also resembled Apollo in physique as well. Most depictions of Hermes show him as a muscular and very handsome man.

He was usually illustrated as wearing his winged sandals and cap given to him by Zeus and dressed in the clothes of a traveler or herald Several images show him carrying his herald's staff, and sometimes a lamb or a ram as well.

ESSENTIALS

As you can see, Hermes had a natural inclination toward music. However, because Apollo already held the title of god of music, Hermes had to settle for a position as a minor patron of poetry.

Bad-Boy Attraction

Though most often thought of as a mischievous little boy, Hermes did grow up to have several adult love affairs. Always the fun-loving, free-spirited, and rather naughty boy in childhood, Hermes didn't grow out of that spirit in adulthood. For this reason, he was popular with the ladies—for flings at least. Hermes never married. Hermes simply loved a challenge and therefore many of his tales of love revolved around his ability to trick the target into submitting to him.

Aphrodite

Aphrodite was one of Hermes' favorite consorts. But even the goddess of love posed a challenge. Hermes made his love for the goddess known, but she refused to return it. This rejection just made Hermes want her all the more. So, as was his style, he came up with a plan to win her love (or at least her consent).

Hermes went to Zeus and asked his help in achieving his goal. Zeus heard the pleas and felt sorry for his son. Therefore, he sent one of his eagles to steal the sandal of the goddess as she was bathing. The eagle returned the sandal to Hermes who offered to give back the sandal in return for a favor of love.

Aphrodite, though a little annoyed, submitted to Hermes advances. Together, they produced Hermaphroditus, who merged with the nymph Salmacis and as a result, possessed both the sexes of a man and of a woman. Priapus became a god of fertility.

Challenging Love

Though the affair with Aphrodite was the most popular tryst, Hermes had several others that made their way into the myths. He fell in love with Herse, a daughter of Cecrops. This time, his obstacle was not the beloved, but the beloved's sister. Herse's sister Aglaurus would not allow the god to gain entrance into Herse's bedroom. This didn't detain Hermes one bit. He simply turned Aglaurus to stone and walked right in. The union between Herse and Hermes produced a son named Cephalus.

Hermes was also in love with Apemosyne, the daughter of Catreus, king of Crete. Apemosyne tried to outrun him, which she did for quite a while, but Hermes didn't give up easily. He threw animal hides down in her path, which caused her to slip. He then trapped and violated her. Apemosyne went to her brother for help, claiming to be pregnant as a product of Hermes raping her. Her brother was so furious that he kicked her to death.

Chione was a very beautiful young girl who had several admirers. Apollo and Hermes were among her would-be suitors. Chione, though disinterested, could not dissuade the gods. They both visited her on the same night, though at different times. Hermes put her to sleep and violated her. That night, Chione conceived twins, one child of Apollo's, one child of Hermes'. Of Hermes, she bore Autolycus who inherited his father's thieving abilities and became known as one of the most famous thieves of ancient Greece.

Hermes had several affairs and several children. Among these children are the famed Pan, Myrtilus, and Echion, all three of which inherited at least one of Hermes' characteristics. Pan was a god of shepherds and fertility. He was also renowned for his musical abilities. Myrtilus was a famous charioteer, best known for his swiftness. Echion was one of the Argonauts, best known as the herald for the Argo.

FACTS

Hermes cared for his children and as a father was crushed when one was harmed. When Myrtilus was killed, Hermes had him placed in the sky as a constellation known as Auriga, or the Charioteer.

Hermes Wins the Prize

Hermes is portrayed in myths more often than any other deity. Granted, he doesn't have several that he can call his own, but he makes an appearance, if only a minor one, in most. Because he was so multitalented, storytellers could easily find a way to fit him in: he could be a bad guy or a good guy, a helper or a troublemaker, and all without explanation needed. Hermes didn't always play the messenger boy. Sometimes, he was just your average bad boy who liked to play tricks. There are several instances in which he used his thieving skills to steal from the other gods. For example, he stole the trident from Poseidon, the scepter from Zeus, the girdle from Aphrodite, and various tools from Hephaestus. Yet he was always able to use his boyish charm to get him out of trouble. It was that boyish charm that made him so popular.

While most of the other Olympian deities could be rather stiff and self-absorbed, Hermes' personality added a playful touch to Mount Olympus. He was well liked by everyone, mortals and immortals alike. Childlike in several of his actions, he could also be very responsible and trustworthy. He kept up with his duties as a god, but had fun in the meantime. Hermes certainly made for a diverse and interesting character, often playing both sides of the coin at once.

CHAPTER 15
Adultery Abounds

In this chapter, you will be introduced to Aphrodite, goddess of love. But as you will soon see, her world revolves more around passion and desire than pure and unadulterated love, making hers some of the juiciest myths of the ancient world. Oh, but we can't forget her husband. Yes, the goddess of love is married. But don't get your hopes up—Hephaestus is a far cry from the hunks on romance novel covers.

The Queen of Hearts

A couple of myths argue over the birth of the goddess of love. The most popular states that Aphrodite actually preceded the rest of the twelve Olympians. If you remember, Cronus was persuaded by his mother to bring about the fall of his father, Uranus. One night, Cronus attacked his father, cutting off his genitals. Not caring to keep a hold of the severed organ, he tossed it into the sea. When it hit, a foam gathered. From this foam emerged a full-grown Aphrodite. She made her way to land and every step she took created a path of flowers. Other myths state that Aphrodite was the daughter of Zeus and Dione, an Oceanid.

Regardless of where she came from, Aphrodite is the undisputed goddess of love. Whereas several of other Olympian deities have multiple (and sometimes unrelated) duties, Aphrodite's only job was to make love. As you will soon see, she put her all into this duty. However, the Greeks seemed to associate several qualities with love, which means that Aphrodite was also the goddess of beauty, desire, and sex. And she had no problem keeping reign over these qualities.

Aphrodite was able to make anyone desire anyone (with the exception of Athena, Hestia, and Artemis whose virginities were protected), including both mortals and immortals. She took great pleasure in helping young mortals obtain their beloved. Aphrodite also enjoyed making the immortals squirm by causing them to fall in love with either each other or a mortal. She, too, wasn't beyond love. As you will soon see, Aphrodite loved a great number of beings, both mortal and immortal, though she had a particular fancy for mortal men.

FACTS

The name Aphrodite has an unknown origin; however, the Greeks claim it means "foam-born." In fact, the Greek word *aphros* is said to be a derivative of Aphrodite and means "foam."

Zeus's greatest weapon was the thunderbolt, Poseidon's greatest weapon was the trident, but Aphrodite's greatest weapon was a girdle. This wasn't an ordinary girdle. Anyone who wore this magic girdle would automatically become irresistibly desirable to all who saw her. Quite a lover's trap! In moments of generosity, Aphrodite lent this girdle to others. She once allowed Hera to borrow the girdle so she could make Zeus once again succumb to her wishes.

One would think that the goddess of love, desire, and sex would never marry. But Aphrodite did. What type of god could possibly be lucky enough to marry this beauty, you're wondering? He must be beautiful, loving, and irresistible, right? Wrong. Aphrodite married Hephaestus, but we'll get to that in a moment. Let's first get to know Hephaestus a little better.

A Master Craftsman

Hephaestus was the fatherless son of Hera. You might as well say he was motherless as well, for when Hera looked down upon her child, she was so disgusted with his ugliness that she threw him out of the heavens. Hephaestus fell into the ocean and was saved by Thetis and Eurynome. They raised him in an underwater cave for nine years, unbeknownst to Hera. It was here Hephaestus learned his art.

This wasn't the only time Hephaestus was thrown from the heavens. After reconciling with his mother, he once took her side in an argument against Zeus. Furious, Zeus picked up the god by his leg and flung him out of the heavens.

Hephaestus was the god of fire, smithing, craftsmanship, and metalworking. He never forgot the cruel treatment by his mother and used his talents to create a golden throne to offer as a gift to Hera. Hera readily accepted the beautiful and luxurious throne. However, as soon as she sat down, the throne imprisoned her. None of the other deities could figure out the trap and therefore could not release her. Hephaestus was invited to Mount Olympus where the gods got him rather drunk. Even so, no one could persuade him to free Hera. Dionysus finally won the trust of Hephaestus and he handed over the key.

Following this episode, the animosity between Hephaestus and the other Olympian deities seemed to subside. They accepted him as one of their own, though they didn't refrain from making fun of him from time to time, for Hephaestus was the least handsome of all the gods. He had several deformities that left him lame and caused him to have a funny walk. But Hephaestus proved himself as a master craftsman and built several of the halls and palaces on Mount Olympus.

Many believed his workshops to be located in the volcanoes of Sicily and Lemnos. Therefore, Hephaestus was also considered to be the god of volcanoes. Some myths say that the Cyclopes, great forgers themselves, worked as Hephaestus's assistants in the volcanic workshops.

There wasn't an idea around that Hephaestus could not fashion into being. He was the one responsible for building the first woman, having fashioned her out of clay. He created chains strong enough to bind Prometheus to the mountainside. He made the arrows for Artemis and Apollo and suits of armor (presumably the best around) as favors for the fellow deities to give as gifts.

Smart and generous, Hephaestus wasn't a bad guy, just not all that much to look at. Even with all his talents as a master craftsman, Hephaestus is best known through his wife, the goddess of love.

ESSENTIALS

Some myths claim that the marriage between Hephaestus and Aphrodite was set up by Zeus as an act of revenge on Aphrodite because she had once refused him as a lover.

Beauty and the Beast

Though quite the unlikely pair, the goddess of beauty married the ugliest of the gods. As one might imagine, this wasn't a happily-ever-after fairy tale. Rather it was a tale of lawful matrimony that could give modern day soap operas a run for their money.

Since Hephaestus was now welcomed into Mount Olympus and served as one of the twelve great Olympian deities, he had made amends with his mother, all acts of disloyalty forgotten. Having seen the beautiful and irresistible goddess of love, he implored his mother to make Aphrodite his wife. Hera agreed, as did Zeus, not leaving much choice in the matter for Aphrodite. The marriage took place, but certainly wasn't one of happiness.

As the goddess of love, it is only natural that she could not be confined to one person. So, it isn't surprising that Aphrodite had a tendency to run around on her husband. The most popular of these extramarital affairs was with Hephaestus's half brother, Ares.

For some unknown reason, Aphrodite was in love with the one god no one else could stand. They had a wild and torrid love affair behind Hephaestus's back. They were able to keep the secret for quite a while, but alas their secret meetings became less discreet; they got sloppy.

Helios discovered the love affair and took the news directly to Hephaestus. Instead of simply confronting his wife, Hephaestus was so angry he decided to take revenge on the couple. Using his talents as a craftsman, he fashioned a trap that would catch the couple in the act.

He built a great bronze net, which only he could handle. He attached the net to his and Aphrodite's bed frame. Making sure it was completely hidden, he told his wife he was going to visit the island of Lemnos for a while. Aphrodite, thrilled at the idea of having her husband gone for an extended period of time, immediately called upon Ares at Hephaestus's departure.

The lovers wasted no time in reaching the booby-trapped bed. However, the net fell and trapped the two of them in the middle of their lovemaking session. Naked and helpless, the couple could do nothing but wait for Hephaestus's return.

The goddess of love could punish just as easily as she could bring pleasure. Aphrodite was a dangerous deity. Her punishments were cruel, and even those she favored didn't always fare well. Read on for Aphrodite's punishment of Helios.

Hephaestus didn't return alone, however. He summoned the rest of the Olympian deities to witness the shameful behavior of the adulterous couple. The other deities ridiculed the couple, but they also ridiculed Hephaestus, which he was not expecting.

Poseidon looked down at the beautiful, naked Aphrodite and pitied her. He begged Hephaestus to reconcile with his wife and set the couple free. Whether it was due to Poseidon's intervention or because Hephaestus was made a fool, he let the couple go.

Of course, this wasn't the only instance in which Aphrodite cheated on her husband. But Hephaestus was so in love with the beautiful goddess, he never wanted to be separated from her. Certainly not an ideal marriage, Aphrodite was still able to maintain her promiscuous ways, and Hephaestus was able to maintain possession of the goddess of love.

A Woman in Love

Just to give you an idea of how well Aphrodite carried out her duties as goddess of love, the following are a few (yes, just a few) of the accounts of her many affairs. Keep in mind, these are her personal love affairs. We haven't even begun to see what else she can do with her powers as a goddess.

Anchises

This love affair was all Zeus's doing. Because Aphrodite made fun of the other deities for succumbing to her love spells, Zeus decided to teach the goddess a lesson. He made her fall in love with the mortal Anchises, king of Dardania.

Aphrodite came across Anchises as he was herding sheep on Mount Ida. Because of Zeus, Aphrodite immediately fell head over heels for the young man. Considering her options, she figured the best approach would be to come before him as a beautiful mortal girl. Anchises had no qualms about giving in to the girl's advances. Their union produced a son, Aeneas.

Aphrodite decided to reveal her true identity to her lover, thinking Anchises would be pleased to know he was a consort of the goddess of love. However, Anchises had a different reaction. He was frightened of the repercussions of making love to a goddess, for there are several stories involving immortals loving mortals and the mortals never come out on the good side. Aphrodite quieted his fears, though, and promised him safety as long as he never spoke of the act. But mating with the goddess of love was just too good a tale to keep to himself. In an act of stupidity, Anchises bragged about this love affair. As punishment, Zeus struck him with a thunderbolt, not killing him, but making him lame. Aphrodite wouldn't come to the aid of Anchises and left him.

FACTS

As an Olympian god, Hephaestus was an important deity. However, he doesn't show up in the myths very often aside from being mentioned as Aphrodite's husband. And even so, the mentioning often involves a phrase such as "Aphrodite was not a faithful wife to Hephaestus."

Butes

Butes was the son of Zeuxippe (the daughter of the river god Eridanus) and either Teleon or Poseidon. He was one of the Argonauts accompanying Jason on his quest for the Golden Fleece. He was also a priest of one of Athena's temples.

While sailing on the Argo with Jason's crew, they came upon the Sirens who sang their beautiful songs, which were known to mesmerize the sailors and cause them to wreck. The entire crew, save Butes, was able to resist the songs of the Sirens. Because the crew refused to steer their ship toward the music, Butes jumped overboard and tried to swim to the Sirens, completely under their spell.

Aphrodite was in love with Butes, and because he was sure to have met his death with the Sirens, she took pity on him and rescued him from the seas. She took him to Sicily and there made love to him.

Immortal Lovers

Though Aphrodite fancied mortal men, she was not beyond trysts with immortals. Of course, you already know about the love affair with

Ares. But some myths claim that this was more than just a physical desire. Aphrodite was truly and deeply in love with this god, though no one can quite figure out why. She bore him four children: Anteros, Deimos, Phobos, and Harmonia. Some myths also claim that Eros was the child of this divine couple.

QUESTIONS?

Who was Priapus?
As the son of the goddess of love and the god of wine, Priapus was a god of fertility. But he had another feature that made him stand out from the rest—his ugly, gnarled body was rarely noticed in light of his unnaturally enormous genitals.

Aphrodite also had love affairs with Dionysus, which produced a son named Priapus, and with Poseidon who sired Eryx. Adding to her list was the unwanted union with Hermes, which you read about in the last chapter. It is even said that Zeus wanted the irresistible goddess of love, but that she refused to have him.

Love's Helping Hand

There are many instances throughout the myths of ancient Greece in which Aphrodite uses her powers of love to help those who couldn't win over their beloveds alone (sometimes even lending a hand when it was unwanted). It was usually mortal men who won her favor and therefore her help.

Paris and Helen

Probably the most noted myth involving Aphrodite was her involvement with Paris, the son of the king of Troy. Paris was quite the handsome young man, but that's not what drew Aphrodite to his side. But let's start from the beginning.

During a wedding ceremony, Eris (Strife) threw down a golden apple that was inscribed with "for the fairest." Three goddesses tried to claim this prize for beauty: Aphrodite, Athena, and Hera. None of the three would budge on her self-proclamation of beauty, so Zeus decided a judge should be called on to settle the dispute. He instructed Hermes to lead the three goddesses to Paris, who was chosen to pick the winner.

The handsome judge had difficulty deciding between the three, so each of the goddesses tried to bribe him. Athena offered him wisdom and victory in battle, Hera promised power and dominion over all of Asia, and Aphrodite promised him the hand of the most beautiful woman in the world. The golden apple was awarded to Aphrodite.

From then on, Aphrodite protected the young man. She also kept her promise and helped him to kidnap Helen, who was already married to King Menelaus of Sparta. Paris made his way to Sparta and was accepted into the king's court. There, Aphrodite worked her magic and caused Helen to fall madly in love with the handsome guest. The couple eloped and this was the cause of the Trojan War.

Milanion and Atalanta

Atalanta was a young woman often compared to Artemis. She was a famous hunter and wanted little to do with men. However, she was so beautiful she had several admirers. Her father insisted that she marry, and to appease him she agreed on one condition: the man she would marry had to first beat her in a foot race; however, any man who participated in the race and lost would be killed. Even though the consequences were harsh, many men tried to outrun Atalanta, and many men died.

FACTS

At birth, Atalanta was abandoned by her father because he didn't want a daughter. She was saved by a mother bear who suckled her and then later was discovered by a band of hunters who raised her to become a great huntress herself. Her skill was so great it was often compared to that of Artemis.

A young man by the name of Milanion was one of the many admirers, but he stood out from the rest; he had Aphrodite on his side. No one could beat Atalanta in a foot race; that much had already been proven. So Aphrodite came up with a plan. She brought three golden apples back from her orchard and gave them to Milanion to use during the race.

Milanion stepped up to the challenge with the apples tucked safely away. With a short burst of speed he managed for a moment to get in front of Atalanta. In position, he tossed one of the apples off course. Atalanta, whether because she was greedy or just curious, followed the apple off course to pick it up. Each time Atalanta got close, Milanion threw another apple. By keeping her distracted, he was able to win the race and thus became the husband of the beautiful Atalanta.

Aeneas and Dido

As you know, Aeneas was the son of Aphrodite. During his travels with the Trojans, he came safely upon a land in Africa, near the land of Queen Dido. Aphrodite was deeply concerned for the safety of her son. She made Dido fall helplessly in love with him so no harm would befall him. Dido's love more than protected his welfare, this tryst allowed the Trojans ample time to rest themselves and replenish their supplies. Meanwhile, Dido and Aeneas were declaring their love physically in a nearby cave.

Though Dido felt the pangs of true love, Aeneas wasn't as responsive as she had hoped. She assumed that their love affair meant marriage, but Aeneas disagreed. Once the troops were ready to leave, Aeneas was right there waiting. They left without a second thought or glance back at Dido. Distraught by the loss of her love, Dido threw herself into a fire and died.

**SSENTIALS** Aphrodite was often portrayed as a rather dimwitted, ridiculous deity who was often cruel in ancient Greek myths. But the Romans (calling her Venus) viewed her as a good-hearted soul, more interested in the seriousness of love than the wantonness of sexual desires.

CHAPTER 16
The Lord of Libation

Congratulations! You have finally reached the last of the introductions to the great Olympian deities. And what better way to celebrate this milestone than to get to know the ultimate party god. Dionysus was the god of wine and revelry and was always up for a good time. Not surprisingly, the mortals came to feel closer to Dionysus than any other deity. So grab a glass of wine, put your dancing shoes on, and get the party started.

The Twice-Born God

Believe it or not, this playboy was a rather complex character. No less complex was the story (or rather stories) of his birth. As with several other deities, no one can seem to agree on exactly where Dionysus came from. The most commonly accepted version of the birth of Dionysus sets him as the son of Zeus and the mortal Semele.

Myth #1

If you remember, Zeus seduced Semele in the disguise of a human male, though Zeus told Semele he was the ruler of the gods. Of course, Zeus had his way with her, and in true form Hera was overcome with jealousy. When Semele became pregnant, Hera sought her out and disguised herself as Semele's nursemaid. As this trusted friend, Hera convinced Semele that the father of her child may have been lying.

To prove she was actually carrying the child of the almighty Zeus, Semele begged him to grant her a wish. Still smitten with the girl, Zeus promised her anything she wanted. When she asked to see Zeus in his true form, Zeus had no choice but to comply. He presented himself to her in all his glory. But the true form of a deity was too much for a mortal to handle and Semele burst into flames.

Zeus called on Hermes to rescue his unborn child. Hermes extracted the baby from the mother while Zeus cut a gash in his thigh. Hermes then placed the child in Zeus's wound and stitched it back up. Three months later Dionysus was born.

Myth #2

If you thought that was a dramatic tale, check out the other version of Dionysus's birth. In this version, Zeus was again the father, but Persephone was the mother. As Zeus was known to do, he had transformed himself into an animal to mate with the woman of his choice. This time he turned himself into a snake to mate with Persephone. From this union a child with a crown of snakes and horns was born, and he was called Zagreus.

As was typical, Hera learned of this act of adultery and went after the illegitimate child. She was able to steal him away and then handed him over to the Titans with instructions to destroy him. The Titans wasted no time in tearing the poor child to pieces, cooking the meat, and devouring him—all save the heart.

Athena stepped in and rescued the heart, turning it over to Zeus. Zeus took the heart to Semele and ordered her to eat it. She did as she was told and thus conceived the already born child. When the child was born the second time, he was named Dionysus.

Dionysus Driven Mad

Regardless of exactly how Dionysus was born, the fact remains that Hera was determined to seek vengeance. Because Zeus knew his wife all too well, he had already taken precautions to protect his son. As soon as Dionysus was born, Zeus placed him in the care of Ino (Semele's sister) and her husband, Athamas, King of Orchomenus.

To hide the child from Hera's watchful eyes, the couple dressed Dionysus as a girl. This trick lasted only so long before Hera saw through the disguise. Instead of immediately attacking the child, Hera decided to first punish the couple who had sheltered him. She drove Ino and Athamas mad, causing them to kill their own sons.

While Hera was preoccupied with this deed, Zeus once again managed to save his son. This time he transformed Dionysus into a young goat and ordered Hermes to take him to Mount Nysa. Once there, Dionysus was placed into the care of the nymphs of the region. The trick worked and Dionysus was raised in a happy and healthy childhood environment.

Dionysus was eventually transformed back into his true form, and Hera, not having given up the search, discovered the young Dionysus and drove him mad as punishment for being the illegitimate son of Zeus. Dionysus wandered the lands in a state of madness for several years. Eventually, his aimless travels led him to the land of Phrygia. Here he was taken in by the earth goddess Cybele. Dionysus was initiated into her religious cult and cured of his madness. He stayed with Cybele for a while, learning her rites and practices. Before long, Dionysus had created his own religious cult, using Cybele's as a foundation.

The Rites of Dionysus

Dionysus had his own religious rites, quite different from those held to honor other Olympian deities. In festivals honoring Dionysus, the people were able to not just honor him, but also to become one with him, whereas in festivals held to honor other Olympian deities, the deity was admired from afar; becoming one with the deity was just as much a sacrilegious thought as an impossible feat. But Dionysus was different, for he participated in the rites himself along with his followers. He loved people; he loved dance; and he loved wine. His festivals were one big party after the other for him.

QUESTIONS?

What is a thyrsus?
A thyrsus is a long pole or rod that was covered in grapevines or ivy adorned with grapes or other berries and topped with a pine cone. The thyrsus was a symbol of the followers of Dionysus.

The other deities had temples in which they were paid reverence, but Dionysus wandered the lands and his cults celebrated him in the woods. He was usually accompanied on his travels by the Maenads, wild women who carried a thyrsus and who helped to incite the people of the towns to join his cult and participate in the festivals. Though everyone was invited to participate, it was most often women who would eagerly join.

As Dionysus was the god of wine, he and his followers were known to celebrate the drink. It was thought that wine gave one the ability to feel the greatness and power of the gods. Wine was able to bring about the relaxation and ecstasy needed to become one with Dionysus. But such excess during his festivals often resulted in a state of frenzy and madness.

During the cult festivities (often held at night), the women would dress in fawn skins, drink wine, and participate in frenzied dances around either Dionysus himself or an image of Dionysus. Sometimes the women would suckle baby animals such as wolves or deer. Other times (or possibly even during the same festival), the women would hunt down an animal, tear it to pieces, and then eat the raw meat.

Having consumed vast amounts of wine, the participants would normally reach a state of ecstasy in which they felt the power of the gods. It is sometimes said that the religious ecstasy was heightened by sexual ecstasy. The nights were wild and the followers in a state of frenzy; anything was possible.

Dionysus Takes a Wife

Ariadne was the daughter of Minos, king of Crete, and in love with the great hero Theseus. She met Theseus when he came to Crete to conquer the Minotaur (see Chapter 18). It was love at first sight for Ariadne, but apparently the feeling wasn't mutual.

She helped her love to accomplish his feat and in doing so alienated herself from her father. Because Theseus was grateful, he had promised to marry her when they reached Athens. They stopped at a few places along the way, and at one of these stops, Theseus left Ariadne while she was sleeping on the shore and sailed away without her.

SSENTIALS

Another myth states that Theseus was indeed in love with Ariadne, but that the Fates would not allow him to marry her. Yet another also says that Theseus loved Ariadne, but that because Dionysus was also in love with her, Theseus backed down and left his love to the god.

Ariadne woke alone and with no one to go to. She was greatly distressed at her position and the loss of her love, but not for long. The great god of wine came upon her and was immediately taken with this beauty. Falling in love instantly, quite as Ariadne had done with Theseus, the god rescued and married her. Some myths say the couple resided on the island of Lemnos, and others claim he took his bride to Mount Olympus.

Ariadne had many children by Dionysus; the best known among them were Oenopion, Phanus, Staphylus, and Thoas. Oenopion became the king of Chios. Phanus and Staphylus were both Argonauts who accompanied Jason on his quest (see Chapter 19). And Thoas became the king of Lemnos.

Madness Unleashed

Not everyone readily accepted the religion of Dionysus. Some even claimed his divinity as false, which stirred the wrath of Dionysus. Perhaps because Dionysus knew firsthand the power of inflicting madness, he chose this as his favorite weapon. Or perhaps, in a twisted sort of way, he simply took pleasure in watching the punished destroy themselves. Regardless of the reason, there are several instances throughout the myths in which Dionysus punished someone by causing him or her to go mad.

Dionysus, though a good-time guy, had a rather short temper and a creative imagination. His punishments were often cruel and brutal, not only for the one being punished, but sometimes for innocents standing by.

The Madness of King Lycurgus

While traveling with his band of Maenads, Dionysus came upon the land of Thrace. Here he was persecuted for his teachings. The king of Thrace, Lycurgus, tried to imprison Dionysus, but Dionysus fled to the sea where he was sheltered by Thetis. Unfortunately, in the process several of his followers had been captured and imprisoned.

Furious with this ill treatment, Dionysus went back to punish the king. Just as he had once been punished, Dionysus inflicted madness upon the king. With the king out of sorts, the imprisoned followers were released. But that isn't the end of the story.

Lycurgus, in his fit of madness got so drunk that he didn't even recognize his own mother and tried to rape her. He regained his senses for a moment and realized what he had done. Because he had been drunk at the time, Lycurgus thought the wine was the problem, so he set out with an ax and began slashing all the vines in the countryside.

Unfortunately, he got a little too slash-happy. Not only did he destroy all the vines, but he also killed his sons and wife in the process, thinking in his madness that they too were vines. To make matters worse, he saw his own legs as vines and hacked them off as well.

Still the punishment did not end. Dionysus plagued the countryside with a famine. An oracle predicted that the famine would not cease until Lycurgus was put to death. So that they wouldn't starve, the people of Thrace captured their king and took him to Mount Pangaeus where he was tossed in among the wild horses known for eating men. King Lycurgus was devoured and the famine was lifted.

A God in Prison

Dionysus took his missionary work to Thebes where he was readily accepted by the women of the city. Climbing Mount Cithaeron, they at once began to take part in his frenzied rites. However, Pentheus, the king of Thebes, refused to recognize the divinity of Dionysus, and he had Dionysus captured and imprisoned in a dungeon. But Dionysus didn't last long there, his chains simply fell off and the doors opened wide for his release.

Using his powers as a deity, Dionysus convinced the king that he would be able to witness spectacular sites (namely sexual acts) if he were to disguise himself as a woman and spy on the rites held on Mount Cithaeron. Taken with the idea, Pentheus followed Dionysus's instructions. Pentheus hid himself behind a tree as he was told, but he wasn't awarded with the excitement he expected.

The women took notice of him, but because they were in a state of frenzied madness, took him for a mountain lion. Pentheus's own mother led the women to his hideout, and then they tore him from limb to limb. In this way, Dionysus exacted his revenge on the disbeliever.

FACTS

Pentheus' mother later came to her senses and realized what she had done. Full of grief she herself buried her butchered son. She, along with her sisters, was then exiled from Thebes.

Not-So-Random Acts of Kindness

Don't get the wrong impression. Yes, Dionysus had a few moments in which he could be rather cruel, but he was after all a deity and he could spread kindness just as effectively. Some wholeheartedly embraced him as a god and welcomed him into their lands. Those who believed in Dionysus were richly rewarded, for Dionysus was just as kind as he could be cruel.

The Gift of Wine

When reaching Attica during his travels, Dionysus came upon a beautiful girl named Erigone. He seduced and loved the girl and then, in gratitude, decided to teach her father, Icarius, the cultivation of the vine and how to make wine.

Icarius took the wine and handed it out to his neighbors as an act of kindness. The neighbors were happy with the wine at first, but they drank in excess and passed out. Waking up with hangovers, the neighbors were convinced that Icarius had tried to poison them. What else aside from poison could make them feel so wretched? The men banded together and beat poor Icarius to death.

Erigone was greatly upset at the disappearance of her father. She, along with her faithful dog Maira, looked all over the countryside for him. She finally discovered her father's beaten and lifeless body, and this was more than she could handle. She hanged herself from a nearby tree.

Of course, Dionysus was not pleased with the ill treatment of his faithful followers. To avenge their deaths, he drove the women of Attica mad. They hanged themselves from trees just as Erigone had done. The men, distressed at the loss of their women, consulted an oracle and discovered the reason behind the contagious acts of suicide. To appease the god, they established a festival to honor Icarius and Erigone. Dionysus restored sanity to the remaining women and all was well once again.

The Golden Touch

Though Dionysus favored giving wine above all else, from time to time he allowed the receiver to choose the gift. This is shown through the story of Silenus.

Dionysus's companion and sometimes tutor, Silenus, was captured by the people of Lydia and taken to King Midas of Phrygia. Midas recognized Silenus as a companion of Dionysus and therefore ordered his release. The king entertained Silenus for a period of ten days and nights, going above and beyond the rules of hospitality. He then had Silenus escorted back into the company of Dionysus.

Silenus was usually depicted as a fat, old man with the tail and ears of a horse. He was known to be very wise and possessed the gift of prophecy. He once stated that the secret of mortal life was to either not be born at all, or if already born, to try to die as soon as possible.

Overjoyed at his friend's return, Dionysus visited the king and offered to bestow upon him anything he chose. Midas wasted no time in requesting that all he touched be turned to gold. Dionysus reluctantly agreed to the king's wish.

Now this may seem like a grand idea, and the king was quite pleased with his abilities at first. He ran around like a giddy school kid touching everything he could and was continuously amazed each time an object turned to gold. But then he became tired (probably a little too much excitement for an aged king) and decided to rest himself. He ordered food and drink, but each time he tried to eat, the food turned to gold. Even the drink was transformed before its refreshing wetness reached his lips. In despair, Midas realized that his gift was going to kill him.

He called on Dionysus to take back this gift, but it was not in his power to do so. However, he advised Midas to wash himself in the River

Pactolus. Midas did as he was told and his gift of the golden touch was cleansed from him. Thereafter, the sands of the River Pactolus were filled with gold dust.

Joining the Olympians

Though Dionysus loved the earth and its inhabitants, he did eventually take his place on Mount Olympus as one of the twelve great deities. But before he left the earth for the heavens, he set himself on a personal quest: to retrieve his mother.

If you remember, Dionysus's mother, Semele, died before actually giving birth; therefore, Dionysus never knew his mother but was always driven to find her. However, this first meeting would be difficult to obtain, for Semele was now in the Underworld.

Having made up his mind to retrieve her, Dionysus wasted no time in getting to the Underworld. He consulted a guide who told him to use the entrance through the Alcyonian Lake, which was much faster than traveling the route by land. The guide wanted sexual favors in return for this information, but Dionysus was in a hurry and promised to give the man anything he wanted on his return.

FACTS

The guide died before Dionysus was able to return and fulfill his promise. Because Dionysus felt sorry for this, he erected a statue of his genitals at the guide's tomb.

In the Underworld, Dionysus had to do some bargaining in order to get his mother back. He ended up handing over the myrtle plant, which was one of his favorites, to Hades in exchange for his mother. Having brought his mother back to life, he then accompanied her to Mount Olympus where he took his place among the great Olympians and settled his mother in for a life of luxury. Having reconciled with Hera, Dionysus had a happily-ever-after ending to his myths.

CHAPTER 17
The Lesser Gods

The Olympian gods weren't the only characters in mythology, you know. There were several other characters who had their own powers and stories, though not as well known as the Greats. In this chapter, you're going to get to know the lesser gods of classical mythology. These may be on a lower rung of power than the Olympians, but they are still quite important to the myths.

The Muses

As you know, the Muses were the daughters of Zeus and Mnemosyne and the goddesses of music, art, poetry, dance, and the arts in general. Their rise to fame was brought about by the many poets and artists who felt their inspiration. Several myths pay tribute to the Muses as the highest supremacy of fine arts.

The Muses were usually considered to be nine in number (due to nine consecutive nights of lovemaking), each with her own artistic domain:

- Calliope: the Muse of epic poetry
- Clio: the Muse of history
- Erato: the Muse of love poetry, lyric poetry, and marriage songs
- Euterpe: the Muse of music and lyric poetry
- Melpomene: the Muse of tragedy
- Polyhymnia (or Polymnia): the Muse of mime and songs
- Terpsichore: the Muse of dance
- Thalia: the Muse of comedy
- Urania: the Muse of astronomy

Always in attendance at celebrations and festivals, the Muses provided singing and dancing for the gods. They were often said to be followers of Apollo, as he was the god of music. Normally only given honor when an artist gained inspiration, the Muses had very few myths of their own. However, they did play a major role in a few stories. For instance, the Muses provided more than just inspiration. They could also inflict punishments.

When the Pierides challenged the Muses to a contest to showcase their own artistic abilities, the Muses were furious with their audacity. Of course, the Pierides lost the contest, but they lost more than just a simple challenge. Because they had insulted the Muses with their presumptions, they were turned into jackdaws. In a similar case, a bard named Thamyris bragged that he was even better than the Muses in the arts of song and poetry. The Muses quickly stifled the man's ego by striking him blind and making him lose his memory.

QUESTIONS?

Who are the Pierides?
The Pierides were the daughters of Pierus, a Macedonian king. While visiting an oracle in Thrace, the king heard about the Muses. Returning to his country, he founded a cult honoring the Muses. It was through this cult that his daughters became so proficient in the arts that they felt they could challenge the Muses.

The Charites

The Charites were also commonly known as the Graces. They were minor goddesses of beauty, grace, and friendship. The myths disagree on who their parents were and even how many Charites there were in total. The most commonly held belief is that they were the three daughters of Zeus and Eurynome.

The Charites usually did not have their own identities (though several storytellers made up names for them), and it was the group as a whole that personified the qualities of gracefulness. They are more often depicted in art than in the myths themselves. However, when they are mentioned in myths, it is usually in the company of Aphrodite. They were said to be the young, beautiful, and constant attendants of the goddess of love.

The most common names for the Charites were Aglaia, Euphrosyne, and Thalia. These names rose to popularity through the works of Hesiod in *Theogony*. Aglaia was said to be the personification of beauty and radiance or splendor; Euphrosyne was the personification of joy or mirth; and Thalia personified blooming or good cheer.

Like the Muses, the Charites were thought to also influence artistic works. They were sometimes seen singing and dancing in the company of the Muses and Apollo. Their characters show up several times in art and sculpture though they were not well known as deities with great power.

The Satyrs

The satyrs were nature spirits, serving as the personification of fertility and sexual desire. Though originally portrayed as looking like mortal men, they later resembled Pan in physique, having a man's torso and face, but with horns, and the legs and feet of goats. (Some myths state that the lower region of the satyr was the body of a horse instead of a goat.)

FIGURE 17-1:
Satyr,
ornament on
a cast-iron
mirror frame,
ca. 1900

The satyrs show up in several myths, but usually as minor characters. Usually seen in the company of the great Olympian deities, the satyrs served as a type of comic relief. They were known for their mischievous behavior and blatant sexual desire. They were often in drunken, amorous pursuit of nymphs. To further emphasize their insatiable lusty appetites, the satyrs were often depicted as modeling their enormous and always erect penises.

FACTS

During the dramatic competitions of the Great Dionysia, the playwrights were required to produce not only three tragedies but a satyr play as well. A satyr play was a comic play that mocked a mythological subject. The satyrs themselves were represented in the chorus.

As followers of Dionysus, the satyrs took part in the many ecstatic festivals that took place in his honor. If there were indeed sexual overtones during these festivals, you can bet it was a satyr's idea. They staggered about in a drunken state, playing music and dancing (if not presently involved in quenching their lust).

The two most popular satyrs were Silenus and Marsyas. If you remember, Marsyas was the one who had the nerve to challenge Apollo to a musical contest and didn't make out very well, having been flayed alive. Silenus was the good friend of Dionysus. Best known for his wisdom and prophecies, he was also Dionysus's tutor and, like his kinfolk, a drunk. In fact, he was normally so intoxicated that he had to ride atop a donkey because he was too drunk to walk.

The Nymphs

You've heard the nymphs referred to several times throughout the myths, but do you really know who they are? Well, if you haven't yet met them, it's time you did—they certainly aren't to be missed.

The nymphs were nature-goddesses (often the daughters of Zeus or another deity). They were depicted as beautiful women, and eternally youthful. They were often seen as attendants to a higher deity or a higher-ranking nymph. As the personification of the fertility and gracefulness of nature, the nymphs resided in caves, trees, or springs, and were quite amorous. Throughout the myths, there are several instances of love affairs with nymphs including both men and gods.

There were several classifications of the nymphs, including:

- Dryads: tree nymphs
- Hamadryads: nymphs who lived in only one specific tree and died when it died
- Meliae: nymphs of the ash trees
- Naiads: water nymphs
- Nereids: sea nymphs
- Oreads: mountain nymphs

Though goddesses in their own right, the nymphs were not immortal. However, they did live very long lives. They are very rarely central to the myths, but pop up in several as minor characters. Fun-loving and playful, the nymphs could also have mean streaks and be rather cruel.

SSENTIALS

The nymphs took great pleasure in amorous affairs. However, if refused, they could be very vindictive. For instance, the river nymph Nais struck her lover blind when she discovered his infidelity. Not able to see, he fell into a river and the other river nymphs allowed him to drown.

Pan

Pan was the son of Hermes and the god of shepherds and flocks. When Pan was born, his mother was so frightened by the sight of the half-man, half-goat child that she ran away, taking the nurse with her. But Hermes was proud of his son and introduced him to all the Olympian deities.

Pan was normally depicted as having two horns on his forehead, and the ears, tail, legs, and hooves of a goat. It is easy to see why the mother was horrified. Pan was raised by nymphs and became a mountain dweller. His physical characteristics made it easy for him to climb rocks and move quickly over the rough terrain.

Being a woodland god, Pan was worshipped primarily in the rural areas. It was thought that he was responsible for the fertility of animals. When animals within a herd did not reproduce, Pan was blamed and statues erected in his honor were debased. (While the deities normally would erupt with anger over such a thing, this didn't bother Pan nearly as much as having his sleep interrupted.)

Having grown up around nymphs, Pan had quite a fondness for them, but not in the sense one might have for a mother figure. Quite the lusty fellow, Pan amused himself by chasing the nymphs in amorous pursuits. One such pursuit existed with nymph, Syrinx.

Syrinx, disinterested in Pan, tried to outrun the goatlike god, but he was quite agile and fast. She was chased to a river's edge, but unable to cross. Afraid of what would happen once Pan caught up to her, she begged the nymphs to transform her into a bed of reeds. Her wish was granted just as Pan reached the scene.

Disappointed, Pan breathed a huge sigh. His breath caught the reeds and made a musical sound. Forgetting his sorrow, Pan was excited at the prospect of a new musical instrument. He cut several of the reeds at different lengths and tied them together, making a set of pipes. This instrument was known as panpipes, or syrinxes.

FACTS

Pan thought himself a great musician and challenged Apollo to a contest. A judge declared Apollo the winner, but King Midas disagreed; he preferred the music of Pan. Apollo was quite upset at this comment and in his anger transformed Midas's ears into those of a donkey.

Hecate

Hecate was a Titaness. Think way back to the war between Zeus and the Titans. If you remember, most of the Titans were imprisoned in Tartarus following their defeat. However, a few were spared from this eternal torture for refusing to fight Zeus's army, including Hecate. She was able to keep her powers over the earth, sky, and sea, though her powers obviously weren't as great as those of Zeus.

At first, Hecate was known as a benevolent goddess, one who was associated with the earth, quite like Demeter. She was said to have the responsibility of overseeing the fertility of the soil. With the honors Zeus gave her after the fall of the Titans, her powers grew in number. She then had the ability to grant orators eloquence in speech, material prosperity to any mortal, and victory for those she favored in battle. She could even reward fishermen with successful catches and farmers with increasing numbers of livestock. She was easily persuaded to grant favors simply by asking, and mortals looked to her for help and blessings quite often.

The Change

Hecate's character gradually changed. The forces of the dark side enveloped her, so it seems. No one can really pinpoint the reason or exact time at which Hecate switched from a benevolent earth goddess to a dark goddess of sorcery and witchcraft. But the change did take place.

In later myths she is considered a goddess of the night, associated with the land of the dead. Some say she was an attendant of Persephone, the Queen of the Underworld. She presided over magic and spells and often presented herself to practicing magicians and sorceresses.

She was sometimes depicted as having three faces, almost always carrying torches, and with a pack of hounds of hell baying at her side. Quite an intimidating presence, Hecate enjoyed the power of lording fear over others. As crossroads were associated with magical rites, it was here that shrines were built to her.

Hecate was also known to haunt graveyards. She would walk along the graves at night in the company of her dogs, searching for souls not yet transported to the Underworld. It was said that if a black dog appeared in a graveyard, it meant that Hecate was soon to approach.

The Importance of Three

Three was a number that showed itself in several descriptions of Hecate. As you know, she was often described as having three faces;

perhaps this is because she was considered a triple goddess. She had control over the three phases of life: birth, life, and death. She had three sacred emblems, which were a key, a dagger, and a rope. And she was said to show herself only at crossroads at which a traveler faced three choices. She was even given three different names to recognize her different godly personalities. As the goddess of the moon, she was known as Luna. As an earth goddess, she was known as Diana. And of course, she was called Hecate as a goddess of the Underworld.

Hecate was a mysterious character. However, her power remained true to those who believed. Certainly, one of the most influential lesser deities, Hecate is still spoken of today by those interested in witchcraft and magic.

Triton

Triton was the son of Poseidon and a minor sea deity. He was half man, half fish and usually regarded as the herald and messenger of his father. However, he had his own powers, namely the ability to calm the seas using a conch shell. He also used the conch shell to instill fear in others. In fact, some myths say he blew into the conch shell to create a loud and penetrating sound to frighten the Giants during their war with the Olympians.

Triton makes an appearance in several myths. During the travels of the Argonauts, a gigantic tidal wave carried their ship inland. They found themselves on Lake Tritonis (though some myths say the wave carried them well into the desert of Libya). The Argonauts searched for days for a way to get back to the sea, but to no avail; no outlet was to be found.

Triton, disguised as a mortal man, introduced himself as Eurypylus to the Argonauts. He was welcomed with great hospitality, and to show his appreciation for this kindness, he showed the men a route that would return them to the sea. Some myths say that Triton himself pushed the ship along the land and all the way back out to sea.

ESSENTIALS Triton gave one man aboard ship (Euphemus) a clod of earth to show his appreciation. Euphemus dropped this clod of earth shortly after the ship had passed the Island of Crete. Out of the place in which the earth landed sprang up the island of Calliste.

Triton wasn't always honorable though. For instance, one myth states that during a festival held in honor of Dionysus, Triton came upon some women who caught his eye. As was custom, the women were bathing nude to cleanse themselves before partaking in the festivities. Triton was unable to restrain himself and made the mistake of harassing these women. Naturally, the women called upon Dionysus for help. The god quickly responded and the two deities fought. Triton didn't come out on the better end of things.

Another myth says that Triton was a thief. He was thought to have come ashore on several occasions with the sole purpose of stealing herds of cattle. However, during one of these trips ashore, he came upon a jug of wine left by Dionysus. Unable to resist the sweet smell, he drank until he passed out. He was then beheaded with an ax.

Triton was also known in myths as the father of Pallas. If you remember, Pallas was the young playmate of Athena who was killed during combat practice with the goddess. Triton wasn't always a single deity. Later the name Triton came to encompass a large number of creatures that attended Poseidon. The name Triton was also associated with the great sea monster that fought with Heracles.

Lesser, But Not Least

Of course there were several other lesser deities spread thinly throughout the myths. Some have already been mentioned in passing, others are a bit more obscure. However, it is only fair to these deities to pay tribute to them in their own chapter. Therefore, the following is a brief rundown of a few more of the lesser deities.

Boreas: god of the north wind. Boreas was often regarded as quite violent and untrustworthy. Like several other gods, he was known to abduct and rape women of his choosing.

Eris: the goddess of discord and strife. She was often seen in the myths accompanying Ares on the battlefield. She was also the one who threw down the golden apple, which created the beauty contest between Aphrodite, Athena, and Hera.

Eros: the god of love, in particular erotic love. He is often depicted as carrying a bow and arrows, the tips of which could either cause undeniable love or the utmost indifference. Sometimes he was described as being blindfolded, which plays up the old adage "Love is blind."

Eurus: the god of the east wind. He was usually described as being very wet and blustery.

The Fates: three goddesses in charge of determining one's fate. As you know, these three goddesses spun, measured, and cut the thread of life for each individual. However, some myths say that they also held the power to determine a man to be good or evil. Even the Olympians were subject to the Fates.

Hebe: the goddess of youth. She was a daughter of Zeus and Hera and, at one time, served as the cupbearer to the gods. Later she became the wife of Heracles, when he joined the deities on Mount Olympus.

Hymen: the god of marriage. He was normally depicted as leading a wedding procession.

Iris: the goddess of the rainbow. She was considered to have the power to connect the sky and earth with the rainbow. She was also a messenger of the gods.

Nemesis: the goddess of vengeance. She was most often called upon to help avenge those who had been wronged. But she was also in charge of limiting all excess. Therefore, those who became too rich or had an unending streak of good luck would have some of their good fortune taken away, so as to not upset the order of the universe.

Nike: the goddess of victory. She is often seen in the company of Zeus, and also visiting those who have conquered and holding a crown of victory over their heads.

Notus: god of the south wind. He was normally associated with the warmth and moistness of the gentle wind. However, in the fall, he was thought to turn angry and bring storms to destroy crops.

Thanatos: the god of death. His role in myth resembles that of an angel of death. He would visit a mortal when the thread of life had run out and cut off a lock of his or her hair. This was supposed to have ensured their shadows to Hades.

Tyche: the goddess of fortune and the personification of luck. She was one of the Oceanids.

Zephyrus: the god of the west wind. He was considered the gentlest of all the gods of the winds. However, if you recall, it was he that was blamed for the death of Hyacinthus, so that description may not hold true at all times.

Never shun a deity, any deity. Even the lesser gods hold power over mortals. So even when caught up in the splendor and power of the Olympians, always keep the lesser deities in mind.

You should now have a good idea of the complexity and confusion Greek mythology possessed as a religion. It would be quite difficult in the hustle and bustle of today to keep all these deities straight. You may think it silly now, but keep in mind that each and every one of these deities, though lesser than the Olympian deities, had his or her own power and domain and were not to be toyed with. A deity is a deity regardless of rank of importance.

CHAPTER 18
Monster Madness

The Greek myths just wouldn't be complete without monsters. Someone, or something, had to challenge the gods and heroes once in a while to keep it interesting. The mythological creatures you are about to meet are a few of the best-known bestowers of terror throughout the ancient Greek myths. Much like the monsters in children's stories, these monsters were added to make the myths more exciting and to instill fear in the members of the audience.

Chimaera

The Chimaera was the daughter of Typhon and Echidna. But this little girl was not little at all, nor did she even remotely resemble the sweet innocence of young girls. The Chimaera was a fire-breathing monster with the head of a lion, the body of a goat, and the tail of a snake. Quite the horrifying spectacle, she played her part well in terrorizing the people of Lycia. Her most popular role was carried out in a myth about Bellerophon.

FIGURE 18-1:
Chimera, from an Etruscan bronze, fifth century B.C.

Bellerophon, a mortal man, was best known for taming the wild Pegasus. His adventures began when he accidentally killed his brother, though some myths say it wasn't his brother at all, but a tyrant. Regardless, following the murder, he was exiled from his land and went to Argos to be purified. The king, Proetus, welcomed Bellerophon into his kingdom and purified him of the murder.

Things were going well for the young man until the king's wife fell in love with him. Being an honorable man, he refused her advances, which only served to upset her. She told her husband that Bellerophon tried to rape her. Of course, the king couldn't let such a crime go unpunished, but he had also taken a liking to the young man. Besides Bellerophon was a guest in his home; it would be breaking the laws of hospitality if he put him to death. He decided to send Bellerophon to his father-in-law's kingdom with a sealed letter condemning him to death.

Bellerophon left King Proetus and made his way to Lycia, where he was greeted warmly by King Iobates. The king entertained his guest for approximately a week before remembering the letter. When he opened it and saw the sentencing, he was placed in the same predicament as Proetus. He didn't want the blood of Bellerophon on his hands, so he ordered the young man to hunt down the Chimaera, which had been terrorizing his kingdom for quite some time.

The king was sure of Bellerophon's defeat; no one could stand up to the Chimaera. The monster was merciless and destroyed everything in its path. An entire army would be hard-pressed to overcome the fire-breathing monster. A single young man wouldn't have a chance for survival.

However, Bellerophon had tamed Pegasus, so he wasn't completely alone in battle. He used Pegasus to fly out of the monster's range of fire-breath (which was her greatest weapon). He swooped down on the Chimaera, showering her with arrows before she had a chance to react. Bellerophon was successful in his feat and returned to King Iobates with news of the monster's death.

Scylla

Unlike several of the other monsters of classical mythology, Scylla wasn't born as a hideous creature. She was originally a beautiful sea nymph, happy and carefree. She enjoyed the company of the other sea nymphs, but did not share their enthusiasm for lust and love. Scylla didn't want anything to do with men and lovemaking. She was happy as she was and was successful at rejecting all suitors. But then she caught the attention of Glaucus.

Glaucus was a sea deity who immediately fell in love with the beautiful Scylla. He knew of her dislike of men, but wanted her anyway. Knowing he would be unable to have her without the aid of magic, he called upon Circe. He wanted Circe to create for him a love potion that would leave Scylla helpless against him. But his plan backfired.

QUESTIONS?

Who was Circe?

Circe was the daughter of Helios. She was a powerful witch and almost always used her powers for evil. Circe, most famous for the role she played in prolonging Odysseus's journey home, was noted for turning her enemies into various animals and was especially cruel to those who rejected her love.

Circe fell in love with Glaucus. When she declared her love for him, Glaucus was repulsed and shunned her. He saw no one but Scylla. Furious, Circe decided to take her rival out of the running. She concocted a poisonous herb-potion and put it in Scylla's bathwater.

The effect of the potion was described differently in the myths. One account says that Scylla was only affected from the waist down, as it was this section of her body that was submerged in the water. So the top half of her remained as a beautiful woman, but the lower half was something altogether different. Apparently, her waist was encircled with the heads of six vicious dogs. These dogs, constantly barking and always hungry for prey, would reach out and attack almost anything that crossed their paths.

Another account states that Scylla's entire body was transformed. No one could detect the slightest trace of her former beauty in the monster that was now Scylla. She had six heads, each with a mouth that had three rows of teeth, and twelve feet. Quite hideous to look at, Scylla invoked fear into all those who had the unfortunate luck to come upon her.

Scylla made her home in the sea between Italy and Sicily. There she lived in a cave and waited for sailors to come by. She was conveniently located next to the whirlpool of Charybdis. While sailors were passing through the strait, they had to maneuver in order to avoid the whirlpool.

This caused them to sail closer to the rocky cliffs in which Scylla's cave was located. While they were preoccupied with avoiding the whirlpool, Scylla would strike from the edge, trying to capture as many men as she could from the decks of the ship.

Charybdis was merciless. Sailors knew to avoid her whirlpool at all costs, for to get near meant certain destruction. Three times a day, the whirlpool would pull in all objects in the surrounding waters. And three times a day, the whirlpool would cast out the very seawater and objects it had pulled in earlier. So not only did the sailors have to be careful of not being sucked in, but they also had to be careful to avoid what was spewed out.

Minotaur

If you remember, King Minos and Poseidon had a bit of a falling out over the sacrifice of a beautiful bull. Poseidon had sent it to Minos as a worthy sacrifice. But Minos was so enthralled by the bull's beauty that he refused to go through with the sacrifice. His wife, Pasiphae, was also taken with the bull. In fact, she was in love with it. (Some myths claim that Poseidon actually was responsible for Pasiphae's love of the bull. He made her fall in love with it to get back at Minos for not making the sacrifice.)

Pasiphae ordered the great architect Daedalus to build a hollowed form of a cow. She hid herself within this form and in this way was mounted by the beautiful bull. As is the norm in mythology, Pasiphae conceived a child through this union. The son was called Minotaur.

Minotaur was a monster with the body of a man, but with the head of a bull. Not quite sure what to do with this creature, Minos finally decided to call upon the aid of Daedalus (he was after all partially responsible for the Minotaur's existence). He ordered Daedalus to construct a great maze underground, which would be the home of the Minotaur.

Daedalus did as he was told and constructed a labyrinth so intricate that no man was able to find his way back out—this was the prison of the Minotaur. Shut away in this underground maze, the Minotaur was left with little to do than wander the various passageways and eat anything that happened in his path.

FIGURE 18-2:
Minotaur,
from a
Corinthian
amphora, fifth
century B.C.

Meanwhile, Minos had made a name for himself throughout the lands as a conqueror. He declared himself ruler of the seas, and was in constant pursuit of new lands. He made war on Athens because his son Androgeus had died there. However, Athens was too strong for King Minos and he was unable to take the city. But this didn't stop him. He prayed and prayed (being the son of Zeus, his prayers were usually well received) for a great plague to sweep over Athens.

His prayers were answered and Athens was struck with a pestilence so fierce, the king was left with little choice than to try to bargain with Minos. King Minos said the plague would be removed if King Aegeus was willing to offer a yearly sacrifice of fourteen youths. After consulting the

Delphic Oracle, which also said that only after promising the yearly sacrifice would the plague be lifted, King Aegeus consented.

Every year, Athens was obligated to send seven boys and seven girls to King Minos. These youths would be thrown into the underground maze, intended as food for the Minotaur. The Minotaur was a feared creature, not because he roamed the countryside destroying everything in his path or because he hunted down those who wronged him. The Minotaur was feared because it was common knowledge that no one was able to escape the labyrinth, and therefore if thrown into it, he was destined to become food for this great beast. The Minotaur instilled fear because with him, more so than any other monster, the chance of escape was next to none.

Sphinx

Sphinx was the monstrous daughter of Typhon and Echidna. She had the head and breasts of a woman, the body of a lion, and the wings of a bird of prey. Though a vicious monster by normal monster standards, she also loved to play the cat and mouse game. She enjoyed batting around her prey before devouring them. Her favorite game was to allow her victims hope of escape by offering a riddle for them to solve. If the riddle was solved, not only would the victim escape death, but the Sphinx would also kill herself. Of course, this only served to raise the hopes of men before they were eaten, for no one was able to solve her riddles.

The Sphinx lived in the mountains on the outskirts of Thebes. The king of Thebes was so distraught by the constant attacks on his people that he offered up the crown and the hand of his recently widowed sister to anyone who could solve the riddle and rid Thebes of the Sphinx forever. Several men tried, but all were devoured by the Sphinx. Finally, one man was able to solve the riddle. Oedipus had wandered in from out of town and offered to help the city.

He approached the Sphinx and she once more proposed her riddle: "What creature walks on four legs in the morning, two at noon, and three in the evening?"

Oedipus wasted no time in answering the monster: "Man." Man crawls on all fours in the morning of life, walks upright on two legs during the afternoon of life, and uses a cane as his third leg during the evening of life.

The Sphinx was so furious that she had been beaten that she threw herself off a cliff and was killed. The city of Thebes was saved, and Oedipus gained the throne and marriage to the beautiful Jocasta.

SSENTIALS This kind act on the part of Oedipus finalized a horrible prophecy that he would kill his father and marry his mother. Before reaching Thebes, he had run into a band of travelers and was insulted. A fight broke out in which Oedipus unknowingly killed his own father, the husband of Jocasta.

Cacus

Cacus was the son of Hephaestus and Medusa. Inheriting the properties of fire from his father and monstrosities from his mother, he was a fire-breathing monster who was sometimes described as a three-headed giant. He lived on human flesh and was rumored to decorate his cave with the bones and skulls of his victims.

His most famous myth involves the quest of Heracles. One of Heracles' labors involved stealing cattle from Geryon (another monster) and driving them back to Greece. Having succeeded in stealing the cattle, he was on his way back when he decided to rest awhile by a river. Cacus spotted the stunning herd and decided he wanted them for himself. However, he knew his attempts at stealing the entire herd would wake the hero, so he settled for abducting just eight—four bulls and four heifers. Just as Hermes had done, he drove the cattle backward to confuse the trail.

When Heracles awoke and discovered the missing cattle, he searched in vain for he was taken with Cacus's trick. Just when he had almost given up, a cow in Cacus's cave answered a call from a member of Heracles' remaining herd.

Cacus, knowing he was caught, placed a giant boulder in front of the cave. But this didn't stop Heracles; he simply broke off the top of the mountain exposing the interior of the cave. Neither the monster nor the hero were willing to give up the stolen cattle. A terrible fight ensued, Cacus fighting with fire, Heracles with arrows. Instead of weakening him, the fight only served to make Heracles even more furious. Fed up with the ineffectiveness of his arrows, he jumped on the back of the great monster and strangled it to death.

Centaurs

The Centaurs were a race of beings with the head and torso of a man and the body and legs of a horse. With the exception of a few noted Centaurs, the race was brutal and savage. They enjoyed devouring raw flesh and were constantly on the hunt for it. They show up in several myths, almost always violent and ready for battle.

FIGURE 18-3:
Centaur battling dragon, from a stone boss, Westiminster Abbey, London, ca. 1250–58

Though they may not seem to fit within the monster category, several mythographers place them here because of the fear they invoked as well as their overall essence of cruelty. They were in fact monstrous and represented savagery and uncivilized life. They were often drunk and ready to fight. This made them a feared race by the mortals, for one was never sure when he would happen upon a Centaur, and if he so did, the outcome was usually not in his favor.

FACTS

There were two Centaurs—Pholus and Chiron—that didn't fit this violent description. Both highly respected Centaurs, they were wise, hospitable, and shunned violence. Some myths account for their drastic difference in character by claiming they were from a different ancestry than the other Centaurs.

Probably the most famous myth involving the Centaurs was the battle with the Lapiths, a human nation in the land of Thessaly. The Centaurs were invited to the wedding of the Lapith king. Things were going rather well until the wine was brought out, at which point the Centaurs got quite drunk and started raping the women, including the bride. A great fight ensued between the Centaurs and the Lapiths, each side losing several. However, the Centaurs lost more than did the Lapiths and were finally driven out. This fight was recounted in both the *Iliad* and the *Odyssey* and is often depicted in ancient Greek art.

More Mythological Monsters

Of course, these weren't the only monsters in myth. There were several others, some conjured up on the spot by bards to make the story more exciting, others having been born during the early years and passed down through the generations. Just in case your hunger for terror has not yet been satisfied, the following are brief descriptions of more monsters of Greek mythology. Use your imagination to create stories around these characters and just wait for the nightmares to begin

Gorgons: The Gorgons were three monstrous sisters. They had serpents for hair, eyes that could turn any being to stone, claws, and long sharp teeth. Some say they even had wings and impenetrable scales covering their bodies (as if their other features weren't enough). Medusa was the most famous of the Gorgons.

Griffins: These monsters were the guardians of treasure and often employed by the gods and goddesses. They had the head of an eagle, the body of a lion, and wings of a predatory bird. Needless to say, when these creatures were on guard, the treasures were almost always kept safe.

FIGURE 18-4: Griffin, from a late medieval drawing

Harpies: These monsters were birds with women's faces. Fierce creatures with sharp claws, they were often sent by the deities to punish criminals. The Harpies were often to blame for anything that had gone missing; this included children.

Hydra of Lerna: A giant serpent that had numerous heads—the myths vary in number from five to one hundred. Each time one of the heads was cut off, two grew in its place. As if this seemingly unstoppable monster needed any help, it also had a giant crab as its sidekick.

FIGURE 18-5:
The Hydra, from a seventeenth-century etching

Stymphalian Birds: These creatures were in fact birds, but with extra long legs, steel-tipped feathers, and razor-sharp claws. They preyed on men, shooting them with their feathers or attacking them with their beaks and claws.

CHAPTER 19
A Hero's Tale

Though a hero today can be practically anyone who proves his sense of bravery, the ancients had set rules for what made a hero. Beyond bravery, a hero must exhibit confidence and ambition, master a skill, be loyal to his family and creed, and participate in an adventure. The characters you are about to meet met all of these set standards. They were the best-known heroes of classical mythology and the central figures in some of the most popular myths.

Heracles

Heracles is probably the most notable hero in Greek mythology. Certainly you've already read quite a bit about him as it is difficult to relay myths without finding it necessary to throw Heracles' name in there once and a while. But now you will be properly introduced to the hero who gains immortality through mortal blood, sweat, and tears.

Going Home

Heracles was on his way back to Thebes, his native city. However, Thebes had been defeated by the Minyans and forced to pay a tribute of one hundred cattle annually. Heracles ran into the group of men sent to collect the cattle and cut off their ears, noses, and hands and tied the severed parts around their necks. He sent them back to their king with the message that Thebes was no longer under his control.

Of course, the Minyans retaliated, but due to Heracles skill in warfare, Thebes was ready. Heracles gathered an army of Thebans and instead of waiting for the Minyans, attacked their city. The Thebans won the war, and in gratitude, the king of Thebes gave Heracles his daughter Megara in marriage.

Megara bore Heracles three sons and he lived a happy life with his new family. However, Hera hadn't given up on her quest to destroy Zeus's illegitimate son and struck Heracles with a fit of madness. Heracles shot his three sons as well as Megera who had tried to shield one of her sons with her body. Heracles then went after Amphitryon, but Athena struck Heracles with a rock, knocking him unconscious. When Heracles came to, he regained his sanity and realized what he had done.

In order to purify himself of the guilt he felt for murdering his family, Heracles consulted the Delphic Oracle. The oracle ordered him to go to Tiryns and perform any ten labors that King Eurystheus asked of him. Not only would Heracles be purified, but he would also gain immortality and take his place among the gods. Heracles, more anxious to atone for his sins than for the immortality, complied.

The Twelve Labors

Though there were originally supposed to be only ten labors, Eurystheus denied the success of two (Heracles was aided twice, thus not completing the labors on his own) so two more were created, totaling twelve labors. The labors created by Eurystheus were as follows:

1. **Kill the Nemean Lion.** This lion was a monstrous beast that had a skin so thick that arrows and spears could not pierce it. Heracles had to fight the beast with his bare hands. Due to his incredible strength, Heracles was able to wrestle the lion to the ground and strangle it.

2. **Kill the Hydra of Lerna.** As you know from the previous chapter, the Hydra was a great serpent with numerous heads. Heracles tried to cut off the heads, but each time he cut one off, two grew in its place. He had to call on his nephew Iolaus for help. Iolaus cauterized the stumps when Heracles chopped off a head, which prevented the growth of two new heads. The Hydra had one immortal head that Heracles buried beneath a rock. This was a success Eurytheus did not grant Heracles, for he had to enlist the aid of another. So basically this labor did not count.

3. **Capture the Cerynitian Hind.** This deer with golden antlers was sacred to Artemis, so Heracles wanted to capture it unharmed. He hunted it for a full year, and was finally able to capture it with a net while it slept.

4. **Capture the Erymanthian Boar.** The boar was a vicious beast that had been plaguing the countryside of Psophis for years. Heracles was able to capture it by standing outside its lair and shouting loudly. The boar ran out of the lair straight into a snowdrift. Heracles caught it in chains and took it back to Eurytheus.

5. **Clean the Stables of Augeas.** These stables were the home of thousands of cattle and hadn't been cleaned in thirty years. A humiliating task indeed, and one that was ordered to be completed in a single day. Heracles diverted the course of two rivers and ran them

through the stables, washing away all the dung and thus completing the task in one day's time.

6. **Drive out the Stymphalian Birds.** Heracles was able to rid the forest of these man-eating birds by using a giant bronze rattle made by Hephaestus. The noise scared the birds and drove them from the forest. Heracles wasn't granted credit for this feat.

7. **Fetch the Cretan Bull.** The Cretan Bull was the beautiful bull given to Minos by Poseidon. Heracles captured the beast after a long struggle, then took it back to Tiryns and released it.

8. **Capture the Mares of Diomedes.** Diomedes' mares were man-eating horses. Heracles succeeded in stealing the mares but while driving them back to Tiryns, he was attacked by Diomedes. Heracles defeated Diomedes and fed him to his own horses. The horses were said to become quite tame after eating their master.

9. **Bring back the Amazon Girdle.** The girdle was owned by the queen of the Amazons, a warring race of women. Heracles simply asked for the girdle and the queen gave it to him—an easy victory for him.

ESSENTIALS

Hera was furious over the ease of this task. Therefore, she tricked the Amazons into thinking Heracles was stealing their queen. When Heracles saw the attack coming, he thought the queen had betrayed him so he killed her and left for Tiryns.

10. **Steal the Cattle of Geryon.** Heracles had to kill a monstrous watchdog, Eurytion (a son of Ares), and Geryon, a three-headed monster, as well as overcome several obstacles on his return home in order to complete this task.

11. **Retrieve the Golden Apples of the Hesperides.** Heracles did not perform this feat himself. He talked Atlas into getting the apples for him since they were in the possession of his daughters. Heracles offered to hold the world up on his shoulders while Atlas performed the task. When Atlas brought the apples back, he wasn't willing to take the world back. Heracles said that was okay, but asked Atlas to take the world for just a moment while he padded his head. Atlas did and Heracles ran away with the apples.

12. **Fetch Cerberus from the Underworld.** To complete this labor, Heracles had to beat Hades himself in combat to get through the gates. Heracles managed to wound him, causing Hades to have to leave for Mount Olympus to be healed. He wrestled Cerberus barehanded and took the monstrous dog back to Eurystheus. However, Eurystheus was frightened of the creature, and Heracles returned him to the Underworld.

Having completed his tasks, Heracles was now purified of his sin. He was also now immortal. But first he had to live out the rest of his mortal life. In so doing, Heracles had several more adventures during the course of his life on earth and suffered a tragic death. His second wife was tricked into giving Heracles a shirt soaked with the poisoned blood of a Centaur. Heracles put the shirt on and immediately began writhing in pain. As he requested, he was placed on a funeral pyre, still alive, and lit on fire. His mortal body burned, but his immortal body ascended to Mount Olympus.

Theseus

Theseus was considered the greatest Athenian hero. He was most often said to be the son of Poseidon but raised by Aegeus, king of Athens, as his own. When Aethra was pregnant with Theseus, Aegeus showed her a great boulder. He said that beneath the boulder he had placed his sword and sandals. He told her that if her child was a boy, he could become heir to the Athenian throne if he could lift the boulder and bring the sword and sandals to him.

When Theseus reached manhood, his mother showed him the boulder. He easily picked it up and removed the sword and sandals from beneath it. Saying good-bye to his mother, he set out across land for Athens to meet his father for the first time.

The Journey to Athens

During his journey to Athens, Theseus came across several obstacles, most of which were monsters or at the very least murderers. The following are a few of the challenges Theseus faced on his way to meet his father:

Theseus came across Periphetes, son of Hephaestus. Periphetes possessed a huge club, which he used to bludgeon passersby to death. Theseus managed to wrestle the club away from Periphetes. Feeling that the only punishment worthy of this beast was to die by his own weapon, Theseus struck Periphetes on the head with the mighty club, killing him instantly. Theseus kept the club with him and it became one of his emblematic weapons.

Theseus next came across a vicious little creature named Sinis. Sinis's tactic was to rob travelers, bend down two pine trees, tie the victim's arms and legs to the tree, and let the trees go, ripping the traveler in half. Theseus easily overcame the highwayman and killed him in the same fashion he used to kill others.

Soon after ridding the world of Sinis, Theseus was attacked by a monstrous sow, which was feared all throughout the lands of Crommyon. Refusing to run away as did most in the face of the beast, Theseus stood his ground and succeeded in killing the sow with his father's sword.

Next to block his path was Sciron. Sciron blocked a narrow path along the edge of a cliff. He told passersby that to gain passage, they had to first humble themselves before him and wash his feet. When the travelers bent down before Sciron, he kicked them over the cliff to feed them to a monstrous turtle waiting in the waters below. Theseus was a step ahead of Sciron though. He pretended to comply with Sciron's request, but as soon as he positioned himself in front of Sciron, Theseus took a hold of Sciron's legs and threw him over the cliff.

Theseus entered a contest with Cercyon, a monster who forced travelers to wrestle with him. Most people died during the match and those who actually survived were killed anyway. Theseus was a great wrestler and won the match. But he didn't leave it at that. He picked up Cercyon and threw him into the ground, killing him.

Theseus happened upon an innkeeper named Procrustes. At first, the innkeeper seemed very kind and hospitable. He put the travelers in their rooms, but forced the tall people to lie on short beds and the short people to lie on long beds. He then made the person fit the bed. The tall people had their legs cut off and the short people were stretched or hammered out until they fit the bed. Procrustes himself was very tall. Theseus decided to do away with him in the same manner he tortured his guests. Theseus put Procrustes on a short bed and cut off his head.

Claiming the Throne

Theseus finally reached Athens. But his trials were not over yet. Though he was welcomed warmly into the kingdom, he had not yet revealed himself to Aegeus. Aegeus was then married to Medea, a skillful witch, who wanted her own son to take over the throne. But no decision had been made yet. Upon Theseus's arrival, Medea immediately recognized him as a threat to the throne. She convinced her husband to distrust the youth.

Aegeus, listening to his wife, sent Theseus on a mission to kill the Cretan Bull, an exploit that was sure to kill the young man. Theseus, always hungry for adventure, eagerly accepted the mission.

Theseus had no problem overcoming the bull by wrestling it to the ground and tying a rope around its neck. He led it back to Athens and presented it to Aegeus. Of course, Medea was furious that the young man was not killed, so she decided to take matters into her own hands. She persuaded Aegeus to allow her to poison Theseus's cup at a banquet honoring his victory over the bull. Just as Theseus was about to place the cup to his lips, Aegeus recognized the sandals Theseus was wearing as his own and dashed the cup from his son's hands.

Medea, knowing she had been beaten, fled Athens and never returned. Aegeus named Theseus as his son as well as his successor.

FACTS

Theseus did not gain the throne very easily. Aegeus had a brother named Pallas who expected to take over the throne himself. When Theseus was named successor, Pallas and his fifty sons rebelled. Theseus had to kill several of his cousins and forced his uncle out of the city.

Perseus

Perseus was more than just a hero; he was called the "most renowned of all men" by Homer. And for a good reason. Perseus was kind-hearted, faithful to his wife (which is certainly not something you see often in the myths), loyal to his mother and family, and on top of all that, a monster-slayer. Perseus was the epitome of a hero and a model man.

Mama's Boy

Perseus was born to Danae and Zeus. Danae had been imprisoned in a tower due to a prophecy that her son would kill her father. But Zeus managed to get to her and together they produced Perseus. The mother and child were then locked in a chest and cast out to sea, but saved by a kind fisherman.

The king of the land, Polydectes fell in love with Danae, but she wanted nothing to do with him. He was relentless in his persecution, though, and Perseus felt it necessary to defend his mother. Because Polydectes was no match for Perseus, he devised a plan to get the young man out of the way. He raised a tax of horses, of which Perseus had none. But Perseus offered to get for the king anything he wished instead. Polydectes declared he wanted the head of Medusa, sure the young man would die in his quest.

FIGURE 19-2:
Medusa, from
a painting by
Caravaggio

However, as you know, Perseus had both Athena and Hermes on his side and was able to succeed in accomplishing this task. When Perseus returned, he found that Polydectes had not given up persecuting his mother. In retaliation for the ill treatment of his mother, Perseus showed Polydectes the head of Medusa, turning him to stone.

A Damsel in Distress

Perseus met his bride in the true fashion of a hero—he rescued her. Andromeda was the daughter of the king of Joppa and Cassiopea. She was a beautiful girl, and her mother was quite proud of that fact. However, Cassiopea took her pride too far when she declared her daughter to be even more beautiful than the Nereids. The Nereids complained to Poseidon who, at their request, sent a giant sea monster to destroy the country.

In great distress, the king consulted an oracle who stated he must give up his daughter as a sacrifice to the monster if it were to subside. It was a tough decision to make, but the king complied. He chained Andromeda to the foot of a cliff and offered her as a sacrifice to the monster. As the monster was approaching, ready to devour the girl, Perseus flew in on winged sandals and killed the beast with Hermes' sword.

Andromeda and Perseus were married and lived a lifetime of happiness together. Unlike most other characters in mythology, Perseus was faithful to his wife for as long as he lived. Together they produced a son, Perses.

FACTS

Andromeda and Perseus stayed together even after their deaths. Athena placed Andromeda along with Perseus, her parents, and the great sea monster in the sky as constellations.

A Prophecy Not Forgotten

Perseus, a family man through and through, went to Argos to visit his grandfather, Acrisius. Even though his grandfather had tried to have the boy and his mother killed, Perseus had no hard feelings toward him. But Acrisius heard about his grandson's journey to Argos and fled in fear for his life.

Perseus wanted to make things right and bring the family back together. He followed Acrisius to Thessaly. However, once he reached Thessaly, he found out that the king's father had died and funeral games were being held. Putting off the reunion in favor of participating in the discus-throwing competition, Perseus had no idea where his grandfather was.

During the competition, a discus got away from Perseus and struck one of the audience members. Yep, you guessed it, the one struck was none other than Acrisius. The prophecy had come true.

With the death of Acrisius, Perseus gained the throne of Argos. But he was so ashamed of the fact that he killed his own grandfather, he wanted nothing to do with Argos. Therefore, he traded kingdoms and became king of Tiryns instead.

Jason

Jason was the son of Aeson, who should have been the king of Iolcus. However, when Aeson's father died, Aeson's half brother Pelias took over the throne. Aeson was forced to live as a citizen with no power of his own. When his son Jason was born, Aeson was afraid for his life since he was the rightful heir to the throne. So he pretended that he had died and faked a funeral for the child. He secretly sent Jason to live with Chiron, a wise Centaur.

Jason learned of his heritage and was determined to reclaim the throne. He left Chiron and journeyed to Iolcus. Meanwhile, Pelias had been warned by an oracle that a man wearing only one sandal would take his life. Jason had to cross a river in order to reach Iolcus. When he came to the river's edge, he met an old woman who begged him to carry her across. Jason, being the good man that he was, complied, but lost a shoe in the process.

The old woman whom Jason carried across the river was actually Hera in disguise. Hera hated Pelias because he had never paid reverence to her as he should have. Therefore, Hera became a benefactress of Jason during his quest to regain the throne.

Reaching Iolcus with only one sandal, Jason wasted no time in blatantly declaring to the king that he had come to reclaim the throne. Pelias could not kill Jason outright because of the laws of hospitality, plus he did not want to start a riot among Aeson's supporters. Therefore, he calmly told the young man that he would be named successor if he could bring back the Golden Fleece, thinking that Jason would never survive. Thus began the famous quest for the Golden Fleece.

The Quest for the Golden Fleece

Jason banded together some of the noblest and greatest heroes of Greece, including Heracles, to join him on his quest. A great ship was built under the direction of Athena, called the Argo, and the group of heroes called themselves the Argonauts. They set sail for Colchis, where the fleece was known to be. But as usual, the journey was riddled with obstacles; however, the crew was such a talented band that they were able to overcome the obstacles and reach Colchis.

Once in Colchis, the game became more difficult. Even though Jason and his crew were favored by Athena and Hera, they would need additional help to get the fleece from King Aeetes, a cruel man who trusted no one except for his children. Athena devised a scheme to make Aeetes' witchy daughter Medea fall madly in love with Jason and therefore do anything she could to help him. Athena called on Eros to cast his spell and Medea did, in fact, become infatuated with the young hero. After Jason vowed to marry Medea, she helped the crew get the fleece by casting a spell on the guardian dragon, causing it to fall asleep. The Argonauts grabbed the fleece and fled, taking Medea with them.

Of course, Aeetes wasn't going to let them get away easily. He sent his son Apsyrtus with a fleet of ships in pursuit of the Argonauts. Apsyrtus's crew might have defeated the Argonauts if not for Medea's intervention. She sent word to her brother that she had been kidnapped and that he must rescue her at a particular location. When he reached the spot Medea spoke of, Jason ambushed and killed him. Meanwhile, the Argonauts succeeded in killing Apsyrtus's crew.

Another, more gruesome, myth states that Medea's brother was just a boy during this time. She kidnapped him, cut him up into tiny pieces, and left his remains in the water as they sailed away. Because Aeetes had to collect all the pieces for a proper burial, the pursuit of the Argonauts was called off.

The crew faced several more challenges on the way home, including navigating through the waters of Scylla and the whirlpool of Charybdis, facing terrible sea storms, finding their way back to the Mediterranean after being thrown way off course, and defeating a terrible Giant. But they did eventually find their way back home to Iolcus.

An Unsuccessful Mission

In their absence, a rumor had spread that the Argonauts and their ship had gone down. Pelias, thinking Jason was dead, killed Aeson as well as Jason's younger brother. Jason's mother was so distraught she killed herself.

Jason knew Pelias would never give up the throne, so he agreed to let Medea get rid of him. She disguised herself as an old woman who wished to restore Pelias's youth. But to do so, she needed his daughters to chop him up into pieces and boil his body. Of course his daughters recoiled at the thought, but after witnessing Medea doing the same to a sheep and restoring it as a lamb, they agreed. Needless to say, Medea did not restore Pelias.

Even with Pelias out of the way, Jason still did not get the throne. He and Medea were exiled from the land due to the ghastly way in which they disposed of Pelias. Instead, they went to Corinth where Medea had the right to the throne since her father had ruled there years before.

Odysseus

Odysseus is probably best known for his long voyage home after the Trojan War. As a hero simply trying to make it home to his faithful wife and son, Odysseus faced ten full years of obstacles and adventures, each and every one of which cannot be recounted here, for there are simply too many (ten years' worth is a lot to take in). However the highlights of his journey are detailed below.

Encountering Polyphemus

Polyphemus was a man-eating Cyclops and the son of Poseidon. Odysseus and his crew landed on his island to rest and find food. After a time, Odysseus took twelve men with him to explore the island. They came upon a cave with a large food storage in the back. The men wanted to take the food and get out of there, but Odysseus did not want to partake in thievery. He ordered the men to stay so they might ask permission of the owner for the food. Unknowingly, Odysseus had settled his men into the cave of Polyphemus.

Around dusk, Polyphemus returned with his flock of sheep. As was his routine, he drove the flock into the cave and barred the entrance. Odysseus politely asked the Cyclops for the hospitality due to him by the laws of the gods. Polyphemus answered Odysseus's request by promptly seizing two of his men and devouring them.

The men could not kill Polyphemus because he was the only one who could open the entrance to the cave, which had been sealed off with a great boulder. In the morning, Polyphemus gathered his flock and before setting out with them, ate two more of Odysseus's men. As he left, he replaced the boulder and the men remained trapped at the mercy of the Cyclops. But Odysseus devised a plan.

That night, Polyphemus returned with his flock and ate two more men. Odysseus gave the Cyclops all the wine he had, which caused Polyphemus to become drunk and pass out. While the monster lay sleeping, Odysseus used a red-hot stake to pierce his one eye, blinding Polyphemus.

In the morning, the Cyclops needed to release his flock, but as he was unable to see, Polyphemus was worried he would allow the men to escape as well. Therefore, he removed the boulder but blocked the entrance with his own body. He petted each sheep as it passed to make sure it was in fact a sheep. Suspecting this, Odysseus and his men had tied themselves to the underside of the sheep the night before. The men were able to escape unnoticed.

If you are going to be traveling by sea, it is best not to upset the god of the seas. Because Odysseus blinded the son of Poseidon, he suffered great torment during his sea voyage home. Poseidon was relentless in his revenge and Odysseus's life was in danger every second.

Never Trust a Giant

Odysseus next came across a land filled with savage man-eating Giants. The men were warmly welcomed by a Giantess who invited them back to the kingdom for a great feast. Not aware of the other Giants, the men did not know that they were to be the main course.

As soon as they reached the palace, the king seized one of the men and devoured him. The others managed to escape and rushed back to their ships. The Giants, in hot pursuit, hurled huge boulders down on top of the ships, causing them to sink, with the exception of Odysseus's ship, which was kept at a distance from the others. The Giants captured the shipwrecked men and took them home to be eaten, and Odysseus's ship was the lone survivor.

Turning Men into Swine

Having only one ship remaining, Odysseus landed on an island wary of the dangers he might encounter. Not wanting to risk the entire crew, they drew lots to see who would get to explore the island. Odysseus was left behind.

The explorers came upon the witch Circe. She invited them to dine with her but then quickly turned them all to swine. One man, who hung back, was able to escape and told Odysseus what had happened. Determined to save his men, Odysseus went ashore alone. Without a plan, Odysseus luckily ran into Hermes who gave him a magic herb that would protect him from Circe's magic. Circe, unable to transform Odysseus, was at his mercy. He made her swear to not harm him or his crew and to turn the swine back into men. She did as she was told, and, surprisingly, proved to be quite the hospitable hostess.

Terrors of the Sea

With all the dangers on land, one would think the sea would be safer. But as we know, Poseidon lay in wait.

Odysseus and his crew were coming close to the island of the Sirens. As you recall, the Sirens' beautiful songs enchanted the sailors and made them forget everything but the music. They would lure the sailors to their island, causing the ship to wreck on the rocks, and then either devour the sailors or allow them to die of starvation. To put it simply, they were bad news for anyone who heard their songs.

Odysseus had prepared his crew, though. He ordered them to stuff their ears with beeswax so they would be unable to hear their music. Out of curiosity, Odysseus wanted to hear the songs so he had his men bind him to the mast with their promise to not release him for any reason. In this way, Odysseus and his crew were able to get by the Sirens unharmed.

FACTS

Odysseus inadvertently rid the world of the Sirens. As the ship passed them by without a single sailor succumbing to their music, the Sirens became severely distraught. Thinking their spells no longer worked, they threw themselves into the sea and were never heard from again.

Odysseus and his men also braved the Strait of Messina, where they had to face both the whirlpool of Charybdis and Scylla. Odysseus thought Scylla was the lesser of the two evils and therefore steered the ship closer to her side. Unfortunately, he got too close and Scylla was able to seize and devour six of the crew.

Next, the ship was tormented by a great sea storm created by Zeus to punish the crew for eating the animals of Helios. The storm was so fierce it tore the ship to shreds. Odysseus was the only survivor.

After building a raft, having the raft destroyed by yet another sea storm, and swimming to the point of exhaustion, Odysseus at last reached his homeland of Ithaca—ten years after leaving Troy.

CHAPTER 20
The Trojan War

As the most renowned event in all of classical mythology, the Trojan War provides a story that has it all: heroes, war, love, passion, crime, and intrigue. It is truly a tale that appeals to everyone on one level or another. It is rich in its descriptions, fascinating in its exploits, and heartbreaking in its tragedies.

Causes of the War

There were several events that led up to the start of the Trojan War. Some of these may seem unrelated, but keep reading. Like a jigsaw puzzle, you will soon see how each of these events fit together to spark a ten-year war. The chain of events, believe it or not, started as a celebration at the wedding of Peleus and Thetis.

A Marriage Celebration Gone Awry

The marriage ceremony of Peleus, a mortal king, and Thetis, a sea goddess, was a grand affair. Sure, mortals and immortals had love affairs all the time, but it wasn't every day that an immortal *married* a mortal. Nearly all the gods and goddesses attended, as well as many mortals. However, one goddess was excluded from the guest list.

Eris, goddess of discord, was not invited to the wedding because she was sure to cause trouble. But this omission backfired; the goddess went anyway, with the express intent of crashing the party. She brought along a golden apple and threw it into the crowd. The apple had an inscription that read "for the fairest." Athena, Aphrodite, and Hera all considered themselves the fairest and therefore the rightful owner of the apple. A fight broke out between the goddesses, and Zeus ordered Hermes to lead them away from the party and to Troy where Paris would settle the dispute.

As you know, Paris chose Aphrodite as the fairest because she had promised him the most beautiful woman in the world—who happened to be Helen of Troy.

Helen of Troy

Helen was the daughter of Zeus and Leda, and always had several suitors trying to outdo one another for her attention. Her foster father, King Tyndareus of Sparta, was afraid this competition for his daughter would start a war among the princes of Greece. Therefore, he made all the suitors swear an oath to stand by Helen's decision, protect both Helen and her husband, and punish anyone who tried to steal Helen away. The suitors complied and Helen chose Menelaus as her husband.

Paris Wants His Prize

Even though Helen was already married, Paris was bound and determined to collect his prize. Against everyone's advice, Paris set out for Sparta. When he arrived at the kingdom, he was warmly welcomed by Menelaus.

By chance, Menelaus had to leave Sparta to attend a funeral and left Helen behind, never thinking she was in danger. Paris saw his chance. He grabbed Helen and fled Sparta. (Some myths say he also stole treasure from the palace.)

Menelaus and Odysseus went to Troy to demand Helen's return. King Priam did not want war with the Greeks, but his fifty sons appealed to him to protect Paris's right (granted by Aphrodite) to Helen. Outvoted, Priam refused to return Helen and the stolen treasure.

ESSENTIALS

Some myths say that Helen wasn't kidnapped at all. She was actually in love with Paris and left with him of her own free will.

Bound for Troy

When Menelaus returned home, he immediately called upon Helen's former suitors who had sworn the oath to protect her. Though wary of the situation, they had sworn an oath and stuck by their promise. Menelaus named his brother Agamemnon as commander in chief of the army sent to recover Helen.

All in all, Menelaus had rounded up an impressive army—more than a thousand ships were ready to set sail for Troy. However, the winds were not in their favor. The ships could not leave the harbor. A seer told Agamemnon that he must sacrifice his daughter to Artemis if the winds were to blow. Agamemnon complied, and killed his daughter Iphigenia as a sacrifice to Artemis. The winds immediately began to blow in their favor and the Greek ships set sail for Troy.

When the Greeks reached Troy, Protesilaus was the first to step ashore. (This is important to note because a prophecy stated that the first Greek to step on Trojan land would be the first Greek to die there.) They decided their best tactic would be to cut off the supply of food and provisions to the city of Troy. Therefore, they waged a war with the surrounding towns. These battles took place over the course of nine years. It was only during the tenth year that the Greeks attacked Troy directly.

The Olympians Enter the War

Yes, even the gods and goddesses were involved in this war. Certainly we know by now that it's a good thing to have a deity on your side, and a bad thing to have one against you. Because the Olympian deities were split—choosing for their own reasons to take one side over the other—neither side in the war was especially favored nor especially denied rights to victory.

Poseidon chose to side with the Greeks because he never forgot the incident in which he helped build the walls of Troy only to be refused his due wages. Poseidon was one known to hold grudges. He didn't fight with the Greeks for the sake of the Greeks but rather to get back at the Trojans. Both Hera and Athena were angry at having been deemed less beautiful than Aphrodite by Paris; they both fought on the side of the Greeks. Hermes and Hephaestus also sided with the Greeks.

Even the deities weren't invincible during wartime. At least two deities were wounded on the battlefield. Ares was struck by Diomedes with a spear, and Aphrodite was hit either by Athena herself or Diomedes as she tried to help Ares leave the battlefield.

Of course, Aphrodite had to stick by Paris (after all, it was partially her fault the war had started in the first place) and fought with the Trojans. Apollo and Artemis also favored the Trojans. Ares had no allegiance but was most often seen fighting with the Trojans, probably because this was the side of his lover, Aphrodite.

The remaining deities—Hades, Hestia, Demeter, and Zeus—remained neutral.

Heroes of the War

A war wouldn't be a war without heroes. Day after day on the battlefields, a few were singled out to receive the highest honor.

Achilles. Achilles was regarded as the greatest Greek warrior of the Trojan War. When Achilles was a baby, his mother dipped him in the River Styx, which made him invulnerable—all except for his heel, which was what his mother held onto as she dipped him. He proved to be quite invulnerable on the battlefield. He killed a great number of enemies, but when Agamemnon took away his concubine, Achilles got angry and left the war. Achilles' best friend Patroclus took up Achilles' armor and took his place in battle. Patroclus had many successes, but was eventually killed by Hector, the eldest son of King Priam. When Achilles heard the news, he was so bereaved and furious that he swore an oath to kill Hector. Therefore he rejoined the war with a fury that drove him to kill countless Trojans. He kept his oath and pursued Hector until he was able to destroy him. After slaying Hector, Achilles defiled the body and laid it down next to Patroclus's tomb.

Hector. Hector was the greatest Trojan warrior of the war. He wasn't quite the warrior Achilles was, but he was noble and brave. At first, Hector wanted to return Helen to the Greeks, but ended up becoming a vigorous warrior on the battlefield. He was responsible for killing the first Greek, Protesilaus (remember the prophecy?). He was also responsible for killing Achilles' friend, which lead to his own downfall. Hector was favored and protected by Apollo, but even Apollo couldn't protect him from Achilles.

Although these heroes are certainly the most famous, don't forget that they weren't the only ones fighting the war. Several others were also noted for their bravery and successes on the battlefield, including Ajax of Locris, Ajax of Salamis, Teucer, and Nestor.

Aeneas. Aeneas, a son of Aphrodite, was second only to Hector on the Trojan side. A valiant warrior with many successes on the battlefield, Aeneas never left the war and fought to the bitter end, even while Troy was burning down around him. He was one of the few Trojans to survive the war and led the other survivors to their new home.

Diomedes. Diomedes was second only to Achilles on the Greek side. He was one of Helen's former suitors and therefore bound by oath to fight with the Greeks. He proved to be a formidable enemy to the Trojans. Diomedes killed the Trojan prince Pandarus, wounded Aeneas, and wounded both Ares and Aphrodite—all in just one day on the field.

The Tenth Year

For nine long years, the Greeks succeeded in conquering the numerous towns of the Trojan region, but were still unsuccessful at conquering the city of Troy. So much blood had already been spilled, the men were missing their families, and the weight of the war was beginning to be felt in the form of exhaustion. Something needed to give. The tenth year was the turning point of the war. Several deciding factors during this year combined to name the victor.

Trojans Ahead

It was during the tenth year that Achilles was killed. Though he was made invulnerable by his bath in the River Styx, his heel was untouched by those waters. Apollo guided the arrow of Paris from behind the fortress walls to pierce Achilles' heel, leaving a fatal wound.

FACTS

The lesson learned from Achilles' death is still known today. No one is perfect, nor is anyone entirely invulnerable. This is why when speaking of a flaw in an otherwise "perfect" person, we refer to this as his *Achilles' heel.*

After Achilles' death, a fight broke out between Odysseus and Ajax of Salamis (another great warrior for the Greeks) over who had the right to wear Achilles' armor. Odysseus was deemed the most deserving of the armor, which sent Ajax into a fit of madness. He went about slaughtering the Greeks' livestock, depleting their provisions. Once he came to, he realized what he had done and took his own life.

The death of two great Greek warriors, combined with the fact that the Amazons had joined the Trojan forces, did not bode well for the Greeks. However, they were far from giving up. If anything, this served to motivate them to become more strategic in their offense.

An Insider's Secrets

The Greeks, led by Odysseus, captured Priam's son Helenus, who was one of the chief prophets of Troy. He revealed to them that they would never succeed in capturing Troy without the help of Achilles' son Neoptolemus, and Philoctetes, who owned the bow and arrows of Heracles. He also told the Greeks that Troy could not fall as long as the Palladium stood within the city.

QUESTIONS?

What was the Palladium?
The Palladium was the sacred statue of Athena. It was erected by Athena to honor the death of her young friend Pallas. It was originally placed in the heavens, but later fell to earth. It landed on the site of the future city of Troy. It was thought that the statue protected the city from destruction.

Odysseus and Diomedes volunteered to fetch Neoptolemus and Philoctetes. They first went to Scyrus to recruit the young Neoptolemus. This was an easy task, for the boy was eager to join the army and live up to his father's honorable name. Recruiting Philoctetes proved to be a bit more difficult. He was bitter toward the Greeks, and especially Odysseus, for abandoning him on the island years before. But he was persuaded to join the forces when the ghost of Heracles visited him and told him it was his duty to help the Greeks.

Following their return, Odysseus and Diomedes wasted no time in devising a scheme to steal the Palladium from inside the city walls. They disguised themselves, and using the cover of night, were able to remove the statue unseen. Though they had accomplished the tasks set by Helenus, Troy did not fall. They still needed a plan.

The Fall of Troy

It was Odysseus who came up with the plan to get the Greeks into Troy. Under Athena's direction, the Greeks built a gigantic wooden horse. Odysseus, along with several other Greek warriors, hid themselves within the hollowed out body of the horse. Their Greek companions left the horse in front of the city gates with an inscription explaining it was dedicated to Athena.

The Greek army then withdrew from sight, pretending to abandon the war. The Trojans weren't quite sure what to do with the horse when they discovered it. Some wanted to destroy it, others wanted to bring it inside, and some could hardly contain their curiosity.

Then a Greek soldier named Sinon appeared. He was dressed raggedly and told the Trojans that the Greek army was planning on offering him as a sacrifice to Athena, but he had escaped. Athena was furious with the Greeks because they had stolen the Palladium, he explained. As if letting out a great secret, Sinon told the Trojans that the Greeks had built the great wooden horse as an offering to Athena, but that they secretly built it to be too big for the Trojans to get inside the gates. The horse would replace the Palladium they stole and bring the Trojans victory, he added.

The Trojans were pretty much in agreement that they would do their best to get the horse inside the city walls. However, one man spoke out against the idea. Laocoon, a prophet, warned the Trojans not to trust the Greeks. He was wary of what the horse would bring. To emphasize his point, Laocoon threw his spear at the horse. Just then a giant sea monster rose up from the sea and devoured Laocoon and his sons.

The Trojans reasoned that Laocoon's death was a direct result of his attack on the horse. To them, this proved that it was indeed an offering to Athena and that it was Athena who sent the sea monster to punish

Laocoon for the desecration of her monument. Athena did in fact send the sea monster to kill Laocoon, but not because he had offended her by spearing the horse; she just wanted to shut him up.

ESSENTIALS

Some myths say that Helen suspected the trick and at night ventured out to inspect the horse. She mimicked the voices of some of the Greek warriors' wives, trying to get the men to respond. Luckily, Odysseus was able to keep his men quiet and they were not discovered.

Now the Trojans were determined to get the horse inside the city. They finally managed to do so and then celebrated their sure victory. Apparently, they partied a little too hard, for no one noticed Sinon as he freed the warriors from within the horse.

The Greek army quickly assembled, and those warriors on the inside opened the gates of the city to allow the entire army into the city of Troy. Needless to say, once inside, there was no stopping the Greek army. After a long night of bloodshed and complete destruction of the city, the Greek army was declared the winner of the Trojan War. And, of course, Helen was returned to her husband.

The Deities Are Disgusted

After having helped the Greeks to take Troy, several of the deities were appalled at the behavior of the Greeks. They were ruthless, merciless, and simply atrocious. For example, Ajax of Locris raped Cassandra on the altar of Athena, causing a statue to topple over. Odysseus threw Hector's infant son from the walls of the city to put an end to Priam's bloodline. Priam himself was slaughtered by Neoptolemos at the foot of an altar.

For these sacrilegious crimes, the gods and goddesses who once supported the Greeks, now punished them. Even though the Greeks were the victors, they didn't fare much better than the Trojans. There weren't very many Greek soldiers who made it home alive.

Poseidon called up a great sea storm, which destroyed several ships of the Greek fleet. Of the ships that managed to survive the storm, several more crashed against the rocky shores of Euboea, where they had been guided by a false beacon. Some ships were simply thrown way off course due to the storm and were lost for years. Some did actually make it home and later wished they hadn't:

- As you know, it took Odysseus ten years to reach his home. Those ten years, though still supported by Athena, were wrought with danger.
- Diomedes returned home to Argos to find that his wife had become the mistress of another. He also lost his rights to the throne and was exiled from the country.
- Teucer arrived home safely, but was not allowed to land. His father forbade him to enter the country because of his deeds during the war.
- In order to arrive home safely, Idomeneus promised Poseidon he would sacrifice the first living creature he came across when he reached his homeland. Poseidon allowed him safe passage, but unfortunately, the first to meet Idomeneus was his son, happy and excited to have his father home. Idomeneus had to keep his promise and killed his son as a sacrifice to Poseidon. For this act, Idomeneus was banished from his homeland.
- Agamemnon returned home to find that his wife, Clytemnestra, had become the mistress of Agamemnon's uncle. Clytemnestra killed Agamemnon with an ax while he was bathing.

ESSENTIALS One man was able to make it home in good time and unharmed. Nestor did not approve of the Greeks' conduct during the sacking of Troy. Therefore, when they departed the city to go home, Nestor sailed off on his own and was allowed a peaceful and safe passage home.

As you can see, the Trojan War benefited no one. It was a long, bloody, and vicious battle that consumed at the very least ten years of the warriors' lives. All were affected, mortal and immortal alike. The losses were great and victory meant very little. Yet it was still the most famous event to have taken place in classical mythology.

CHAPTER 21

When in Rome . . .

Until now, the mythology we've covered has been primarily that of the Greeks. However, much of Roman mythology was borrowed from the Greeks. But while the stories remain essentially the same, the names have been changed. The Romans also have myths of their own, completely separate from those of the Greeks. In this chapter, you will get to know the deities as the Romans knew them, as well as read the myths that are exclusively Roman.

Greek Versus Roman

The early ancient Romans had a religion that was completely their own. However, throughout time, extensive changes took place in this religion. The assimilation of Greek mythology to fill in gaps led to the adaptation of Greek myths into Roman mythology on a much broader scale.

While the Romans did take a heavy hand in borrowing from the Greeks, they maintained their own names for the gods and goddesses. If you want to have a very basic knowledge of Roman mythology, all you have to do is memorize the following Roman names with their Greek counterparts. The stories and myths are quite similar. Just plug in the Roman name where the Greek name should be, and you've got Roman mythology (of course, it gets to be a little more complicated than that, but you'll have a good start).

Greek Name	Roman Name	Greek Name	Roman Name
Aphrodite	Venus	Hephaestus	Vulcan
Apollo	Sol	Hera	Juno
Ares	Mars	Heracles	Hercules
Artemis	Diana	Hermes	Mercury
Athena	Minerva	Hestia	Vesta
Cronus	Saturn	Muses	Camenae
Demeter	Ceres	Odysseus	Ulysses
Dionysus	Bacchus	Pan	Faunus
Eos	Aurora	Persephone	Proserpine
Eris	Discordia	Poseidon	Neptune
Eros	Cupid	Rhea	Ops
Fates	Morae	Zeus	Jupiter
Hades	Pluto		

The Journey to Italy

The Romans couldn't borrow everything from the Greeks. They had to have their own foundation and beginning. So they took a hero from the Trojan War and continued his myth, making him the forefather of the

Romans. Of course, they couldn't very well use a Greek hero, so they choose Aeneas, an enemy of the Greeks and a Trojan hero.

As you recall, Aeneas was one of the few to survive the Trojan War. He was placed in charge of the few Trojans who managed to escape the war with their lives. Obviously, they would need a new home, but where? They traveled to several places, none suiting them, until they received a prophecy to make their home in the place of their "ancient mother." At first, the prophecy was interpreted as Crete, but suffering a famine there made them think again.

Finally, they realized that the prophecy spoke of Italy, the homeland of Dardanus, and ancestor of the Trojans. However, their journey there was not an easy one. At first they suffered terrible sea storms and an encounter with the Harpies. As if this wasn't enough, they also had Juno (Hera) to deal with.

Juno's Wrath

As you know, Juno could be quite ruthless, especially when a situation struck her personally. She was on the side of the Greeks during the Trojan War and never quite got over her enemy relations with the Trojans.

Though she may not have hated the Trojans from the get-go, she certainly had a pretty big grudge against them. The Trojans were descendants of Dardanus, as you know. Well, Dardanus happened to be the illegitimate son of a love affair between Jupiter (Zeus) and Electra.

Juno was no doubt going to do whatever she could to see the Trojans fail. She first tried to get the winds to destroy the Trojans' ships. But without the cooperation of Neptune (Poseidon), there was little to be done as far as damage was concerned. But the winds did manage to throw the fleet way off course, taking them even further from their destination.

On their way back, the fleet stopped at several places along the way. Most were tired of traveling and simply wanted to settle (they had been traveling for several years already). Juno found an opportunity to riot some of the women against Aeneas and his plans for Italy.

When they stopped in Sicily, Juno convinced the women to set fire to the ships. If all the ships were destroyed, they could never continue their journey. Some of the ships were in fact destroyed, but Jupiter intervened and saved the rest. Aeneas wasn't going to give up though. Because the remaining ships couldn't carry everyone, he allowed some to stay in Sicily, but took the others and continued his journey.

Reaching Italy

Finally, more than seven years after the fall of Troy, Aeneas and his companions landed in Italy. Having reached their destination, they weren't sure what to do next. Aeneas had relied on visions and prophecies up until this point, but now he was at a loss and needed further guidance.

He decided to travel to the Underworld and seek out the advice of his father. Sibyl, an aged prophetess, agreed to be his guide. She instructed him to first pluck a Golden Bough, and then led him to the Underworld.

The Golden Bough was sacred to Proserpine (Persephone) and because Charon saw it as a gift to his queen, he allowed Sibyl and Aeneas passage across the River Styx. Aeneas met his father in the Elysian Fields. His father told him that Aeneas would found the Roman race and his descendants would found the city of Rome.

Aeneas returned to the world of the living and set out once again. This time they landed in Latium, a region of land on the Tiber River. Latium was ruled by King Latinus, a son of Faunus (Pan). He had received an oracle stating that his daughter, Lavinia, would marry a man from abroad. Aeneas was recognized as this man, so he and his companions were given a warm welcome.

Juno Steps in Again

Latinus and his wife, Amata, had already promised their daughter in marriage to the King of the Rutulians, Turnus—who also happened to be

Amata's nephew. Oracle or no, Turnus wasn't about to be pushed aside for some stranger.

Of course, Juno couldn't let the Trojans rest easy. She decided to stir up trouble between the Trojans and the Latins by taking advantage of this prearranged marriage. She sent a Fury to incite Amata's anger and turn her against the marriage between Aeneas and Lavinia. Having won over Amata, the Fury then turned to Turnus and talked him into declaring war.

Yet another war for the Trojans, they fought valiantly against the Rutulains for Latium. The war went back and forth with many casualties on both sides. Because each commander was losing so many men, they decided to meet face to face, just the two of them, to battle it out. Aeneas was a better fighter than Turnus, and Juno knew this. She persuaded Turnus to back out of the deal at the last minute.

Furious, Aeneas launched a vicious attack on the Rutulains. So many men were killed during this attack that a rumor began that Turnus was one of the slain. Amata, distraught over the death of her nephew, killed herself.

Once again, the two agreed to meet in one-on-one combat. Juno was nowhere to be seen this time. Aeneas, being the greater warrior, easily defeated Turnus and ended the war.

FACTS

Aeneas did not kill Turnus right away. When it was evident that Aeneas was the winner, Turnus begged for mercy. Aeneas almost conceded, but then he noticed his slain friend's sword-belt around the waist of Turnus. He killed him on the spot.

Founding of the Roman Race

Following the war with the Rutulains, Aeneas made his peace with the Latins. The Latins agreed to follow the Trojans' rule and to worship their gods. In return, the Trojans agreed to call themselves Latins and learn the Latin language.

Fulfilling the prophecy, Aeneas married Lavinia. Together, they produced a son named Silvius, who was known as the first born into the Roman race. However, Silvius would not succeed his father as ruler of Latium. Aeneas had a son from his first marriage named Ascanius, though his name later changed to Iulus.

Iulus wandered further inland and founded a city called Alba Longa. This city would become the capital of the Latins and remain so for several years. Each descending ruler took his place on the throne in Alba Longa. Throughout the first twelve generations of rulers (all descendants of Aeneas), the Latins enjoyed peace and prosperity.

It was this combination of Trojans and Latins that would begin the new Roman race. However, they weren't called Romans just yet.

Peace Disrupted

Though the Latins enjoyed a peaceful succession of rulers for several years, that contentment was too good to be true and sure to end. And it did end with the succession of Numitor to the throne. But Numitor was usurped by his brother, Amulius, who, pleased with his position of power, was unwilling to allow anyone to challenge him. Therefore, he killed the two sons of Numitor, and forced Numitor's only daughter, Rhea Silvia, to become a Vestal Virgin.

Content with his security of power, Amulius was quite angered to find that Rhea Silvia had given birth to twin boys. Though a Vestal Virgin, she was unable to protect herself from the amorous advances of Mars (Ares), and thus became pregnant with his sons. Furious, Amulius had Rhea Silvia imprisoned and ordered his servants to drown the two boys in a nearby river. However, the servants couldn't bring themselves to kill two infants and instead set them on a plank and pushed them down the river.

Mars came to the rescue of his sons, or they surely would have died. He sent a wolf to suckle the boys, and when they were weaned from the breast, he sent a woodpecker to provide them with food. Eventually, Faustulus found them and took them home to raise in secret.

The boys, named Romulus and Remus, grew up to be well educated, strong, and brave. They soon became friends with the local shepherds, who looked to the two young men as their leaders. Their foster-father eventually revealed to them the details of their infancy. He let on that he suspected they were the lost twins born to Rhea Silvia and, therefore, heirs to the throne.

Who was Faustulus?
Faustulus was King Amulius's chief shepherd. Even though Faustulus was in the service of the king and he suspected these were the children, who the king had disposed of, he braved the penalty of treason and raised the two boys as his own.

Romulus and Remus visited Numitor and after discovering their true identity, formed a plan to remove Amulius from the throne. The two organized a rebellion backed by those faithful to Numitor and the twins' shepherd friends. They were successful in killing Amulius and set Numitor back on the throne.

Founding Rome

Too adventurous to just sit back and wait for the throne, the two young men ventured out to found their own city. They agreed on a location (near the Tiber River where they had been rescued by the wolf), but that's where the agreements ended. Every other detail created a huge argument: Who would oversee the design of the city? Who would name the city? And most importantly, who would rule?

The brothers were at a standstill; they simply couldn't agree on anything beyond location. Therefore, they decided to let the deities decide by a divination by birds. Each positioned himself on a hill overlooking the location of the city. Remus saw the first six vultures, but Romulus saw twelve vultures. Each proclaimed himself as the winner. The argument became heated and a fight broke out. Remus was killed in the battle (some myths say that it was Romulus who delivered the deadly blow).

Romulus was named ruler of the city that he was constructing and called it Rome.

Where Are the Women?

A city wouldn't be a city without people, so Romulus encouraged fugitives and runaways to take refuge in Rome. The city quickly grew in population, but there was a problem—virtually no women chose to live there. Romulus came up with a solution. Because no man from the surrounding area would allow his daughter to marry the rogues who inhabited Rome, Romulus would have to take women by force.

He planned a great festival, complete with games and theatrical performances, and invited the neighboring villages and tribes to attend. Once the guests were inside, the Romans barred the gates to the city. They attacked their guests, seizing the women and girls, and wounding or killing the men and boys. Once they had a nice supply of women, they drove the remaining men out of the city.

Of course, the men weren't willing to give up their wives and daughters so easily and several attacks were made on Rome. However, these groups were so small in number and so disorganized that the Romans had little difficulty in defeating them. But the Sabine tribe was a different story.

Romulus didn't allow the frenzy to last long. Though the women were terrified of what had taken place, Romulus made a great speech using soothing words and sounds and won over the women who were to become the wives of his citizens. Whether it was the attractive, bad-boy image of the rogues or Romulus's speech, the women did become content to stay in Rome.

The Sabine men banded together and organized themselves with a strategic plan of attack. Under their king, Titus Tatius, the Sabine men blockaded the city and were able to bribe the daughter of a Roman commander to open the gates to the citadel. The Sabines were winning the war.

But during what may have been the final battle, the abducted women placed themselves between the two armies. The fighting stopped as no one wanted to harm the women. Of course, the women did not want to see their fathers on the Sabine side harmed, but neither did they want to see their new husbands on the Roman side harmed.

Unable to continue fighting without killing the very thing they were fighting for, the two armies had little choice but to call a truce. The two sides agreed to merge their populations to create a single federation. Both Romulus and Titus Tatius would rule jointly.

The Death of Romulus

Romulus and Titus Tatius expanded the Roman Empire and built a powerful army. The city was growing and flourished in peace and prosperity. After nearly forty years of success, Romulus suddenly disappeared.

During one of Romulus's routine inspections of his army on the Campus Martius, a violent thunderstorm opened up the sky. Romulus was surrounded by a cloud and vanished from sight.

Those who witnessed the disappearing act claimed that the gods had reached down and lifted him up to heaven. Most of Rome accepted this as truth and honored Romulus's divinity. He was thereafter worshipped as Quirinus, a god of war.

FACTS

Not all accepted this account of the king's disappearance. Some believed that a conspiracy had taken place to have the king murdered. Rumor had it that the senators standing next to the king on the field murdered him and tore his body to pieces as a cloud moved over and hid them from view. As the storm produced high winds, the men threw the king's body pieces into the air and the wind scattered them.

The Age of Kings

Roman mythology continues with the reign of six kings following Romulus. Rome was indeed a great city; no one can dispute that fact. The Romans contributed this greatness to all but the last of these ruling kings. Each in his own way played a role in expanding the city and making the city's influence known throughout the world.

Numa Pompilius

Numa was the son-in-law of Titus Tatius. A peaceful man, Numa was known as "the Lawgiver." He instituted several new laws and kept the peace with the neighboring cities and tribes. Celebrated for his wisdom and piety, Numa credited his mistress, the nymph Egeria, as giving him counsel. He claimed that though he would propose new laws, he would not introduce them until Egeria had looked them over and given her approval.

Tullus Hostilius

Following Numa was Tullus Hostilius. Whereas Numa encouraged peace, Tullus was more interested in expansion. He worked hard to train and exercise Rome's army. His hard work paid off. Under Tullus's rule, Rome conquered several cities, making the power of Rome famous. He also managed to conquer Alba Longa and forced the people to live in Rome. This doubled Rome's population.

Tullus ruled for thirty-two years, during which time Rome's expansion was his main concern. He neglected to pay proper tribute to the gods and suffered for it. Rome suffered a plague brought on by the gods. Ill and close to death, Tullus tried to appease the gods, but was instead struck by lightning and finished off.

ALERT

To neglect a god in the first place is bad enough. But then to try to insincerely win the gods' favor during a time of need is considered a slap in the face to the deities. Death is the only answer for such a show of disrespect.

Ancus Marcius

Ancus Marcius was the grandson of Numa and inherited his notions of peace. He was best known for building the first wooden bridge over the Tiber River. He also established Ostia as a port at the mouth of the Tiber.

Though known as a peaceful ruler, Ancus, like his predecessors, managed to expand the kingdom of Rome. He pushed the city boundaries further south and west, gaining the land of Latium.

Lucius Tarquinius Priscus

Lucius Tarquinius Priscus was actually born Lucumo. As an Etruscan, he had no blood right to the throne, but changed his name to Lucius Tarquinius Priscus and proved himself indispensable to King Ancus. When the king died, Tarquinius was elected king despite the fact Ancus had left behind two sons.

During the thirty-eight years Tarquinius ruled, he was credited with having improved Rome in several ways. Of course, as was expected, he expanded the kingdom even further, conquering several Latin towns. He began the construction of a great stone wall to surround the city, as well as the construction of the temple Capitoline Jupiter. He is also believed to have drained the marshy land that would later become the Roman Forum.

Tarquinius was never forgiven by the sons of Ancus. They felt they were the rightful rulers of Rome and therefore hired two shepherds to murder Tarquinius.

Servius Tullius

Servius Tullius was born of a slave woman in the service of the queen. However, the queen recognized his greatness and, along with Tarquinius, plotted to have him placed on the throne. When Servius was of age, he married the daughter of Tarquinius and therefore was placed next in line for the throne.

Servius was a successful ruler. He was openly admired and respected by the people of Rome. Like his predecessors, Servius expanded the kingdom; he also built a wall called the Servian Wall around the boundaries of the city. He was said to have divided the citizens into classes based on ownership of property and introduced Diana (Artemis) as a goddess to be worshipped.

Servius was murdered by his son-in-law, Lucius Tarquinius Superbus, who wanted the throne for himself. Legend has it that Superbus removed Servius from his throne and threw him out of the Senate House. He then sent his hit men to stab Servius to death.

Some myths say that Servius's daughter was the mastermind behind the plot to overthrow her father. When Servius was killed, Superbus would not allow for a burial and Servius's daughter drove her carriage over her father's corpse.

Lucius Tarquinius Superbus

Lucius Tarquinius Superbus simply wasn't the ruler his predecessors were. He wasn't interested in winning the respect of the people; he merely wanted to rule. He managed to keep the throne for twenty-five years through a reign of terror. He expanded Rome's kingdom even further by conquering several Latin states and Rutulian towns. However, his son, who would have next taken the position as king, caused an uproar and essentially the end of the monarchy.

Superbus's son, Sextus, was just as ruthless as his father. Sextus took what he wanted with little regard for anyone else. One night he decided he wanted the wife of his friend. He visited Lucretia's home while her husband was away and made his advances. Lucretia denied him, but Sextus threatened to dishonor her family by claiming he found Lucretia and her servant in bed together. Fearing for the honor of her family, Lucretia gave in.

When her husband returned, Lucretia relayed the whole story. Lucretia made her husband, her father, and a friend, Lucius Junius Brutus, swear that they would avenge her death and then she killed herself. The men gathered a small army of rebels and killed Sextus. They drove Superbus from Rome and abolished the monarchy altogether. This was the beginning of the Roman Republic.

CHAPTER 22

Thank the Gods and Goddesses!

Now that you have all this great newfound knowledge, what can you do with it? Take a look around. Classical mythology surrounds you in your everyday life. From public speeches to art to commercials, references to mythology are everywhere. Now that you know what you're looking for, you will be able to see the gods and goddesses living in today's world.

The Myth in Everyday Language

You may not realize it, but several words and phrases that are commonly used in the English language allude to the ancient myths of Greece and Rome. Perhaps you have used some of these yourself. Well, let's hope you haven't had to use the first one anyway.

Words and Phrases

The phrase *Oedipus complex* was coined by Sigmund Freud, an Austrian neurologist, to describe the sexual feelings one may have toward his or her parent of the opposite sex as well as the feelings of jealously felt toward the parent of the same sex. This phrase was taken from the myth of Oedipus, a man who unknowingly fulfilled a prophecy that stated he would kill his father and marry his mother.

The term *narcissism* means to be in love with one's self. This refers to the myth of Narcissus, a boy who fell in love with his own reflection and eventually turned into the narcissus flower.

FACTS

The Olympic Games we have today are little more than a variation on the festivals held in ancient Greece to honor the gods. During these festivals, sports and artistic contests were held. Even then, winning during the Olympic Games was an admirable and respected feat.

The term *panic* is thought to have been a derivative of Pan. According to legend, during battle, Pan would let out a piercing shriek that made the enemy lose control in their terror.

A hermaphrodite is an animal born with the reproductive organs of both sexes. This term comes from the offspring of Aphrodite and Hermes, a double-sexed child named Hermaphroditus.

The phrase *Pandora's box,* normally used to describe a source of many troubles, is taken directly from the myth of Pandora, the first woman. Unable to control her curiosity, Pandora inadvertently released all of the world's troubles by opening a box.

For all of you who detest spiders, *arachnid* may be a frightening word for you. The spider is associated with the myth of Arachne. Arachne was a foolish young girl who had the audacity to challenge Athena to a weaving contest. When Athena saw that the girl's skill matched her own, she tore the cloth from the girl's hands. Arachne hung herself and was changed into the spider, who kept her skill of weaving.

You can even find references to the myth on the Periodic Table. *Titanium* is a metallic element known for its strength. Think it is a coincidence the word titanium is a form of the word *titan?* The Titans in mythology were, after all, known for their great strength.

Written in the Stars

Of course, we also have the constellations, many of which were made up of characters in the myths who were honored following their deaths. For example, the great hunter Orion was placed in the sky after being slain.

There are also the zodiac signs. Aries was the golden-fleeced ram. Taurus was the white bull who carried Europa to Crete. Gemini was the twins Castor and Pollux. Cancer was the crab that Heracles faced. Leo was another enemy of Heracles, the Nemean Lion. Virgo was the Roman goddess of justice, Astraea. Libra was the scales of Astraea. Scorpio was the scorpion who killed Orion. Sagittarius was the great archer Chiron. Capricorn was the goat Amalthea who nursed Zeus. Aquarius was Ganymede, the cupbearer to the gods. And Pisces was the fish that both Aphrodite and Eros used to disguise themselves.

SSENTIALS

Did you happen to notice in the last chapter the names of the Roman gods and goddesses? Most of our planets are named after these Roman deities.

The Myth in Literature

As the myth is a story in itself, it only makes sense that it is alluded to in literature. Its influence is evident in nearly all ages of literature. More than any other channel, literature keeps classical mythology alive in the world today.

Some works of literature simply use mythological characters or scenes as an analogy to add flavor to their own characters and scenes. This is a popular tactic and, for those who are familiar with the myths, quite a delicious one at that. Writers will sometimes copy the style of the myths. Several have recreated the epic adventures of the *Odyssey* or the *Iliad* to fit a modern-day scenario and style. Others simply tell modern stories in the very same style used in the epic poems. Allusions are made all the time; it makes reading a lot more interesting and fun if you are able to pick out and understand these allusions.

Because there are way too many works of literature that make reference to the ancient myths, this section will focus on only a few. But don't let this stop you from exploring further. While searching for allusions to mythology, you are certain to happen upon some fantastic works.

Percy Bysshe Shelley's *Prometheus Unbound* (1819) is a classic. As if the title doesn't tip you off, this work makes several references to the classical myths. In fact, his characters are several of the same as those in the myths. He takes a humanistic approach with this work and turned it into a fascinating tale full of symbolism.

 **SSENTIALS**

Even Shakespeare with all his genius turned to classical mythology for inspiration. For those of you who favor the eroticism of romance novels, you will certainly enjoy Shakespeare's *Venus and Adonis* (1593).

James Joyce's *Ulysses* (1922) takes a different approach in using classical mythology. He uses the plot of the *Odyssey* to create a story paralleling characters and themes. Though *Ulysses* is set in Dublin and takes place over the course of a single day instead of twenty years, it is remarkably reminiscent of the *Odyssey*. The characters, though having different names, are the equivalents of the main characters of the *Odyssey*. A brilliant novel that stands on its own is made even better when recognizing the numerous comparisons to the famous epic poem.

Honk If You Love Aphrodite (1999) by Daniel Evan Weiss is a Homeric-style, *Odyssey*-driven tale of the youngest son of Aphrodite making his journey through Brooklyn. To prove his bravery to (and to win the love of) his mother, the young god travels to earth to check things out. Set in modern day with an ancient character, this work sets us up for a wild ride. Analogies are constantly made, such as the subway being the Underworld of earth. Though an enjoyable story in itself, the genius of Weiss comes alive when you understand the characters and places as they are portrayed in classical mythology.

Undoubtedly, *The Power of the Myth* (1988) by Joseph Campbell with Bill Moyers must make the list. This book is set up as a conversation taking place between Campbell and Moyers. Discussing everything from Darth Vader to marriage, the two explore the various roles that the symbols of mythology play in our everyday lives. If you truly want to open your eyes to mythology in the modern world, this book is simply a must-read.

The Myth in Art

Nearly every museum you visit will have at least one piece of art depicting classical mythology, whether it's a painting, sculpture, or engraving. Since mythology was a religion, piety was quite often expressed through art. Statues were erected in the deities' honor, carvings adorned temple walls, and images were painted on household items such as cups, vases, and plates.

If you enjoy ancient art, there are several ancient Greek and Roman buildings that are adorned with carvings depicting scenes and characters from mythology. Several of these have been quite well preserved and with a little imagination, one can bring to mind the scene as it was seen at the height of its popularity.

Several statues and sculptures have managed to survive the years (though several are missing limbs such as arms and sometimes penises). Perhaps one of the best-known sculptures is the Venus de Milo, which dates back to around the first or second century B.C. If you haven't guessed, this is a sculpture of the almighty Venus (or Aphrodite), goddess of love.

With the birth of Christianity, mythology slowly fell by the wayside. It was considered sacrilegious and paganistic to possess or, heaven forbid, create art that depicted the ancient myths. Classical imagery diminished and art featuring Jesus, the Virgin Mary, and the Saints took a stronghold. However, classical mythology was not forgotten altogether.

If you are appalled at nudity in art, it would be wise to stay away from the art of the eighteenth and nineteenth centuries. Artists often used figures from classical mythology to depict sexuality. What better source for this than the ancient myths, which took the subject of sex and seduction and ran wild with it.

Mythology in art is continued throughout the centuries. During the Renaissance, artists brought the deities back to life in their works. From the Renaissance on, there are several famous works of art that focus on the characters and scenes taken directly from the Greek and Roman myths. Perhaps you have heard of:

- *The Birth of Venus* by Sandro Botticelli
- *Venus and Adonis* by Peter Paul Rubens
- *Apollo and Daphne* by Gian Lorenzo Bernini
- *Judgement of Paris* by Lucas Cranach
- *Bacchus and Ariadne* by Titian
- *School of Pan* by Luca Signorelli
- *Rape of Proserpine* by Peter Paul Rubens

If you haven't heard of these, all the better. Like a child tasting sugar for the first time, you will undergo a shock that is both sweet and addicting at the same time. Check them out and experience the excitement of seeing the myths come alive in visual representation.

Of course, mythology in art doesn't stop with the Renaissance period. Throughout the eighteenth and nineteenth centuries, classical mythology was displayed everywhere in every art form. This time period owns such works as *Cupid and Psyche* by Antonio Canova and *Olympia* by Edouard Manet.

Unfortunately, new schools of art such as impressionism and cubism made the imagery of classical mythology withdraw from view. However, classical mythology is still quite a popular subject to artists of all mediums and is sure to come back into focus before long.

QUESTIONS?

What are impressionism and cubism?
Impressionism is a practice in painting in which the artist uses dabs and strokes to stimulate reflected light in order to depict a natural appearance. Cubism is a style of art that emphasizes abstract structure by fragmenting the form of objects or showing several aspects of one particular object simultaneously.

The Myth in Movies

Filmmakers are always in search of compelling stories to bring to the big screen. With the variety of subjects, themes, and plots offered within classical mythology, it's surprising that very few movies have been made that closely adhere to the storyline of the myths. Several make allusions to characters or scenes from mythology, but few tell the stories themselves.

The movie that came closest to staying true to classical mythology was *Helen of Troy* (1956), an adaptation of the Trojan War directed by Robert Wise. A sincere attempt at recreating the famous mythological event, *Helen of Troy* illustrated how Hollywood didn't hold back with costumes, special effects, and scenery to make the film as authentic as possible. The movie focuses on Helen (Rossana Podesta) and her love affair with Paris (Jacques Sernas) and, of course, features the Trojan War. Though not as rich as the story itself, the movie was an impressive gesture made to honor one of the greatest stories ever told.

A more recent attempt to capture classical mythology on film was *Clash of the Titans* (1981) directed by Desmond Davis. Starring Harry Hamlin, Laurence Olivier, and Maggie Smith, this movie was a popular adaptation of the myth of Perseus, the famed hero. Action-packed, the film features several monsters, the rescue of a damsel in distress, and of course the greatness (and sometimes cruelty) of the gods. It has added to the original story somewhat to add color and isn't always true to the myth. However, it is a great flick if you aren't fanatical about sticking to the original storyline.

Other movies based on the stories of classical mythology include:

- *Jason and the Argonauts* (1963) directed by Don Chaffey
- *Ulysses* (1955) directed by Mario Camerini
- *Orpheus* (1949) directed by Jean Cocteau
- *Hercules* (1957) directed by Pietro Francisci
- *Mighty Aphrodite* (1995) directed by Woody Allen
- *O Brother, Where Art Thou?* (2000) directed by Ethan Coen and Joel Coen

FACTS

Though sometimes having a storyline differing from classical mythology altogether, several movies make reference to the stories or scenes of mythology in their dialogue and/or actions. For instance, in *Monty Python and the Holy Grail*, the crew flubs up their attempt at re-creating the wooden horse from the Trojan War.

The Myth in Cartoons

Yes, mythology is even portrayed in cartoons. If you think about it, the heroes of classical mythology lend themselves to the superheroes of today's animated world. The action, the villains, the monsters, the heroes—all these elements combine to create an action-packed adventure story well suited for an animated feature. Even so, there aren't too many cartoons featuring the ancient myths, but perhaps that is about to change. It seems as though the cartoons with mythological characters and storylines are becoming rather popular.

Disney, in particular, seems to be a big fan of classical mythology. They have brought the myths back to life in the form of an animated film. *Hercules* (1997), an entertaining cartoon, bases its storyline on the myth of, you guessed it, Hercules. Although cartoons have a tendency to skip over the gruesome parts of the original stories, *Hercules* did manage to keep the essence of the myth. Granted, it didn't show Hercules' horrible death or even some of the more thrilling parts of his labors, but it did portray the hero as the ancients did—a man able, through his ambition and accomplishments, to achieve the highest reward: immortality.

ESSENTIALS

Another Disney animated film alluding to mythology is *Fantasia*. Set to music, *Fantasia* features characters from Greek mythology ranging from Centaurs to Zeus.

If you want to focus on popularity, *Hercules & Xena: The Battle for Olympus* makes a good show. This full-length animated film is a spin-off of the popular television show. Even though Xena isn't a mythological character, she is paired with the greatest of heroes to overcome the Titans in a battle for Mount Olympus. Featuring the voices of the characters of the television show, this film was a little bonus to those who are fans of Hercules and Xena. Unfortunately, it strays quite a bit from the original myth, but isn't that what creativity is all about?

Another cartoon that refers to classical mythology is the older *Metamorphoses*, released in 1978 by the Sanrio Company. This feature, though animated, doesn't hold back in its subject matter. Scenes depict the killing of Medusa by Perseus, the creation story, and the death of Actaeon. Though not as popular as the aforementioned animated films, it is certainly true to the essence and stories of classical mythology.

The Myth in Television

Television. We all know television. While the ancient Greeks and Romans relied on oral traditions for entertainment, we rely on television (well, for at least one source). Fortunately, those same oral traditions ensured our knowledge of the ancient myths, and therefore we are able to depict these myths on television, passing on the knowledge to future generations. Unfortunately, television depictions don't always stay true to the original myth. But maybe, just maybe, those television renderings will encourage people to dig further and discover the myths for themselves.

Perhaps the best-known television program based on classical myths is *Hercules: The Legendary Journeys*. This program is actually a spin-off of *Xena: Warrior Princess*. Obviously, the mythological element raised enough interest to pursue further programming. The show maintains the characters and their relationships (such as the constant battles between Hera and Hercules), but from there branches out into its own storylines.

FACTS

Although Xena is portrayed in stories featuring characters from classical myths, including Hercules and the Olympian gods and goddesses, Xena herself wasn't a mythological figure.

There have also been a few television miniseries based on the stories and characters of classical mythology. Francis Ford Coppola brought us *The Odyssey*, a two-part miniseries dedicated to the myth of Odysseus. This feature, though only three hours in length, followed the story of Odysseus quite closely. Of course, due to time constraints, the story had to be condensed. It would be rather hard to fit ten years' worth of wanderings in three hours, wouldn't you say? But don't worry, it managed to hit on the key points, including the exciting voyage of the ship between the two evils: Scylla and the whirlpool of Charybdis.

Jim Henson added a touch, or rather a handful, of fun to the classical myths by bringing us Jim Henson's *Storyteller: Greek Myths*. In honor of the ancient tradition, the myths are presented to us through the use of a storyteller. Stories included in this series of four shows included the myth of Perseus and Medusa and the myth of Theseus and his battle with the labyrinth and the Minotaur. Not only was this depiction of classical mythology fascinating and fun for adults, it intrigued children as well, helping them to gain an interest in classical materials.

APPENDIX A
Cast of Characters

Achilles Greatest Greek warrior of the Trojan War; killed Hector, among others.

Acrisius Grandfather of Perseus; accidentally killed by Perseus, fulfilling a prophecy.

Actaeon Grandson of Apollo; great hunter; killed when he came across Artemis bathing naked.

Admetus King of Pheres; neglected to sacrifice to Artemis and found his bedchamber filled with snakes on his wedding night.

Adonis A beautiful young boy loved by Aphrodite and killed by Ares out of jealousy.

Aeacus Son of Aegina and Zeus; fair ruler of the island Aegina; became a Judge of the Dead.

Aeetes Father of Medea.

Aegeus King of Athens; foster father of Theseus.

Aegina Daughter of the river god Asopus; mother of Aeacus by Zeus; namesake of the island Aegina.

Aeneas Trojan warrior; founder of the Roman race.

Aerope A lover of Ares; died giving birth to Ares' son.

Aether Air; born to Nyx and Erebus.

Aethra Daughter of the king of Troezen; wife of Aegeus.

Agamemnon Commander in chief of the Greeks during the Trojan War; killed by his wife upon his return from the war.

Aglaia A Charite; the personification of beauty and radiance or splendor.

Aglaurus Daughter of Cecrops; mother of Alcippe by Ares.

Agrius A Giant; killed by the Fates and Heracles during the war with the Olympians.

Alcmene Mother of Heracles by Zeus.

Alcyoneus A Giant; one of the leaders of the Giants during the war with the Olympians; killed by Athena and Heracles.

Amalthea A goat-nymph who suckled Zeus; is turned into the constellation Capricorn.

Amata Wife of Latinus.

Amazons A race of warrior women; said to be descendants of Ares.

Amphitrite Daughter of Nereus; wife of Poseidon; mother of Benthesicyme, Rhode, and Triton.

Amphitryon Heracles' foster father.

Amymone One of the fifty daughters of King Danaus; mother of Nauplius by Poseidon.

Anchises King of Dardania; father of Aeneas by Aphrodite.

Ancus Marcius Fourth king of Rome.

Andromeda Daughter of the king of Joppa; wife of Perseus.

Anteros God of passion; son of Aphrodite and Ares.

Antiope Daughter of the king of Thebes; mother of Amphion and Zethus by Zeus.

Apemosyne A daughter of the king of Crete; loved and impregnated by Hermes; killed by her brother when he found out about her pregnancy.

Aphrodite Goddess of love; one of the twelve great Olympians.

Apollo God of archery, music, and poetry; brother of Artemis; son of Leto and Zeus; one of the twelve great Olympians.

Apsyrtus Brother of Medea; killed when Medea fled with Jason.

Arachne A young woman who challenged Athena to a weaving contest; was turned into a spider.

Ares God of war; son of Zeus and Hera; one of the twelve great Olympians.

Arges One of the three Cyclopes; known as the Shiner or Thunderbolt.

Argus A giant monster with a hundred eyes; placed as guardian of Io by Hera; killed by Hermes to rescue Io.

Ariadne Daughter of King Minos; helped Theseus to escape the labyrinth; wife of Dionysus.

Artemis Virgin goddess of the hunt; sister of Apollo; daughter of Leto and Zeus; one of the twelve great Olympians.

Asclepius Son of Apollo; god of healing.

Asteria Sister of Leto; provided Leto refuge from Hera.

Atalanta A famous hunter; would only marry if a man could beat her in a foot race; wife of Milanion.

Athamas King of Orchomenus; husband of Ino; driven mad by Hera for having sheltered Dionysus, causing him to kill his own children.

Athena Goddess of wisdom, war, crafts, and skill; born out of the head of Zeus; one of the twelve great Olympians.

Atlas A Titan; condemned to hold the heavens up on his shoulders.

Atropos One of the Fates; responsible for cutting the thread of life; daughter of Zeus and Thetis.

Aurora Roman goddess of the dawn; counterpart of Eos.

Autolycus Son of Hermes and Chione; one of the most famous thieves of ancient Greece.

Bacchus Roman god of wine; counterpart of Dionysus.

Battus A shepherd who witnessed Hermes stealing Apollo's cattle; was turned to stone when he betrayed Hermes.

Bellerophon Mortal man who tamed Pegasus.

Boreas The North wind.

Brontes One of the three Cyclopes; known as Thunder or Thunderer.

Butes An Argonaut; a priest of one of Athena's temples; fell victim to the Sirens and saved by Aphrodite.

Cacus Son of Hephaestus and Medusa; a fire-breathing, three-headed monster.

Cadmus Founder of the city of Thebes; was made Ares' slave for eight years; husband of Harmonia.

Calliope The Muse of epic poetry.

Callisto An attendant of Artemis; raped by Zeus and bore him a son, Arcas.

Camenae Roman counterpart of the Muses.

Campe A monster appointed by Cronus to guard the Hecatoncheires and the Cyclopes in Tartarus.

Cassandra Daughter of King Priam and Hecuba; tricked Apollo into granting her the gift of prophecy.

Cecrops Half man, half serpent; son of Gaia; first king of Attica.

Centaurs A savage race of beings with the head and torso of a man and the body and legs of a horse.

Cerberus The dog of Hades; guarded the Underworld, not allowing the living to enter, nor the dead to exit.

Cercyon A monster killed by Theseus.

Ceres Roman goddess of agriculture; counterpart of Demeter.

Cerynitian Hind Deer with golden antlers sacred to Artemis; captured by Heracles.

Ceto A deity of large marine beasts; daughter of Gaia and Pontus.

Charites Known as the Graces; minor goddesses of beauty, grace, and friendship; three daughters of Zeus and Eurynome.

Charon The ferryman of the dead across the River Styx.

Charybdis A monster that swallows ships by creating a whirlpool.

Chimaera Daughter of Typhon and Echidna; fire-breathing monster with the head of a lion, the body of a goat, and the tail of a snake.

Chione Lover of Hermes and Apollo; mother of Philammon by Apollo; mother of Autolycus by Hermes.

Chiron A wise Centaur; tutor of several heroes.

Chryse Mother of Phlegyas by Ares.

Circe Daughter of Helios; powerful witch who used her powers for evil.

Clio The Muse of history.

Clito An orphan girl who became a lover of Poseidon; bore five pairs of twin sons to Poseidon, including Atlas.

Clotho One of the Fates; responsible for spinning the thread of life; daughter of Zeus and Thetis.

Clytemnestra Wife of Agamemnon; killed her husband.

Clytius A Giant; killed by Hecate and Heracles during the war with the Olympians.

Coeus A Titan; husband of Phoebe; father of Leto.

Coronis A mortal lover of Apollo; was unfaithful to Apollo and shot and killed by Artemis.

Cretan Bull Sacrificial bull given to King Minos by Poseidon; father of the Minotaur.

Crius A Titan; husband of Eurybia; father of Astraeus, Pallas, and Perses.

Cronus A Titan; ruler of the universe following Uranus; husband of Rhea; father of the original Olympians.

Cupid Roman god of love; counterpart of Eros.

Cybele An earth goddess; taught Dionysus religious rites and practices.

Cyclopes Three sons of Gaia and Uranus (Brontes, Arges, Steropes), giants with only one eye centered in the forehead.

Cyparissus Grandson of Heracles; loved by Apollo; changed into the cypress tree when his best friend was killed.

Cyrene A nymph; mother of Diomedes by Ares.

Daedalus A great architect; built the labyrinth underground that held the Minotaur prisoner.

Danae Daughter of the king of Argos; mother of Perseus by Zeus.

Danaides The fifty daughters of Danaus; forty-nine killed their husbands on their wedding night.

Daphne A mountain nymph who turned into the laurel tree to escape Apollo's advances.

Deimos Personification of fear; son of Aphrodite and Ares.

Demeter Goddess of fertility and agriculture; one of the twelve great Olympians; daughter of Cronus and Rhea.

Diana Roman moon goddess; counterpart of Artemis.

Dido Queen of Carthage; fell in love with Aeneas and when he left, committed suicide.

Dike Personification of justice; daughter of Zeus and Thetis.

Diomedes Greek warrior during the Trojan War; king of Aetolia.

Dionysus God of the vine, wine, and revelry; one of the twelve great Olympians.

Discordia Roman goddess of discord; counterpart of Eris.

Dryads Tree nymphs.

Echidna Monster with the body of a woman and a serpent's tail instead of legs; mother of several monstrous offspring.

Echion Son of Hermes; the herald for the Argo.

Egeria A nymph who was a lover of and counseled Numa Pompilius.

Eileithyia A goddess of childbirth; daughter of Zeus and Hera.

Eirene Personification of peace; daughter of Zeus and Thetis.

Elais Daughter of King Anius; could turn anything into oil with just a touch.

Electra Daughter of Atlas; mother of Dardanus by Zeus.

Enceladus A Giant; killed by Athena and Heracles during the war with the Olympians.

Endymion King of Elis; lover of Selene; wished for eternal youth and was granted immortal sleep.

Enyo Goddess of the battle; often seen in the company of Ares.

Eos The Dawn; sister of Helios and Selene; mother of the Winds.

Eosphorus The Morning Star.

Ephialtes A Giant; killed by Apollo and Heracles during the war with the Olympians.

Epimetheus A Titan; the brother of Prometheus; the husband of Pandora.

Erato The Muse of love poetry, lyric poetry, and marriage songs.

Erebus Darkness; one of the first five elements born of Chaos.

Ericthonius Son of Gaia and Hephaestus; half man, half serpent; raised by Athena as her own son.

Erigone Daughter of Icarius; loved by Dionysus; committed suicide when she discovered her father's dead body.

Eris Goddess of discord; born to Nyx.

Eris Strife.

Eros Love; one of the first five elements born of Chaos.

Erymanthian Boar Vicious boar captured by Heracles during his labors.

Erysichthon Son of the king of Dotion; disrespected Demeter's sacred trees and died a horrible death.

Eunomia Personification of law and order; daughter of Zeus and Thetis.

Euphrosyne A Charite; the personification of joy or mirth.

Europa Daughter of the king of Phoenicia; lover of Zeus.

Eurus The East wind.

Eurybia Daughter of Gaia and Pontus; wife of Crius; mother of three Titan sons: Astraeus, Pallas, and Perses.

Eurydice The wife of Orpheus; died from a snakebite and was almost retrieved from the Underworld by her husband.

Eurynome Daughter of Oceanus; wife of Ophion; lover of Zeus; mother of the Graces.

Eurystheus The king of Tiryns; commanded the twelve labors of Heracles.

Eurytus A Giant; killed by Dionysus and Heracles during the war with the Olympians.

Euterpe The Muse of music and lyric poetry.

Fates Three goddesses in charge of determining one's fate.

Faunus Roman counterpart of Pan.

Faustulus King Amulius's chief shepherd; raised Romulus and Remus.

Gaia Mother Earth; one of the first five elements born of Chaos.

Ganymede Son of the royal Trojan family; kidnapped by Zeus; a cupbearer to the gods.

Geras Old Age; born to Nyx.

Geryon A three-headed monster killed by Heracles during his labors.

Giants A race of monsters; battled the Olympians for control of the universe and lost.

Glaucus A sea deity; loved Scylla and inadvertently caused her transformation into a monster.

Gorgons Three monstrous sisters who had serpents for hair, eyes that could turn any being to stone, and sharp claws and teeth.

Gration A Giant; killed by Artemis and Heracles during the war with the Olympians.

Griffins Monsters with the head of an eagle, the body of a lion, and the wings of a predatory bird; guardians of treasure.

Hades Ruler of the Underworld; son of Cronus and Rhea.

Halirrhothius Son of Poseidon and Euryte; was killed by Ares for raping his daughter.

Hamadryads Nymphs who lived in only one specific tree and died when it died.

Harmonia Daughter of Aphrodite and Ares; wife of Cadmus, king of Thebes.

Harpies Monstrous birds with the faces of women; sent by deities to punish criminals.

Harpinna Daughter of the river-god Asopus; mother of Oenomaus by Ares.

Hebe Personification of youth; cupbearer to the gods; daughter of Zeus and Hera.

Hecate A Titaness; a triple goddess presiding over magic and spells; an attendant of Persephone.

Hecatoncheires The three, hundred-handed, fifty-headed sons of Gaia and Uranus (Cottus, Briareus, and Gyges).

Hector Greatest Trojan warrior of the Trojan War; killed Protesilaus.

Hecuba Wife of King Priam; mother of Troilus by Apollo.

Helen Daughter of Zeus and Leda; most beautiful woman in the world; was kidnapped by Paris.

Helenus Son of Priam; chief prophet of Troy.

Helios The Sun; brother of Eos and Selene.

Hemera Day; born to Nyx and Erebus.

Hephaestus God of fire, smithing, craftsmanship, and metalworking; one of the twelve great Olympians.

Hera Queen of the heavens and the gods; goddess of marriage and childbirth; sister and wife of Zeus; one of the twelve great Olympians.

Heracles Son of Zeus and Alcmene; one of the greatest heroes of Greek mythology; underwent the Twelve Labors.

Hercules Roman counterpart of Heracles.

Hermes Messenger of the gods; the god of commerce and flight; son of Zeus and Maia; one of the twelve great Olympians.

Herse A daughter of Cecrops; mother of Cephalus by Hermes.

Hesperides Nymphs who lived in the Garden of Hesperides and protected the golden apples; three in number: Aegle, Erythia, and Hesperarethusa.

Hestia Goddess of the hearth and home; one of the three virgin goddesses; daughter of Cronus and Rhea.

Hippolytus A Giant; killed by Hermes and Heracles during the war with the Olympians.

Hyacinthus A beautiful young man loved by Apollo; was killed during a game of discus-throwing.

Hydra of Lerna A giant serpent with numerous heads; had a giant crab as its sidekick.

Hymen God of marriage.

Hyperion A Titan; husband of Theia; father of Helios, Selene, and Eos.

Hypnos Sleep; born to Nyx.

Iacchus Son of Demeter and Zeus; a minor deity associated with the Eleusinian Mysteries.

Iambe Daughter of Pan; servant in the house of Celeus along with Demeter.

Iapetus A Titan; husband of Themis; father of Prometheus, Epimetheus, Menoetius, and Atlas.

Iasion Son of Zeus and Electra; lover of Demeter; killed by a thunderbolt thrown by Zeus.

Icarius Taught cultivation of the vine and how to make wine by Dionysus; was killed when his neighbors thought he was trying to poison them.

Idas Son of Poseidon; chosen by Marpessa over Apollo.

Idomeneus A Greek warrior during the Trojan War.

Ino Semele's sister; driven mad by Hera for having sheltered Dionysus, causing her to kill her own children.

Io Virgin priestess of Hera's; lover of Zeus; turned into a white heifer; persecuted by Hera.

Iphigenia Daughter of Agamemnon; sacrificed by her father to Artemis.

Iphimedia Wife of Aloeus; seduced Poseidon and bore him two Giant sons, Ephialtes and Otus.

Iris Goddess of the rainbow.

Iulus Son of Aeneas; founder of the city Alba Longa.

Ixion A king of Thessaly; condemned to Tartarus for trying to seduce Zeus's wife.

Jason A great hero; led the Argonauts on the quest for the Golden Fleece; husband of Medea.

Juno Roman goddess of marriage and childbirth; counterpart of Hera.

Jupiter Roman god of the heavens; counterpart of Zeus.

Keres Female spirits of death, sometimes said to be the same as the Furies; born to Nyx.

Lachesis One of the Fates; responsible for measuring the thread of life; daughter of Zeus and Thetis.

Ladon A hundred-headed dragon; the prime guardian of the golden apples in the Garden of Hesperides.

Laocoon A prophet; warned the Trojans about the wooden horse; was devoured by a sea monster.

Laomedon King of Troy; father of Priam and Hesione.

Latinus King of Latium; son of Faunus.

Lavinia Daughter of Latinus; wife of Aeneas.

Leda Daughter of the king of Aetolia; mother of Polydeuces and Helen by Zeus.

Leto Daughter of Coeus and Phoebe; mother of Apollo and Artemis by Zeus.

Leucothoe Loved by Helios; buried alive by her father when he found out about the affair.

Lucius Tarquinius Priscus Fifth king of Rome.

Lucius Tarquinius Superbus Seventh and final king of Rome; father of Sextus.

Lycurgus King of Thrace; punished by Dionysus for refusing his religious teachings; put to death by his own people.

Macris The nymph who nursed the baby Dionysus.

Maenads Wild women followers of Dionysus.

Maia The eldest daughter of Atlas; mother of Hermes by Zeus.

Marpessa Daughter of the river-god Evenus; chose a mortal man over Apollo.

Mars Roman god of war; counterpart of Ares.

Marsyas A satyr; challenged Apollo to a musical contest and lost his life.

Medea A powerful witch; aided Jason on his quest for the Golden Fleece.

Medusa A Gorgon; monster with snakes for hair and a stare that could turn any being into stone; a lover of Poseidon.

Megara Daughter of the King of Thebes; first wife of Heracles.

Melampus A great seer; cured the women of Argos from madness inflicted upon them by Dionysus.

Meliae Nymphs of the ash trees.

Melpomene The Muse of tragedy.

Menelaus King of Sparta; husband of Helen.

Mercury Roman counterpart of Hermes.

Metis An Oceanid known for her wisdom; the first wife and cousin of Zeus.

Midas King of Phrygia; granted by Dionysus a touch that could turn anything to gold.

Milanion Young man who beat Atalanta in a foot race, winning her hand in marriage.

Mimas A Giant; killed by Hephaestus and Heracles during the war with the Olympians.

Minerva Roman goddess of wisdom and warfare; counterpart of Athena.

Minos Son of Zeus and Europa; King of Crete; became a Judge of the Dead.

Minotaur A monster with the body of a man and the head of a bull; trapped in the labyrinth and fed sacrifices of young children.

Mnemosyne A Titaness; known as Memory; mother of the Muses.

Momus Sarcasm; born to Nyx.

Morae Roman counterpart of the Fates.

Moros Doom; born to Nyx.

Muses The daughters of Zeus and Mnemosyne; goddesses of music, art, poetry, dance, and the arts in general.

Myrtilus Son of Hermes; a famous charioteer, known for his swiftness.

Naiads Water nymphs.

Narcissus A beautiful young man who fell in love with his own reflection and was turned into the narcissus flower.

Nauplius An Argonaut; founder of the town of Nauplia; famous for his knowledge of the seas and astronomy.

Nemean Lion Monstrous lion strangled by Heracles during his labors.

Nemesis Goddess of vengeance; born to Nyx.

Nemisis Retribution.

Neptune Roman god of the sea; counterpart of Poseidon.

Nereids Sea nymphs.

Nereus A marine deity known as the "Old Man of the Sea"; father of the Nereids; son of Gaia and Pontus.

Nike Goddess of victory.

Niobe The first of Zeus' mortal lovers; daughter of Phoroneus (the first mortal man); mother of Argus by Zeus. Also the wife of Amphion; her children were killed by Artemis and Apollo because she bragged that her children were greater than Leto's.

Notus The South wind.

Numa Pompilius Second king of Rome.

Nymphs Nature goddesses; the personification of the fertility and gracefulness of nature; often daughters of Zeus.

Nyx Night; one of the first five elements born of Chaos.

Oceanus A Titan; husband of Tethys; god of the rivers.

Odysseus A great hero; warrior during the Trojan War; famous for his ten-year journey home following the war.

Oedipus King of Thebes; unknowingly fulfilled a prophecy by killing his father and marrying his mother.

Oino Daughter of King Anius; could turn anything into wine with just a touch.

Oizys Pain; born to Nyx.

Oneiroi Dreams; born to Nyx.

Ops Roman counterpart of Rhea.

Oreads Mountain nymphs.

Orestes Son of Agamemnon and Clytemnestra; killed his mother to avenge the murder of his father.

Orion A great hunter; placed in the sky as a constellation after his death.

Orpheus Son of Apollo; talented musician; visited the Underworld to retrieve his dead wife.

Otrere A queen of the Amazons; mother of Penthesilea by Ares.

Otus A Giant; son of Poseidon and Iphimedia.

Pallas Daughter of Triton; a childhood friend of Athena; was accidentally killed by Athena.

Pallas A Giant; killed by Athena and Heracles during the war with the Olympians.

Pan Son of Hermes; a minor god of shepherds and flocks.

Pandia Daughter of Selene and Zeus.

Pandora The first mortal woman; wife of Epimetheus; her curiosity drove her to open a box that released all the plagues and ills on the world.

Paris Prince of Troy; judged the beauty contest between Hera, Athena, and Aphrodite; kidnapped Helen.

Pasiphae Wife of King Minos; fell in love with a sacrificial bull and gave birth to the Minotaur.

Patroclus Achilles' best friend; killed during the Trojan War.

Pegasus A winged horse, born from the blood of Medusa's severed head.

Peina Personification of hunger.

Pelias King of Iolcus; killed by Medea to place Jason on the throne.

Pentheus King of Thebes; punished by Dionysus for refusing his religious teachings; killed by women taking part in a Dionysiac festival.

Periphetes Son of Hephaestus; killed by Theseus.

Persephone Queen of the Underworld; daughter of Demeter and Zeus; abducted by Hades.

Perseus Great Greek hero; son of Zeus and Danae; killed Medusa.

Phlegyas Son of Ares and Chryse; shot and killed by Apollo; condemned to spend eternity in Tartarus.

Phobos Personification of terror; son of Aphrodite and Ares.

Phoebe A Titaness; wife of Coeus; mother of Leto; first goddess of the moon.

Phorcys A sea deity; father of the Sirens; son of Gaia and Pontus.

Pierides The daughters of Pierus, a Macedonian king; challenged the Muses to a contest, lost, and were turned into jackdaws.

Pluto Roman god of hell; counterpart of Hades.

Polybotes A Giant; killed by Poseidon and Heracles during the war with the Olympians.

Polydectes King of Seriphus; loved and persecuted Danae; turned to stone by Perseus.

Polyhmnia The Muse of mime and songs.

Polyphemus A man-eating Cyclops; son of Poseidon; blinded by Odysseus.

Pontus Sea; born to Gaia during creation.

Porphyrion A Giant; one of the leaders of the Giants during the war with the Olympians; killed by Zeus and Heracles.

Poseidon God of the sea; one of the twelve great Olympians; son of Cronus and Rhea.

Priam King of Troy; father of Paris.

Priapus God of fertility; son of Aphrodite and Dionysus.

Procrustes A murdering innkeeper killed by Theseus.

Prometheus A Titan; the champion of mankind; thought to be the creator of man; stole fire from the heavens to give to man.

Proserpine Roman counterpart of Persephone.

Protesilaus The first Greek to step ashore in Troy; the first Greek to fall during the Trojan War.

Python A great serpent sent by Hera to persecute Leto; strangled to death by Apollo.

Remus Son of Rhea Silvia and Mars; brother of Romulus; killed during the fight with his brother over Rome.

Rhadamanthys Son of Zeus and brother of Minos; became a Judge of the Dead.

Rhea A Titaness; a mother-deity and earth goddess; wife of Cronus; mother of the original Olympians.

Rhea Silvia Mother of Romulus and Remus by Mars.

Rhode Daughter of Poseidon and Amphitrite; wife of Helios.

Romulus Son of Rhea Silvia and Mars; brother of Remus; founder of Rome.

Saturn Roman counterpart of Cronus.

Satyrs Nature spirits; the personification of fertility and sexual desire; half man, half goat.

Sciron A highwayman killed by Theseus.

Scylla A sea nymph who was transformed into a monster.

Selene The Moon; sister of Helios and Eos.

Semele Mortal lover of Zeus; mother of Dionysus by Zeus; was killed when she asked to see Zeus in his true form.

Servius Tullius Sixth king of Rome.

Sextus Son of Superbus; raped Lucretia and brought about the downfall of the Roman monarchy.

Sibyl An aged prophetess who aided Aeneas in his journey to the Underworld.

Silenus A satyr; tutor and companion of Dionysus; possessed the gift of prophecy.

Silvius Son of Aeneas and Lavinia; first to be born into the Roman race.

Sinis A highwayman killed by Theseus.

Sinon A Greek soldier during the Trojan War; convinced the Trojans to take in the wooden horse.

Sinope A nymph; pursued by both Zeus and Apollo; tricked the gods into granting her eternal virginity.

Sisyphus Considered the cleverest of mortal men; outwits Death; commits several crimes against the gods; sent to Tartarus.

Smyrna Daughter of the king of Cyprus; fell in love with her father because of Aphrodite and was changed into a myrrh tree to escape his wrath.

Sol Roman Sun god; counterpart of Apollo.

Spermo Daughter of King Anius; could turn anything into corn with just a touch.

Sphinx Daughter of Typhon and Echidna; monster with the head and breast of a woman, the body of a lion, and the wings of a bird of prey.

Steropes One of the three Cyclopes; known as Lightning or the Maker of Lightning.

Stymphalian Birds Monstrous birds with long legs, steel-tipped feathers, and razor-sharp claws; preyed on men.

Syrinx A nymph loved by Pan; transformed into a bed of reeds to escape Pan's amorous advances.

Taygete A daughter of Atlas; mother of Lacedaemon by Zeus.

Terpsichore The Muse of dance.

Tethys A Titaness; first goddess of the sea; wife of Oceanus; mother of the Oceanids and all the rivers.

Teucer A Greek warrior during the Trojan War.

Thalia The Muse of comedy.

Thalia A Charite; the personification of blooming or good cheer.

Thamyris Son of Philammon; the first homosexual.

Thanatos Death; born to Nyx.

Thaumas A sea deity; father of the Harpies; son of Gaia and Pontus.

Theia A Titaness; wife of Hyperion; mother of Helios, Selene, and Eos.

Themis A Titaness; a mother-deity or earth goddess; wife of Iapetus; mother of Prometheus, the Hours, and the Fates.

Theopane Mother of the ram with the Golden Fleece by Poseidon.

Theseus The greatest Athenian hero; son of Poseidon and Aethra.

Thoas A Giant; killed by the Fates and Heracles during the war with the Olympians.

Thoosa Daughter of Phorcys; lover of Poseidon; mother of the Cyclops Polyphemus.

Tiresias A mortal who had lived as both a man and a woman; one of the greatest prophets of classical mythology; blinded by Hera for taking the side of Zeus during an argument.

Titus Tatius King of Sabine; ruled jointly with Romulus.

Tityus A Giant who tried to rape Leto; was killed by Artemis and Apollo.

Triton Poseidon's herald and son; half man, half fish; a sea deity.

Tullus Hostilius Third king of Rome.

Turnus King of the Rutulians; battled Aeneas for the hand of Lavinia.

Tyche Goddess of fortune and the personification of luck.

Typhon A monster with a hundred serpentine heads, wings, and a body encircled with snakes.

Ulysses Roman counterpart of Odysseus.

Urania The Muse of astronomy.

Uranus Sky; born to Gaia during creation.

Venus Roman goddess of love; counterpart of Aphrodite.

Vesta Roman goddess of the hearth; counterpart of Hestia.

Vestal Virgins The priestesses of the Temple of Vesta.

Vulcan Roman god of fire; counterpart of Hephaestus.

Zagreus The first name of the infant Dionysus; a child with a crown of snakes and horns.

Zephyrus The West wind.

Zeus Ruler of the heavens, gods, and men; one of the twelve great Olympians; son of Cronus and Rhea.

APPENDIX B
Resources

CLASSIC SOURCES

Aeschylus
  Oresteia
  Persians
  Prometheus Bound
  Seven Against Thebes
  Suppliants
Apollodorus
  The Library
Apollonius Rhodis
  Argonautica
Euripides
  Andromache
  Hecuba
  Iphigenia at Aulis
  Bacchants
  Alcestis
  Medea
  Children of Heracles
  Hippolytus
  Suppliants
  Electra
  Madness of Heracles
  Ion
  Trojan Women

  *Iphigenia Among the
    Taurians*
  Phoenician Women
  Helen
  Orestes
Herodotus
  History
Hesiod
  Theogony
  Works and Days
Homer
  Iliad
  Odyssey
Horace
  Odes
  Epodes
Livy
  History of Rome
Ovid
  Metamorphoses
  Amores
  Heroides
  Fasti
  Tristia
  Epistulae ex Ponto

  Ibis
Pausanias
  Description of Greece
Sophocles
  Oedipus the King
  Oedipus at Colonus
  Antigone
  Ajax
  Trachinian Women
  Philoctetes
  Electra
Statius
  Thebaid
Virgil
  Aeneid
  Eclogues
  Georgics

BOOKS ON MYTHOLOGY

Avery, Catherine B. (ed.). *The New Century Classical Handbook*. Appleton-Century-Crofts, Inc.

Bulfinch, Thomas. *Bulfinch's Mythology*. Modern Library.

Burkert, Walter. *Ancient Mystery Cults.* Harvard University Press.

Campbell, Joseph and Bill Moyers (Contributor). *The Power of Myth.* Anchor.

Colum, Padraic. *Myths of the World*. Grosset & Dunlap.

Gayley, Charles Mills. *The Classic Myths in English Literature and in Art*. Ginn & Company.

Grant, Michael and John Hazel (Contributor). *Who's Who in Classical Mythology*. Oxford University Press.

Grant, Michael. *Myths of the Greeks and Romans*. The World Publishing Company.

Guerber, H. A. *The Myths of Greece and Rome*. British Book Centre.

Hamilton, Edith. *Mythology*. Back Bay Books.

Hamilton, Edith. *Mythology: Timeless Tales of Gods and Heroes*. Warner Books.

Highet, Gilbert. *The Classical Tradition*. Oxford University Press.

Kirk, G. S. *The Nature of Greek Mythology*. Penguin.

Morford, Mark P. O. and Robert J. Lenardon. *Classical Mythology, Sixth Edition*.

Murray, Alexander S. *Manual of Mythology*. Tudor Publishing Company.

Rose, H. J. *A Handbook of Greek Mythology*. Dutton.

Seltman, Charles. *The Twelve Olympians and Their Guests*. Apollo Editions, Inc.

Vernant, Jean-Pierre and Linda Asher (Translator). *The Universe, the Gods, and Men: Ancient Greek Myths*. HarperCollins.

Warner, Rex. *Men and Gods*. Random House.

Zimmerman, John Edward. *Dictionary of Classical Mythology*. Bantam Books.

WEB SITES ON CLASSICAL MYTHOLOGY

4Mythology: *http://4mythology.4anything.com*

Ancient Greece Mythology: *www.ancientculture.com/mythology*

Ancient Greece: *www.earlygreece.com*

Ancient/Classical History: *www.ancienthistory.about.com*

Bulfinch's Mythology: *www.bulfinch.org*

Classical Myth: *http://web.uvic.ca/grs/bowman/myth*

Greek Mythology: *www.greekmythology.com*

Greek Mythology: *www.messagenet.com/myths*

Greek Mythology: *www.mythweb.com*

Greek Spider: *www.greekspider.com*

Mythography: *www.loggia.com/myth*

Olympians: *www.temple.edu/classics/olympians.htm*

Perseus Digital Library: *www.perseus.tufts.edu*

Roman Mythology: *www.paralumun.com/mythroman.htm*

The Ancient Gods: *www.hol.gr/greece/ancgods.htm*

The Encyclopedia Mythica: *www.pantheon.org*

Index

The EVERYTHING Series!

BUSINESS & PERSONAL FINANCE

Everything® Budgeting Book
Everything® Business Planning Book
Everything® Coaching and Mentoring Book
Everything® Fundraising Book
Everything® Get Out of Debt Book
Everything® Grant Writing Book
Everything® Home-Based Business Book
Everything® Homebuying Book, 2nd Ed.
Everything® Homeselling Book, 2nd Ed.
Everything® Investing Book, 2nd Ed.
Everything® Landlording Book
Everything® Leadership Book
Everything® Managing People Book
Everything® Negotiating Book
Everything® Online Business Book
Everything® Personal Finance Book
Everything® Personal Finance in Your 20s
    and 30s Book
Everything® Project Management Book
Everything® Real Estate Investing Book
Everything® Robert's Rules Book, $7.95
Everything® Selling Book
Everything® Start Your Own Business Book
Everything® Wills & Estate Planning Book

COOKING

Everything® Barbecue Cookbook
Everything® Bartender's Book, $9.95
Everything® Chinese Cookbook
Everything® Cocktail Parties and Drinks
    Book
Everything® College Cookbook
Everything® Cookbook
Everything® Cooking for Two Cookbook
Everything® Diabetes Cookbook
Everything® Easy Gourmet Cookbook
Everything® Fondue Cookbook
Everything® Gluten-Free Cookbook

Everything® Grilling Cookbook
Everything® Healthy Meals in Minutes
    Cookbook
Everything® Holiday Cookbook
Everything® Indian Cookbook
Everything® Italian Cookbook
Everything® Low-Carb Cookbook
Everything® Low-Fat High-Flavor Cookbook
Everything® Low-Salt Cookbook
Everything® Meals for a Month Cookbook
Everything® Mediterranean Cookbook
Everything® Mexican Cookbook
Everything® One-Pot Cookbook
Everything® Pasta Cookbook
Everything® Quick Meals Cookbook
Everything® Slow Cooker Cookbook
Everything® Slow Cooking for a Crowd
    Cookbook
Everything® Soup Cookbook
Everything® Thai Cookbook
Everything® Vegetarian Cookbook
Everything® Wine Book, 2nd Ed.

CRAFT SERIES

Everything® Crafts—Baby Scrapbooking
Everything® Crafts—Bead Your Own Jewelry
Everything® Crafts—Create Your Own
    Greeting Cards
Everything® Crafts—Easy Projects
Everything® Crafts—Polymer Clay for
    Beginners
Everything® Crafts—Rubber Stamping
    Made Easy
Everything® Crafts—Wedding Decorations
    and Keepsakes

HEALTH

Everything® Alzheimer's Book
Everything® Diabetes Book
Everything® Health Guide to Controlling
    Anxiety

Everything® Hypnosis Book
Everything® Low Cholesterol Book
Everything® Massage Book
Everything® Menopause Book
Everything® Nutrition Book
Everything® Reflexology Book
Everything® Stress Management Book

HISTORY

Everything® American Government Book
Everything® American History Book
Everything® Civil War Book
Everything® Irish History & Heritage Book
Everything® Middle East Book

HOBBIES & GAMES

Everything® Blackjack Strategy Book
Everything® Brain Strain Book, $9.95
Everything® Bridge Book
Everything® Candlemaking Book
Everything® Card Games Book
Everything® Card Tricks Book, $9.95
Everything® Cartooning Book
Everything® Casino Gambling Book, 2nd Ed.
Everything® Chess Basics Book
Everything® Craps Strategy Book
Everything® Crossword and Puzzle Book
Everything® Crossword Challenge Book
Everything® Cryptograms Book, $9.95
Everything® Digital Photography Book
Everything® Drawing Book
Everything® Easy Crosswords Book
Everything® Family Tree Book, 2nd Ed.
Everything® Games Book, 2nd Ed.
Everything® Knitting Book
Everything® Knots Book
Everything® Photography Book
Everything® Poker Strategy Book
Everything® Pool & Billiards Book
Everything® Quilting Book
Everything® Scrapbooking Book

All Everything® books are priced at $12.95 or $14.95, unless otherwise stated. Prices subject to change without notice.

Everything® Sewing Book
Everything® Test Your IQ Book, $9.95
Everything® Travel Crosswords Book, $9.95
Everything® Woodworking Book
Everything® Word Games Challenge Book
Everything® Word Search Book

HOME IMPROVEMENT

Everything® Feng Shui Book
Everything® Feng Shui Decluttering Book,
$9.95
Everything® Fix-It Book
Everything® Homebuilding Book
Everything® Lawn Care Book
Everything® Organize Your Home Book

EVERYTHING® *KIDS'* BOOKS

All titles are $6.95

Everything® Kids' Animal Puzzle & Activity
Book
Everything® Kids' Baseball Book, 3rd Ed.
Everything® Kids' Bible Trivia Book
Everything® Kids' Bugs Book
Everything® Kids' Christmas Puzzle
& Activity Book
Everything® Kids' Cookbook
Everything® Kids' Crazy Puzzles Book
Everything® Kids' Dinosaurs Book
Everything® Kids' Gross Jokes Book
Everything® Kids' Gross Puzzle and
Activity Book
Everything® Kids' Halloween Puzzle
& Activity Book
Everything® Kids' Hidden Pictures Book
Everything® Kids' Joke Book
Everything® Kids' Knock Knock Book
Everything® Kids' Math Puzzles Book
Everything® Kids' Mazes Book
Everything® Kids' Money Book
Everything® Kids' Nature Book
Everything® Kids' Puzzle Book
Everything® Kids' Riddles & Brain Teasers Book
Everything® Kids' Science Experiments Book
Everything® Kids' Sharks Book
Everything® Kids' Soccer Book
Everything® Kids' Travel Activity Book

KIDS' STORY BOOKS

Everything® Fairy Tales Book

LANGUAGE

Everything® Conversational Japanese Book
(with CD), $19.95
Everything® French Phrase Book, $9.95
Everything® French Verb Book, $9.95
Everything® Inglés Book
Everything® Learning French Book
Everything® Learning German Book
Everything® Learning Italian Book
Everything® Learning Latin Book
Everything® Learning Spanish Book
Everything® Sign Language Book
Everything® Spanish Grammar Book
Everything® Spanish Practice Book
(with CD), $19.95
Everything® Spanish Phrase Book, $9.95
Everything® Spanish Verb Book, $9.95

MUSIC

Everything® Drums Book (with CD), $19.95
Everything® Guitar Book
Everything® Home Recording Book
Everything® Playing Piano and Keyboards
Book
Everything® Reading Music Book (with CD),
$19.95
Everything® Rock & Blues Guitar Book
(with CD), $19.95
Everything® Songwriting Book

NEW AGE

Everything® Astrology Book, 2nd Ed.
Everything® Dreams Book, 2nd Ed.
Everything® Ghost Book
Everything® Love Signs Book, $9.95
Everything® Numerology Book
Everything® Paganism Book
Everything® Palmistry Book
Everything® Psychic Book
Everything® Reiki Book
Everything® Tarot Book
Everything® Wicca and Witchcraft Book

PARENTING

Everything® Baby Names Book
Everything® Baby Shower Book
Everything® Baby's First Food Book
Everything® Baby's First Year Book
Everything® Birthing Book
Everything® Breastfeeding Book
Everything® Father-to-Be Book
Everything® Father's First Year Book
Everything® Get Ready for Baby Book
Everything® Get Your Baby to Sleep Book,
$9.95
Everything® Getting Pregnant Book
Everything® Homeschooling Book
Everything® Mother's First Year Book
Everything® Parent's Guide to Children
and Divorce
Everything® Parent's Guide to Children
with ADD/ADHD
Everything® Parent's Guide to Children
with Asperger's Syndrome
Everything® Parent's Guide to Children
with Autism
Everything® Parent's Guide to Children with
Bipolar Disorder
Everything® Parent's Guide to Children
with Dyslexia
Everything® Parent's Guide to Positive
Discipline
Everything® Parent's Guide to Raising a
Successful Child
Everything® Parent's Guide to Tantrums
Everything® Parent's Guide to the Overweight
Child
Everything® Parent's Guide to the Strong-
Willed Child
Everything® Parenting a Teenager Book
Everything® Potty Training Book, $9.95
Everything® Pregnancy Book, 2nd Ed.
Everything® Pregnancy Fitness Book
Everything® Pregnancy Nutrition Book
Everything® Pregnancy Organizer, $15.00
Everything® Toddler Book
Everything® Tween Book
Everything® Twins, Triplets, and More Book

All Everything® books are priced at $12.95 or $14.95, unless otherwise stated. Prices subject to change without notice.

PETS

Everything® Cat Book
Everything® Dachshund Book
Everything® Dog Book
Everything® Dog Health Book
Everything® Dog Training and Tricks Book
Everything® German Shepherd Book
Everything® Golden Retriever Book
Everything® Horse Book
Everything® Horseback Riding Book
Everything® Labrador Retriever Book
Everything® Poodle Book
Everything® Pug Book
Everything® Puppy Book
Everything® Rottweiler Book
Everything® Small Dogs Book
Everything® Tropical Fish Book
Everything® Yorkshire Terrier Book

REFERENCE

Everything® Car Care Book
Everything® Classical Mythology Book
Everything® Computer Book
Everything® Divorce Book
Everything® Einstein Book
Everything® Etiquette Book, 2nd Ed.
Everything® Inventions and Patents Book
Everything® Mafia Book
Everything® Philosophy Book
Everything® Psychology Book
Everything® Shakespeare Book

RELIGION

Everything® Angels Book
Everything® Bible Book
Everything® Buddhism Book
Everything® Catholicism Book
Everything® Christianity Book
Everything® Jewish History & Heritage Book
Everything® Judaism Book
Everything® Koran Book
Everything® Prayer Book
Everything® Saints Book

Everything® Torah Book
Everything® Understanding Islam Book
Everything® World's Religions Book
Everything® Zen Book

SCHOOL & CAREERS

Everything® Alternative Careers Book
Everything® College Survival Book, 2nd Ed.
Everything® Cover Letter Book, 2nd Ed.
Everything® Get-a-Job Book
Everything® Guide to Starting and Running a Restaurant
Everything® Job Interview Book
Everything® New Teacher Book
Everything® Online Job Search Book
Everything® Paying for College Book
Everything® Practice Interview Book
Everything® Resume Book, 2nd Ed.
Everything® Study Book

SELF-HELP

Everything® Dating Book, 2nd Ed.
Everything® Great Sex Book
Everything® Kama Sutra Book
Everything® Self-Esteem Book

SPORTS & FITNESS

Everything® Fishing Book
Everything® Golf Instruction Book
Everything® Pilates Book
Everything® Running Book
Everything® Total Fitness Book
Everything® Weight Training Book
Everything® Yoga Book

TRAVEL

Everything® Family Guide to Hawaii
Everything® Family Guide to Las Vegas, 2nd Ed.
Everything® Family Guide to New York City, 2nd Ed.
Everything® Family Guide to RV Travel & Campgrounds

Everything® Family Guide to the Walt Disney World Resort®, Universal Studios®, and Greater Orlando, 4th Ed.
Everything® Family Guide to Cruise Vacations
Everything® Family Guide to the Caribbean
Everything® Family Guide to Washington D.C., 2nd Ed.
Everything® Guide to New England
Everything® Travel Guide to the Disneyland Resort®, California Adventure®, Universal Studios®, and the Anaheim Area

WEDDINGS

Everything® Bachelorette Party Book, $9.95
Everything® Bridesmaid Book, $9.95
Everything® Elopement Book, $9.95
Everything® Father of the Bride Book, $9.95
Everything® Groom Book, $9.95
Everything® Mother of the Bride Book, $9.95
Everything® Outdoor Wedding Book
Everything® Wedding Book, 3rd Ed.
Everything® Wedding Checklist, $9.95
Everything® Wedding Etiquette Book, $9.95
Everything® Wedding Organizer, $15.00
Everything® Wedding Shower Book, $9.95
Everything® Wedding Vows Book, $9.95
Everything® Weddings on a Budget Book, $9.95

WRITING

Everything® Creative Writing Book
Everything® Get Published Book
Everything® Grammar and Style Book
Everything® Guide to Writing a Book Proposal
Everything® Guide to Writing a Novel
Everything® Guide to Writing Children's Books
Everything® Guide to Writing Research Papers
Everything® Screenwriting Book
Everything® Writing Poetry Book
Everything® Writing Well Book

Available wherever books are sold!
To order, call 800-258-0929, or visit us at *www.everything.com*
Everything® and everything.com® are registered trademarks of F+W Publications, Inc.